Preserving Whose City?

Preserving Whose City?

Memory, Place, and Identity in Rio de Janeiro

Brian J. Godfrey

ROWMAN & LITTLEFIELD
Lanham • Boulder • New York • London

Published by Rowman & Littlefield
An imprint of The Rowman & Littlefield Publishing Group, Inc.
4501 Forbes Boulevard, Suite 200, Lanham, Maryland 20706
www.rowman.com

6 Tinworth Street, London SE11 5AL, United Kingdom

Copyright © 2021 by The Rowman & Littlefield Publishing Group, Inc.

All rights reserved. No part of this book may be reproduced in any form or by any electronic or mechanical means, including information storage and retrieval systems, without written permission from the publisher, except by a reviewer who may quote passages in a review.

British Library Cataloguing in Publication Information Available

Library of Congress Cataloging-in-Publication Data

Names: Godfrey, Brian J., author.
Title: Preserving whose city? : memory, place, and identity in Rio de Janeiro / Brian J. Godfrey.
Description: Lanham : Rowman & Littlefield, [2021] | Includes bibliographical references and index.
Identifiers: LCCN 2021058725 (print) | LCCN 2021058726 (ebook) | ISBN 9781538136546 (hardcover) | ISBN 9781538136621 (paperback) | ISBN 9781538136638 (epub)
Subjects: LCSH: Historic sites—Conservation and restoration—Brazil—Rio de Janeiro. | Historic preservation—Social aspects—Brazil—Rio de Janeiro. | Natural monuments—Social aspects—Brazil—Rio de Janeiro. | Cultural landscapes—Brazil—Rio de Janeiro. | Cultural property—Protection—Brazil—Rio de Janeiro. | Collective memory—Brazil—Rio de Janeiro. | Rio de Janeiro (Brazil)—Cultural policy.
Classification: LCC F2646.5.A2 G63 2021 (print) | LCC F2646.5.A2 (ebook) | DDC 981/.53—dc23
LC record available at https://lccn.loc.gov/2021058725
LC ebook record available at https://lccn.loc.gov/2021058726

Ao grande amigo,
Jurandyr Florentino Miguez, Carioca da gema,
Que tanto inspirou este livro

Contents

Preface	ix
1 Uses of Memory: Preserving Whose Rio de Janeiro?	1
Narratives of Historic Placemaking	6
"Civilizing" Rio through Urban Design	12
The "Land of the Future" Discovers Its Past	16
Memory, Preservation, and Heritage	22
Approaching Place Memory and Identity	26
2 Preservation Politics	35
Postcolonial Urbanism in Rio de Janeiro	38
Entrepreneurial Preservation	47
November 15th Square: Placemaking on the Praça	57
Adaptive Reuse of the Imperial Palace	65
Reinvention and Continuity	70
3 Little Africa: Afro-Brazilian Heritage and Historic Placemaking	77
Counter-Memory and Cultural Reinvention	80
Slave Port and Divided City	84
Valongo Wharf: Making a World Heritage Site	92
Little Africa and the African Heritage Circuit	100
Community Identity and Cultural Politics	109
4 Resilient Favelas: Pride of Place, Memory of Resistance	115
Contested Origins: Invention of the Favela	119
Favela Expansion, Removal, and Resistance	127

	Favela as Spectacle: "They Don't Care about Us"	135
	The Rise of "Favela Chic"	143
	Favelas As Informal Urbanism	149
5	Environmental Heritage: Protecting Carioca Landscapes	157
	Carioca Landscapes: Making a World Heritage Site	160
	Tijuca National Park: One Park, Many Symbols	165
	Guanabara Bay: Conservation Turns to Environmental Justice	174
	Copacabana and Ipanema: Democratic Beaches?	180
	Environmental Heritages: Protecting Carioca Landscapes	191
6	Remembering Rio	197
Bibliography		205
Index		221
About the Author		237

Preface

> The city which cannot be expunged from the mind is like an armature, a honeycomb in whose cells each of us can place the things he wants to remember. . . . Between each idea and each point of the itinerary an affinity or a contrast can be established, serving as an immediate aid to memory.
>
> —Italo Calvino, 1974[1]

Like Calvino's *Invisible Cities*, our own cities of memory stand like personal landmarks amid the ongoing passages of life. As we recall events of the past, associations with particular people and places inevitably come to mind, even if the specific circumstances now seem vague, even dreamlike. Similarly, the collective memories of people and places tend to become ambiguous with the passage of time, as cities and nations reference the past in oblique and ambiguous ways. Personally, the writing of this work provided an opportunity to revisit and study Rio de Janeiro, which I began to explore decades ago. As I studied the city's history, placemaking, and planning, personal recollections of my travels, friends, and acquaintances I have known over the years came back to me. This project on the making of historic places soon became a meditation on my own place memories.

After receiving an undergraduate degree in history, I had the good fortune to receive a Thomas J. Watson Fellowship to study patterns of colonization in Latin America. I focused my travels mainly on Brazil. When I first visited Belém, Fortaleza, Ouro Preto, Recife, Rio de Janeiro, Salvador, São Paulo, and other Brazilian cities during the 1970s, the historic downtowns and waterfronts captivated me. Although rapid urbanization was already transforming the cities into sprawling metropolitan areas, the lively city centers remained vibrant centers of social diversity. Wealthy families had already abandoned residence in crowded inner cities, but the central areas retained middle-class families along with the less privileged. Outlying shopping malls had not yet proliferated, so downtown commerce still attracted a broad clientele. I enjoyed wandering these old streets and taking in the historic surroundings, observing the passers-by in the main squares, the lively street life, and mixture of people from different walks of life. No doubt my memories have aged with nostalgia, but these cities provided an intensely urban and culturally distinctive experience for a child of postwar suburban Southern California.

Brazilian cities always intrigued and often surprised me. I had previously traveled through Spanish-American countries, so right away I was struck by the regional and cultural differences with Brazil. With their hills, their characteristic upper and lower quarters, their distinctive architecture, and their Portuguese language, Brazilian cities recalled my earlier visits to Lisbon and Porto. Despite problems of poverty and deterioration, the city centers of Brazil retained a formidable built heritage and a dramatic sense of place. Historic places evoked local pride—perhaps an old marketplace, a central square or park, the municipal theater, a colonial fortress, or the metropolitan cathedral—but residents still frequented these structures as part of daily life. Tourists also visited these heritage sites, but the monuments were not regarded primarily as tourist destinations. The Brazilian cities of my youth seemed historical without notable self-consciousness or marketing.

During many trips over the years for graduate and professional work, my early impressions evolved in ways I did not anticipate. By the turn of the twentieth century, the historic downtowns had lost much of their high-end commerce to suburban shopping malls, but heritage-based revitalization programs attempted to restore a sense of place and to beckon affluent customers and tourists. Long dubbed the "land of the future," Brazil suddenly seemed enamored of its past. Where modern development and urban renewal precluded the sort of architectural cohesion of the World Heritage cities, municipal legislation carved out historic districts, most notably in Rio de Janeiro's innovative "Cultural Corridor," begun in about 1980. Similar programs of historic preservation and adaptive reuse followed in other major cities. In all these Old Towns, I noticed the appearance of new cultural centers and commercial establishments catering to the arts and cultural tourism. Although I initially intended this work to chronicle the rise of cultural heritage as a placemaking strategy in several major cities of Brazil, I soon realized that such a large-scale project would exceed the available time and budgetary constraints.

Given the centrality of Rio de Janeiro in Brazilian history, as the former national capital, I soon realized that the "Cidade Maravilhosa" would in itself serve as an excellent site to study memory formation, historic preservation, and urban planning. In 2015, as Rio approached the 450th anniversary of its

Portuguese founding in 1565, issues of historical and collective memory assumed a particular relevance. Rio retains by far the country's largest concentration of national landmarks, along with two UNESCO World Heritage sites. Political events and protests have long taken place at the city's landmarks, including the country's declaration of independence in 1822, abolition of slavery in 1888, and declaration of the republic in 1889. This particular city of memory thus became the platform from which to draw national and international comparisons. While my own observations naturally inform this work, historical-geographical methods deepened this study of preservation planning, urban redevelopment, and environmental heritage. Research methods emphasize visual assessment and photography (contemporary and historical), archival documentation on historic landmarks and public spaces, historical descriptions and images of places, walking tours of historic districts, and conversations with longtime residents. I have interspersed my own recollections of these cities as they evolved with more structured historical research and landscape analysis. In more theoretical terms, Rio also shows the evolution of collective memory from its origins in the preservation of prominent monuments to broader conceptions of historic districts, natural landmarks and threatened environments, and multicultural and low-income communities.

As I immersed myself in the vast literatures on sense of placemaking, memory and heritage, and historic preservation, I saw parallels in global economic restructuring and neoliberal policies. While historic-landmark legislation may go back to the early twentieth century, the rising contemporary popularity and the steady broadening of heritage to incorporate new ethnic, racial, and regional perspectives have been notable. Efforts to revitalize and renovate the deteriorating city centers were widespread by the turn of the millennium, and the transformations underway transfixed Brazilian scholars and institutions. The "cultural turn" in academia made studies of heritage increasingly popular. Naturally, I asked myself what I, as a foreign observer, could contribute to the discussion of the country's cities. Gradually I realized that my perspective as a Brazilianist might add useful elements to ongoing debates. For one thing, the impressive Brazilian scholarship remains largely inaccessible to those outside the country, so my work would make the Portuguese-language literature on cities of Brazil available in English. Furthermore, going back to Alexis de Tocqueville's much-quoted *Democracy in America*, foreign observers may see a country from a comparative perspective and thereby contribute original insights.[2] I hope that this book can add useful perspectives to the ongoing debates on collective memory, heritage, and historic preservation in Brazil and elsewhere.

This project reflects the help of many people and institutions along the way. The Vassar Committee on Research awarded me several grants over the years to carry out field research in Brazil. I received generous grants from the Elinor Nims Brink Fund; a grant from the Frances D. Fergusson Faculty Technology Exploration Fund allowed the purchase of digital boundary files and graphics software to prepare maps; and the Environmental Research Institute funded my project on the environmental heritages of Rio de Janeiro. Most recently, I received a grant from the President's Office to engage a development editor to help me sharpen the focus and condense what had become a sprawling manuscript: Jenny Gavacs gave useful suggestions to strengthen the argument and to reorganize the chapters. At Rowman & Littlefield, editor Susan McEachern has been a pleasure to work with, always friendly, helpful, generous, and amazingly prompt in responding to my inquiries.

I have appreciated the collegiality and insights of colleagues and students, who in different ways have all contributed to this long-term project. At Vassar, special thanks go to Joseph Nevins, Katherine Hite, Leslie Offutt, Tyrone Simpson, Pinar Batur, Sarah Pearlman, Yu Zhou, Mary Ann Cunningham, Kirsten Menking, and my other colleagues in the Earth Science and Geography, Environmental Studies, Latin American and Latinx Studies, and Urban Studies programs. I also benefited from the assistance of dedicated student research assistants over the years: Olivia Arguinzoni, Debra Bergman, Samuel O'Keefe, Sam Thypin-Bermeo, Laurel Walker, Zack Zeilman, and Túlio Zille. Thanks to all!

Conversations with other academic colleagues helped deepen my interests in Brazilian cities, just as their scholarship inspired me. I particularly appreciate the assistance of the late Maurício de Almeida Abreu, historical geographer of Rio de Janeiro; Daniel Arreola of Arizona State University; Colin Crawford of Tulane University; James Freeman of Concordia University; Christopher Gaffney of New York University; James Green of Brown University; anthropologist and photographer Milton Guran in Rio; Lawrence Herzog of San Diego State; Alan Marcus of Towson University; Maureen Hays-Mitchell of Colgate University; Vicente del Rio of Cal Poly, San Luis Obispo; Janice Perlman, a former professor of mine at Berkeley, whose work on favelas inspired me from a young age; Joseph Scarpaci, formerly of Virginia Tech; Betina Schurmann of the Federal University of Brasília; Daryle Williams of the University of Maryland; and Theresa Williamson, founder of Catalytic Communities and editor of the *RioOnWatch* community newspaper. Theresa, a tireless advocate for Rio's favelas, has generously shared her insights over the years. During the summer of 2020, when I could not travel because of the COVID-19 pandemic, *RioOnWatch* provided current information that I could not obtain through planned interviews. The American Geographical Society kindly gave me permission to repurpose parts of an article on Rio's beaches as public space, published originally in the *Geographical Review*.

Over the nearly four decades that I have studied Brazil, I have been personally overwhelmed by the generosity and warmth of many Brasileiros. I fear I that can never adequately repay their kind attentions, though this book is an attempt to do so. Casual conversations and structured interviews with people in the cities studied mounted over the years to the point that I cannot remember all the names. The professional staffs at the archives and libraries of the Noronha Santos Archives of the National Institute of Historic and Artistic Patrimony (IPHAN), the Pereira Passos Institute (IPP/RIO), and the National Library in Rio all generously assisted me in research for this work. I feel particular gratitude to several close Brazilian friends who have helped, inspired, or played other supportive parts in this work. Jurandyr Florentino Miguez proved to be an intrepid explorer of his native city; he hosted many of my visits to Rio and patiently helped me to improve my Portuguese, despite my stubborn resistance to irregular verbs and the genders of words. Carlos Oliveira, Olyntho Resende, Fernando Francelino, Sadakne Biroundi, and other *carioca* friends also made me welcome in the *Cidade Maravilhosa.*

Ultimately, I came to feel that I had to write this book to be true to the many friends, family members, teachers, and institutions to whom I owe so many debts, and of course to Rio de Janeiro, which so beckoned and fascinated me over the years. I heartily thank the individuals and institutions above, and many others whom I cannot remember by name now. Despite their generosity, of course, only I remain responsible for what follows here. Furthermore, I personally translated all subsequent Portuguese-language quotations in this text, unless otherwise noted, so I must be held accountable for these as well.

NOTES

1. Italo Calvino, *Invisible Cities* (New York: Harcourt, 1974), 15–16.
2. Alexis de Tocqueville, *Democracy in America* (New York: J. & H. G. Langley, 1841).

Chapter 1

Uses of Memory

Preserving Whose Rio de Janeiro?

1808. The Royal Family disembarked here.
Rio. The only imperial capital in the Americas.
The City is going to rescue the landscape of this place.

—Commission for the Bicentennial Commemorations of the Arrival of
Dom João and the Royal Family in Rio de Janeiro, 2008[1]

In Rio de Janeiro, founded over 450 years ago and long the national capital, collective memory pervades the cityscape. This historic sense of place has fascinated me since a chance encounter with city branding in early 2008. Walking through November 15th Square (Praça XV), beside the restored Imperial Palace, I came upon a billboard with the proclamation in the epigraph above (see photo 1.1). Sponsored by a civic bicentennial commission, the sign referred to the Portuguese monarchy's arrival in Rio on March 8, 1808, after fleeing Lisbon in the royal fleet, accompanied by a British naval escort, to escape the impending Napoleonic invasion. Along with the royal family came the treasury, a library and printing press, officials and aristocrats, military forces, and other hangers-on. By commemorating this dramatic episode, "the only imperial capital in the Americas" laid claim to the legacies of an empire and the origins of a nation.

The bicentennial program featured the presidents of Brazil and Portugal, who met for a ceremony at Rio's Royal Portuguese Reading Library on March 8, 2008, exactly two centuries after the royal family set foot in the city. Historian José Luis Cardoso noted that "multiple educational, cultural and recreational activities, ranging from the most erudite lectures to the popular parade of samba schools at the Rio Carnival, guaranteed a commemorative program of enormous symbolic importance and undeniable public repercussions."[2] Indeed, the two-hundredth anniversary of the Bragança dynasty's

Photo 1.1. A billboard in downtown Rio announced the bicentennial of the Portuguese monarchy's arrival in 1808: "The City is going to rescue the landscape of this place." Photo by the author.

transatlantic odyssey provided an opportune occasion to reevaluate the legacy of Portuguese rule, rethink the origins of national independence, and reconsider Rio's historic role as a global city. Even if the commemorative events at times smacked of imperial nostalgia, they served the strategic purpose of enhancing the city's long-term status. As M. Christine Boyer aptly notes, "The past, being over and done with, falls prey to invention."[3]

Rio's imperial rebranding program was not just symbolic, but also proposed tangible changes in the urban built form. As the Luso-Brazilian bicentennial campaign proclaimed: "The City is going to rescue the landscape of this place." This nostalgic rhetoric of rescue, commonly deployed to redevelop historic centers, raised questions of causes and consequences—for whom or from what would the cityscape be saved? While the general goal probably centered on reversing the city center's socioeconomic decline and improving its visual appearance, more specific objectives might have been left unstated. One might wonder if street venders and the homeless were to be removed, or if dilapidated buildings were to be renovated? Such goals may have been implicit, but the bicentennial billboard provided clues for the immediate target: at top, the elevated expressway blocked the historic panorama of the bay; below, free of the towering viaduct, the square enjoyed a clear view of the spectacular scene. The juxtaposition of these images suggested that the city's rescue would involve, at least in part, removal of the expressway built between 1956 and 1962, thereby restoring a clear visual connection with Guanabara Bay. Indeed, authorities subsequently embarked on just such a transformation. By the time Rio hosted the Summer Olympics of 2016, the seven-kilometer freeway had disappeared, replaced by an underground tunnel, broad boulevards, and expanded plazas. What began as an evocative visual imaginary "to rescue the landscape of this place" ultimately led to an urban renewal program that transformed Rio's waterfront.

This book examines the uses of memory in reinventing such historic places in Rio. By representing the city's past in its complexity, rather than according to the fictive authenticity of an urban theme park, heritage sites become more fully educational and socially inclusive. Even as cities market their heritage, they still may communicate socioeconomic, cultural, and ethnic solidarity. Taking a critical preservationist stance, I focus on how Rio's sense of place derives from the designation, adaptive reuse, and representation of historic sites. The point is not so much to endorse or take issue with particular narratives of the past, but to enrich our understanding of the city's diverse imaginaries, identities, and places. I ask whose heritage is to be preserved, and why? For a city of memory exists in the present and is subject to current needs and anxieties about the future. As Brian Graham and his colleagues have noted, "Heritage is a view from the present, either backward to a past or forward to a future."[4]

As such, heritage involves historical fact, compelling narrative, and creative reinvention. Despite common assumptions that heritage sites should to be preserved or restored to preexisting states of "authenticity," someone chooses the central historic moment to be commemorated—but who makes the choices? After all, places evolve along with political, economic, and cultural circumstances. As historic cities are reimagined to serve new purposes, memory construction in turn involves periods of continuity interspersed with moments of instability and rupture. Dominant historical representations often gain their strength from the ideological appeals of state institutions and media depictions. When historian Eric Hobsbawm coined the term "invention of tradition," for example, he called attention to the promotion of certain values and norms "to establish continuity with a suitable historic past."[5] In this sense, we need to consider how governmental institutions, international agencies, commercial enterprises, and community groups invent traditions and inscribe places with meaning. Such memory brokers often select compelling place narratives to enhance their own social status, well-being, and identity.

Place memory and built heritage take many forms, but central to them all is the question of who participates and ultimately makes the important decisions. Building on Henri Lefebvre's seminal work on "the right to the city" for all citizens, not just elites, David Harvey famously restated the concept as "not merely a right of access to what already exists, but a right to change it after our heart's desire."[6] Assertion of rights is no panacea, of course, since resulting conflicts still require political resolution, but widespread public participation enhances urban equity and social justice. As a result, Harvey and others have emphasized collective rather than individual rights, along with democratic engagement in the design and use of urban space.[7] This principle of human rights has been widely applied to urban housing, public transit, health care, planning, community-police relations, and other issues. Historic preservation also reflects social status and political-economic power, so I extend the right to the city to include heritage conservation and placemaking: beyond governmental bodies and social elites, ideally citizens should retain collective rights to shape their built heritage, public space, and cultural landscape.

Since heritage sites have been so unevenly distributed, a broadly conceived right to remember can serve social justice by recognizing a variety of historical periods and styles, social strata, and ethnic backgrounds. At first glance, considering remembrance and heritage as human rights may seem like an absurd tautology ("Of course, everyone can remember!") or an unnecessary luxury ("What does it really matter?"). To the first objection, I would reiterate that remembrance does not merely comprise gratuitous mental recollection, but also refers to collective identity and sense of place. In the case of Rio's historic waterfront, for example, heritage-based redevelopment became a tool to reshape the urban landscape. To the second reservation, I would respond that heritage constitutes an essential aspect of human existence: the ability to recognize communities of affinity, based on common bonds, and to appreciate diverse social groups. In fact, although official heritage has long emphasized society's ruling elites, a broadening to include marginalized groups, often seeking to reclaim their imperiled memory and cultural identity, has begun to provide greater social balance around the world.

The right to heritage—*le droit du patrimoine*—has received growing attention as wars and ethnic conflicts have targeted the material culture of adversaries. Emphasizing universal rights to cultural heritage, both the Fribourg Declaration on Cultural Rights and the Council of Europe's Framework Convention on the Value of Heritage for Society have recognized the importance of cultural identity as a basic human need. Yet this right to heritage has proven to be a persistent source of contention and conflict, given the material and symbolic stakes involved. Thus, negotiation among those with different cultural heritages has become increasingly important in contemporary global society. As historian Gabi Dolff-Bonekamper has observed, "While heritage construction goes transnational, heritage preservation and protection still have to be achieved locally. The object will always be located in one place. But whether it is robust or frail, it needs attention, wherever it happens to be."[8]

Rights to heritage can and should play important roles in the construction of urban community, inter-group understanding, and social justice. Rio certainly serves as an excellent study site, given the city's rich array of cultural imaginaries, dramatic historical narratives, alternative counter-memories, and multiple human environments under threat. This book examines whose city has been preserved, by whom, and the consequences for sense of place. Processes of remembrance and heritage, I propose, shape distinctive identities, political conflicts, and place memories in this spectacular but highly unequal megacity. By focusing this study on the city of Rio de Janeiro, the Brazilian past and present also come into view. After all, Rio has by far the country's largest concentration of historic landmarks, boasting 147 federally protected sites—14 percent of the country's total, about as many as the second- and third-ranked cities combined.[9] In my opinion, the world has much to learn from Rio de Janeiro about conserving a historic city, cultural diversity, and urban environments.

Focusing on the origins and uses of Rio's distinctive sense of place, this study examines how, and why, the remembrance of heritage sites and landscapes has come to define the city, and to a significant degree the nation, given Rio's long oversized prominence in Brazil. Of particular importance are the dynamics of historic placemaking: Who has sponsored heritage projects, what have been their impacts, and how have they reflected particular political-economic agendas? Instead of simply taking placemaking narratives at face value, I strive to interrogate them in terms of social promotion and political power. This analytical approach both broadens and differentiates Rio's wide range of heritage projects according to different types of memory and ultimately power relations. I propose that the contemporary city has juxtaposed three different and sometimes conflicting place-based imaginaries:

1. Official historic sites rebrand the city with reference to glorious pasts.
2. Grassroots sites of counter-memory strive for a more inclusive society.
3. Environmental heritage promotes conservation, sustainability, and resilience.

NARRATIVES OF HISTORIC PLACEMAKING

In general terms, *placemaking* refers to the social, spatial, and symbolic processes that give rise to a distinctive sense of place. While the term has now come into vogue, the phenomenon is nothing new. People have long created places through the circulation of narratives, based on group experience, social networks, governmental programs, news media, tourist promotion, and so on. Cultural geographer Michael Curry has explored the ways in which people construct places: naming them, selecting symbols to represent them, telling stories about them, and performing a wide range of rituals and activities within them. If place memory incorporates stories of origin to justify heritage sites and to preserve landmarks, one can refer to this more specifically as "historic placemaking." When state institutions and commercial forces appropriate narratives of place, vernacular styles and local identities may even jump scale to become what Benedict Anderson calls the "imagined communities" of nationalism.[10]

Considering historical narratives of European colonization in the New World, placemaking began as an imperialistic project five centuries ago. The chronicles of Portuguese exploration in South America date from April 1500, when navigator Pedro Alvares Cabral made landfall on the mid-Atlantic coast of Brazil. Cabral began by duly claiming the new lands for Portugal. Since the fleet was on its way to India around South Africa's Cape of Good Hope, perhaps Cabral's expedition was blown off course by prevailing winds and ocean currents. Or possibly Cabral's expedition had some prior knowledge and intended to stop in South America on the way to Asia so as to establish a Portuguese presence along the strategic sea lanes of the South Atlantic. Cabral named the colony "Land of the True Cross" (Terra de Vera Cruz), although it soon became known for its first exploitable resource, Brazil-wood, a valuable source of dyes for European textile production.[11]

The expedition's written account became a notable chronicle of discovery, often called the "founding document" of Brazil. The "Letter of Pedro Vaz de Caminha to King Manuel," dated May 1, 1500, at Porto Seguro, vividly describes the Portuguese encounter with Tupí-Guaraní peoples and environments. From a series of signs by the natives, known on the mid-Atlantic Brazilian coast as Tupinambás, the Portuguese deduced the possibility of finding gold and minerals. The Tupian natives also seemed open to religious conversion, according to Caminha, "because they do not have or understand any belief, as it appears." In a depiction resembling a "Noble Savage" trope, the Tupinambás appeared naked and innocent, as if they lived harmoniously with a bountiful nature. Caminha even admitted coyly that the unclothed native women "were not displeasing to the eye." But central to this vision of Eden were the "very beautiful" lands, lush forests as far as the eye could see, and a "very good climate." Caminha emphasized: "Its waters are quite endless. So pleasing is it that if one cares to profit by it, everything will grow in it because of its waters."[12] Soon images of Brazil as an idyllic tropical paradise began to circulate in Europe.

After Cabral's discoveries, Portugal sent a three-ship squadron to conduct further exploration in 1501–1502, under the command of Gonçalo Coelho. This expedition probably included Italian explorer and cartographer Amerigo Vespucci—Americus Vespucius in Latin—whose name cartographers later attached to the New World in the feminine form of "America." That Europeans could bestow an enduring identity on the Western Hemisphere speaks volumes about the power relations of colonial placemaking. Rio de Janeiro owes its name to an alleged geographical mistake by these early explorers. On January 1, 1502, the three ships arrived at a great bay, which they named Rio de Janeiro (River of January). According to tradition, the mariners mistook the bay's entrance for the mouth of a large river, but commentators have since suggested that it was simply a habit of early Iberian explorers to refer to estuaries and bays as "rivers." Now known as Guanabara Bay—literally "breast of the sea" in the Tupian language—the body of water receives tributary streams, but none very big or navigable. Still, the Portuguese name remained attached to the site. City residents subsequently got their "Carioca" nickname from a native expression for the "White man's house," which a Portuguese sailor apparently built in 1503, after being stranded when the expedition left without him. The city's original source of water, descending from Corcovado Mountain, became known as the Carioca River.

Although Rio's geographic location had been claimed and named by a Portuguese expedition in 1502, actual settlements only materialized decades later, under foreign threat. Initially preoccupied with colonizing the Brazilian Northeast, where sugar cane plantations proved immensely profitable, Portugal was slow to occupy Guanabara Bay. The indigenous peoples there, known locally as Tamoios, proved to be fierce warriors and, like other Tupinambá groups, practiced ritualistic cannibalism of captured adversaries. French forces first won over the Tamoios, who became fierce foes of the Portuguese. King Henry II of France approved a private colonization initiative comprising largely French Huguenots in South America. Led by Admiral Nicolas Durant de Villegagnon, the group established a foothold on Guanabara Bay in 1555, as a base for La France Antarctique. The settlement of Henriville, named after their patron, along with Fort Coligny, grew to some three thousand residents. In response, Portuguese forces under Estácio de Sá attacked and after two years of battle, expelled the French intruders.[13]

Amid these French-Portuguese battles, European perceptions of the native peoples began to shift away from the friendly and innocent depictions of Pedro Vaz de Caminha. The ritualistic cannibalism against rival warriors and occasionally European intruders gave rise to threatening images. In fact, such negative portrayals served to rationalize the conquest and evangelism of the Tupinambás, even as European invasions displaced and infected the indigenous peoples with new diseases. Being treated with an ambivalent mixture of fascination, paternalism, fear, and loathing would become routine among the "others" subjected to Luso-Brazilian colonization—native peoples, Afro-descendant slaves, and dwellers of urban favela communities. In modern Brazil, this submerged counter-memory has encouraged "cannibalist" readings of national culture, a trope dating from works of modernist intellectuals of the 1920s. It rose again with an avant-garde film school known as "New Cinema" (Cinema Novo) during the 1960s: a classic film in this genre is *How Tasty Was My Little Frenchman* (1971), a satire directed by Nelson Pereira dos Santos, which depicts the Tupinambá's capture and cannibalism of a stranded Frenchman.[14] Symbolically, the film can be read as cultural resistance to imperialism through the digestion, recycling, and appropriation of foreign technologies and neocolonialist images. This penchant for counter-narratives of national history goes back to the early Portuguese settlements in Rio and other cities.

The Portuguese colonizers founded São Sebastião do Rio de Janeiro—named for the patron saint as well as the reigning king of Portugal—on March 1, 1565. Rio's initial cramped site was at an improvised fortress on Dogface Hill (Morro Cara de Cão), beside Sugar Loaf Mountain at the entrance to Guanabara Bay. After a prolonged siege, the Portuguese forces expelled the

Figure 1.1. Ground plan of built-up Rio de Janeiro, circa 1812, now the city's historic center. Adapted by the author.

French in January of 1567. The victors transferred their colony to a prominent peninsula with a convenient harbor on the bay's western side (see figure 1.1). Rio's first religious and military institutions arose here on Castle Hill (Morro do Castelo): the Fortress of St. Sebastian, Jesuit churches and schools, the city jail, and other structures. Early Rio de Janeiro's hills featured irregular, winding streets adapted to the steep topography, but the lower-lying areas were more regular in their ground plans. While more or less linear, the lower city's streets accommodated the topography—not strictly rectilinear as in the gridiron pattern favored by Spain in the Americas. As Maurício Abreu has argued, colonial Rio did not follow formal plans, like those of the Spanish "Laws of the Indies," but the practice of laying out streets goes back to the city's origins, directed by the Portuguese governors, "according to modern urban norms, but not too rigidly, which some authors now call 'Portuguese urbanism.'"[15]

In fact, urban historians have often contrasted the colonial cities of Brazil unfavorably with the more regular Spanish-American forms. Historian Robert C. Smith famously argued: "The Portuguese discoverers and early colonists were men of the Renaissance, but as town planners they belonged to the Middle Ages. Continuously they rejected the regular gridiron plan that came to Europe with the Renaissance and to America with the Spanish conquerors."[16] Smith held that Portugal projected a less centrally planned pattern for overseas settlements, since the kingdom had fewer resources, a smaller population, and a stronger orientation toward profitable commerce than land colonization. Sérgio Buarque de Holanda's classic *Raizes do Brasil* (Brazilian Roots) similarly emphasized Portugal's prevailing commercial motivation for exploration and the irregularity of city forms in Brazil, as opposed to the Castilian focus on conquest and colonization. Given the initial Portuguese emphasis on maritime trade, the first wave of colonial towns in Brazil, such as Rio de Janeiro, featured sites with sheltered harbors and prominent hills for defensive fortification.[17]

Satisfying these requirements, colonial Rio de Janeiro proceeded to expand in an orderly but adaptive fashion, set among several high hills and Guanabara Bay. Growth was greatest in the lower city, where development intensified near the port's main landing on Palace Square—the city's main center of administration, commerce, and social life. While defense against attacks by the French and Dutch prompted new fortifications during the eighteenth century, gradually an open city prevailed as settlement extended along the waterfront and in low-lying areas.[18] Still, Castle Hill long dominated Guanabara Bay's spectacular tableau. An English visitor, Lieutenant Henry Chamberlain, enthused in 1819 or 1820: "It is impossible to describe the Variety, the Beauty, or the Magnificence of the Prospects from almost every part of this Hill, which commands uninterrupted Views of the City and Shipping, the Bay and its numerous islands as far as the Organ Mountains. Nothing surely can exceed them!"[19]

The eighteenth-century gold and diamond boom in the inland region of Minas Gerais (General Mines) created vast new riches, which increased Portuguese oversight, stimulated urban growth and planning, and encouraged more regular city forms. These efforts intensified under the Marquis of Pombal, the dominant minister from 1750 to 1777, who led the rebuilding of Lisbon after the devastating earthquake of 1755. The Pombaline emphasis on mercantile trade and baroque architecture echoed back and forth across the Atlantic Ocean, as the mining wealth permitted the beautification of urban design, formal squares, and administrative buildings. Skilled artisans and artists—most famously, Antônio Francisco Lisboa, or "Aleijadinho" (circa 1730–1814)—crafted extraordinary sculpture, painting, and architecture in baroque churches. This tendency toward urban embellishment was not simply aesthetic, but reflected the rise of Portuguese political absolutism, commercial aspirations, and Enlightenment philosophies in eighteenth-century Brazil. Although several routes served to export the mineral riches, the Portuguese crown favored the passage through Rio de Janeiro so as to monitor more closely the export of gold and later of diamonds. In 1763, the improved political-economic situation and urban growth prompted the transfer of the colonial capital from Salvador to Rio. As geographer Preston James once noted: "Gold made Rio de Janeiro, as surely as sugar made São Salvador and Recife and, as later, coffee made São Paulo."[20]

The Bragança dynasty's hasty migration from Lisbon to Rio de Janeiro in 1807–1808, after fleeing the Napoleonic invasion of Portugal, transformed colonial Brazil. The arriving royal family included Queen Maria I, who had been declared insane in 1792; Prince Regent Dom João, later crowned King João VI; his Spanish-born wife, Carlota Joaquina; and their sons Pedro and Miguel and six daughters. Rio also received an influx of Portuguese refugees for whom the city was ill prepared. The in-migration included thousands of nobles, officials, attendants, and others. After the initial festivities to welcome the new residents, Rio faced a severe housing shortage. The crown decreed that the arriving Portuguese nobles could seize the homes of local residents. These colonial masters firmly held the "right to the city." In an early historical case of gentrification and displacement, the infamous "PR" (which stood for the ruling prince regent) painted on confiscated homes became an eviction notice derisively known by local residents as "get yourself out into the street" (*ponha-se na rua*).[21]

Rio de Janeiro had a population of about 60,000 to 70,000 (about a fifth of it enslaved) by the time of the monarchy's arrival, as compared to 180,000 in Lisbon. Late-colonial Brazil had already surpassed Portugal in economic importance, however, and soon after his arrival the prince regent ended centuries of mercantilism by opening Brazilian ports to foreign trade. The sudden role reversal remade a sleepy outpost into the nerve center of a far-flung world empire scattered across four continents. Seemingly overnight, Rio became a teeming city, where diverse groups, social classes, and races interacted with various degrees of accommodation and conflict. After authorities opened the port to international trade, the influx of foreign goods mounted. In the early 1820s, Maria Graham, an English visitor, stated: "Most of the streets are lined with English goods: at every door the words *London superfine* meets the eye: printed cottons, broad clothes, crockery, but above all, hardware from

Birmingham, are to be had little dearer than at home, in the Brazilian shops, besides silks, crapes, and other articles from China."[22]

Amid the uncertainties of a city in flux, power geometries of social status and cultural difference strained the early nineteenth-century city. As Luciana Martins and Maurício Abreu have argued, "Members of the Portuguese nobility, the existing Brazilian elite, European immigrants, freepersons and slaves used and interpreted the spaces of the city in different ways."[23] The Portuguese king's tropical idyll fostered resentments among the Brazilian subjects, particularly local elites, who grew increasingly dissatisfied with their treatment as second-class citizens and confiscation of the better residences by members of the royal court. Local merchants resented the competition of British, French, and other immigrant merchants. The burgeoning city experienced a wave of popular resentment and protest, which anticipated a recurrent historical pattern of urban displacement and social conflict.

"CIVILIZING" RIO THROUGH URBAN DESIGN

Besides setting in motion events that ultimately led to Brazilian independence, the Portuguese sovereign's thirteen-year overseas move remade the imperial capital. While formal urban plans began earlier during the late eighteenth century, the discourse and practice of urban "civilization" arrived in full force with the royal family. As historian Nireu Cavalcanti has noted, late colonial cities modeled "civilized" behavior in Brazil: "To urbanize meant to make urban, to civilize."[24] With the presence of the royal court, Rio served as a cultural hearth for elite aspirations during a time of political transition. Alternatively called a "New Rome" and a "tropical Versailles," the imperial city witnessed increasing attention to urban design with a flurry of new projects. Although efforts to "civilize" and "discipline" the city are often traced to the massive urban renewal of the early twentieth century, in fact an increasing formalism of urban design arose during the late-colonial and early-imperial periods.[25]

By the time of the royal family's residence in Rio, the settlement's core had shifted from the initial stronghold on Castle Hill to the low-lying commercial and residential areas near the port. From this central area, the city spread beyond the four hills that had long bounded the city—Hills of the Castle, Saint Benedict (São Bento), Saint Anthony (Santo Antônio), and the Conception (Conceição). Rio's population increased greatly during the royal stay. With the end of mercantilist restrictions and opening of commerce to foreign trade in 1808—a move favored by British allies—the prince regent in 1815 renamed his realm the United Kingdom of Portugal, Brazil, and the Algarves. Writing in about 1820, Henry Chamberlain described Rio as growing vigorously: "Since the arrival of the Royal Family from Portugal, in 1808, new buildings have started up along the water's edge, and indeed in all directions where the ground is favourable, so that the City now extends on every side much beyond the limits before mentioned." Chamberlain added, "The Population is not accurately known, but may perhaps be taken at about 120,000, including Blacks."[26]

The natural panorama of Rio de Janeiro, with its sweeping views of a vast protected bay, sandy beaches, and luxuriant green mountains, has long enraptured visitors. Yet the colonial city seemed unworthy of nature's bounty to some observers. Writing later in the 1930s through a modernist lens on urban progress, Luiz Edmundo opined: "The ugly houses and the narrow dirty streets made a blot on the surrounding landscape."[27] This sentiment must have been widespread, as late colonial authorities made concerted efforts to beautify Rio through formal city planning and architectural design. Living in Rio from 1821 to 1825, Bavarian painter Rugendas applauded these efforts: "In truth, the current government works with great activity in beautifying the city and its buildings, but not without great difficulties, as everywhere it becomes necessary to skip rocks and to open new streets and wharves to give more regularity than now exists."[28] A concern with formal urban design became increasingly apparent in the greater regularity of urban squares and building façades.

After the death of the unstable queen mother in 1816, João VI's coronation occasioned a memorable civic celebration. Jean-Baptiste Debret's painting *View of the Palace Square, the Day of the Acclamation of Dom João VI* depicted the pageantry-filled event on February 6, 1818. Debret served as a court painter in France, and his monarchist stance no doubt influenced his sympathetic portrait of the Portuguese king. In his magisterial *Voyage Pittoresque et Historique au Brésil*, Debret recounted that the monarch—after serving for so many years as prince regent—appeared on a balcony to greet the people and receive tributes from the assembled dignitaries, before proceeding to the royal chapel to be formally crowned. Although protected by platoons of infantry and cavalry in the large crowd, according to Debret, the military presence did not fully reassure the king. The painter suggested that "the king feared the explosion of some popular movement, fueled by the Portuguese malcontent, resentful of his long stay in Brazil, despite the promise that he would return to Lisbon immediately after the conclusion of general peace."[29]

On becoming the king of Portugal, Brazil, and the Algarves, Dom João resisted insistent calls for his return to Lisbon. The monarch preferred life in Rio, but he finally relented when threatened with the loss of his Portuguese crown by the Liberal Revolution of 1820. Queen Carlota Joaquina, often at odds with the king, left separately with their daughters on April 21, 1821. Debret's painting *The Departure of the Queen for Portugal*, set on the waterfront of Palace Square, depicted the crowds assembled to see her off. The artist acknowledged the queen's widely known frustration at being relegated to distant Brazil for so long, away from the courts of Europe. On the parapets of the port, the stony silence of the Brazilians contrasted with the lively emotion of the Portuguese sailors and soldiers, who also longed to return to their European homeland. In a show of her dislike for Brazil, the queen triumphantly screamed: "I'm finally going to be in a country inhabited by men!"[30]

For his part, King João allegedly advised his eldest son and heir to the throne, "Pedro, I fear that Brazil might separate itself from Portugal; if so, place the crown on your head rather than allow it to fall into the hands of an adventurer."[31] Departing Rio for Lisbon on April 25, 1821, the king left Pedro to rule Brazil as regent. The crown prince, in turn, later refused to leave his adopted land and with this decision to stay, he declared Brazil independent on September 7, 1822. After quickly defeating loyalist forces, Pedro I became the first emperor of Brazil on October 12, 1822. As a result, Brazil emerged as an independent country without the prolonged and bloody revolutionary wars experienced elsewhere in the Americas. The preexisting colonial administration and elite classes generally stayed in place after independence, while most of the population remained illiterate, enslaved, or impoverished. Without a rupture of the social hierarchy or international dependencies, a neocolonial structure and mentality continued intact during nineteenth-century Brazil.

Opinions have diverged on the fledgling city of Rio during this period. Chronicler Luiz Edmundo bemoaned "the old colonial capital, sad and dirty in those days, far different from the clean, modern and beautiful city of Rio de Janeiro of today."[32] English lady Maria Graham, on the other hand, visiting in 1821–1823, was favorably impressed: "The city of Rio is more like a European city than either Bahia or Pernambuco; the houses are three or four stories high, with projecting roofs, and tolerably handsome."[33] Bavarian painter Johann Moritz Rugendas, who lived in the city during the early 1820s, applauded the city's increasing orderliness: "In the old part of the City the streets are straight and regular; they are cut at right angles and almost all are paved and provided with sidewalks."[34] A view from São Bento church and monastery, which Rugendas painted from 1820 to 1825, shows a lively public space with a cosmopolitan crowd of military personnel, wealthy ladies, foreign merchants, street venders, and others (see figure 1.2).

During the First and Second Empires (1822–1889), elites continued to emulate European styles. After a bitter dispute with his cabinet in 1831, Pedro I abdicated and returned to Portugal. He left behind in Brazil his son and heir, five-year-old Pedro de Alcântara, with regents to govern until Pedro II reached

Figure 1.2. View of Rio de Janeiro from São Bento Hill, by Johann Moritz Rugendas, c.1820–1825.

adulthood in 1840. As coffee surpassed sugar as the country's major export, Rio, São Paulo, and other gateway cities grew steadily. New systems of transportation and communication—the railroad, steamship, and telegraph—favored such cities as centers of foreign investment with their own regional hinterlands. Additionally, improved urban services made the leading cities images of modernity, which attracted both foreign immigrants and regional in-migrants from the interior. Amid such modernizing influences, the abolition of slavery in 1888 weakened the tottering monarchy and aristocratic order.

After the monarchy's fall in 1889, a republican government emblazoned its ideology of "Order and Progress" on the new national flag. Although Brazil remained economically dependent on cash crops (sugar, coffee, rubber, and other primary commodities), the new regime sought to eliminate vestiges of the colonial past: to be "civilized" now meant to follow the aesthetic sensibilities and industrial standards of Europe and North America. As David Underwood has observed, fin de siècle Rio de Janeiro "was a city marked by its commercial and cultural dependency on Europe: a society dominated by its infatuation with French fashion, by its lust for British capital, and by the inferiority complex of the Brazilian elite, who continued to prefer London and Paris to their own cities."[35] Indeed, Rio's republican elites considered their capital city backward, lagging behind rival Buenos Aires, and in need of massive redevelopment.

THE "LAND OF THE FUTURE" DISCOVERS ITS PAST

Although federal landmark legislation dates from the 1930s in Brazil, only in the 1980s did cultural and built heritage become widely popular, as evidenced by the appearance of World Heritage sites and local heritage programs. Rio de Janeiro began an influential public-private program of historic preservation known as the "Cultural Corridor" program during the 1980s, for example, which popularized heritage-based programs of urban revitalization. This heightened concern with public history and remembrance reflected a significant broadening of national discourse. Previously, the country's aspirations centered primarily on economic development and modernization. The past long seemed like a colonial legacy of underdevelopment, while the future of a country with such abundant natural resources surely promised greatness—*grandeza!* The conception of Brazil as a country of the future with a still unrealized potential dates from at least 1941, when expatriate Austrian writer Stefan Zweig, who fled Europe during the rise of Hitler, published his famous *Brazil: A Land of the Future.*[36]

After reviewing the history, economy, and culture of Brazil, the book recounts a travelogue through the vast interior, the stunning landscapes of Rio, the progress of São Paulo, and the colonial mining towns of Minas Gerais. Zweig depicted his adopted country as a fertile tropical land of rich resources, refreshingly free from ethnic prejudice, and a "new type of civilization." In Zweig's view, "the country is only at the beginning of its development. Brazil's importance for the coming generations cannot be assessed even by the most daring calculations."[37] The book's outlook verges on utopian in its portrayal of a country with countless possibilities, a model of racial harmony, a peace-loving refuge from the global hostilities of World War II. Despite his optimistic view of Brazil, the state of the world weighed heavily on Zweig, particularly with the spread of Nazism. On February 23, 1942, he and his wife committed suicide in the Brazilian city of Petrópolis.

Along with Zweig's impassioned book, the rise of Brazilian modern art and architecture also emphasized an optimistic future, which culminated in the spectacular design by Lúcio Costa and Oscar Niemeyer of the central "Pilot Plan" of Brasília, inaugurated in 1960 and the current national capital. While the federal protection of national historic and artistic patrimony began during the 1930s, official heritage long remained primarily the domain of elites, intellectuals, and governmental institutions. While the growing popularity of cultural heritage generally accompanied international trends, it faced the authoritarian restrictions of a military regime (1964–1985), before benefiting from a democratic transition. Given this political context, urban analysis long stressed social criticism, policy diagnosis, and spatial inequality rather than questions of urban form, history, and preservation. As John Dickenson once argued: "Driven perhaps by political expediency and a predilection for the 'new' geography of the 1970s, Brazilian geographers have treated their cities as places without form or history."[38]

By the turn of the millennium, this situation changed significantly. Following Rio's Cultural Corridor, ambitious programs to renovate historic city centers spread widely. Heritage tourism emerged as means of urban reinvention and economic development under neoliberal regimes. As the urban past became a resource for development programs, international agencies made heritage conservation a source of funding. Indeed, the contemporary quest for heritage stresses historic cities: bookstores carry photographic volumes of changing cityscapes, magazines run regular columns on *memória da cidade*, academic panels analyze urban history, governments rush to create historic districts, community groups struggle to protect venerable buildings and open spaces, and developers renovate deteriorated mansions, warehouses, factories, military bases, and waterfronts into historically themed commercial or residential spaces.[39] As Maurício Abreu observed in 1998:

> After a long period of cultivating only the new, resulting in a constant and systematic attack on the legacies of former times, we now find everyday urban life in Brazil pervaded by speeches and projects preaching the restoration, the preservation, or the revalorization of the most diverse vestiges of the past. The justification invariably presented is the need to preserve "urban memory."[40]

The rival claims of the past, present, and future have long been contested in Rio. Not only has the past been present in this venerable city, but the lengthy tenure as national capital made it a model for the latest trends in architecture and urban renewal. In his *Rio de Janeiro: Carnival under Fire*, journalist Ruy Castro acknowledges the city's enduring "stockpile of memory" and "embrace of the past," but he also points to a long-term infatuation with modernism. "The presence of the past might have been more all-embracing," he argues, "were it not for the mania of Brazilians—an eternally 'young' nation, frivolous and playful—for despising everything that's more than fifteen years old." The contemporary preference has often been to efface historical styles and embrace new modern designs. During the two centuries as the Brazilian national capital, Rio was subject to the dictates of the federal government, which even appointed the mayor. With each change of political regime, Rio experienced "a thorough reform so that the new rulers could show their own style off. Almost always, this meant demolishing the past."[41]

The untimely burning of the National Museum at Rio's Quinta da Boa Vista on September 2–3, 2018, reportedly from an electrical fire in the decrepit wiring, sadly supports Castro's argument. An avoidable tragedy resulting from years of neglect and budget cutting, the fire spread quickly as firefighters found local hydrants without water. Over two centuries old, the imposing Palace of Saint Christopher was an imperial residence under the monarchy and became a public museum after the proclamation of the republic in 1889. With its world-class collections of natural history, archeology, and linguistics, the National Museum has long been a leading center for postgraduate studies in social anthropology and botany. Besides the tragic losses in the collections, just as important may be the institutional loss of national history and cultural heritage. Seduced by such shiny new modernist structures as the Museum of Tomorrow, leaders virtually ignored such core institutions as the National Museum. To many Brazilians, the museum's disastrous fire symbolized the country's decay amid a prolonged economic recession and political crisis.[42] It would be unfair, however, to let this tragic episode obscure the keen public interest in heritage conservation. In fact, the widespread anguish over losses at the National Museum attests to a commitment to protect and maintain historic monuments.

A turning point in attitudes toward the past became evident in 2001–2002, when the City Archives sponsored an exhibition, "Memory of Destruction: Rio—A History of What Was Lost (1889–1965)." With an impressive array of historical photographs, newspaper reports, political cartoons, and architectural and urban plans, the exhibition documented the destructive side of urban renewal. By so vividly displaying "the principal urban interventions carried out by public power and the real-estate speculation that afflicted the physiognomy of the city," this exhibition made pointed criticisms of urban renewal's destructive effects. Accompanied by a printed catalogue, the exhibition became a major event, attended by public figures, academics, and concerned citizens. The dominant emotion was a sadness for "what was lost," including fin de siècle destruction of downtown tenements, the city's birthplace on Castle Hill in the 1920s, the former congressional building at Monroe Palace in 1975, and of course favela communities in the way of urban redevelopment. That the city government would sponsor such a sharp critique, after previously collaborating in large-scale destruction in the name of planning and progress, spoke to a significant shift in dominant attitudes, if not always in official policy. While recognizing the ongoing need for change in dynamic cities, the exhibition asked the big question: What should be preserved in an iconic Brazilian city like Rio?[43]

Given Rio's long history, dynamic multiculturalism, and stunning environmental setting, I long wondered why the United Nations Educational, Scientific, and Cultural Organization (UNESCO) had never approved a World Heritage site in the city. In 2012, "Carioca Landscapes between the Mountain and the Sea" joined the World Heritage list. This site features a series of famous sites—Tijuca National Park, the Botanical Garden, Flamengo Park, the entry to Guanabara Bay, and Copacabana Beach—and "includes all the best view points to appreciate the way nature has been shaped to become a significant cultural part of the city."[44] Rio's second UNESCO World Heritage site recognizes a tragic heritage—remnants of the transatlantic slave trade, rediscovered at the buried site of Valongo Wharf in early 2011. Long forgotten or ignored, the preservation of this historic site became a cause célèbre among civil-rights activists and spiritual groups, along with supportive archeologists and the public at large. In 2017, UNESCO listed the Valongo Wharf Archaeological Site, called "the most important physical trace of the arrival of African slaves on the American continent," where about a million enslaved Africans arrived during the early nineteenth century.[45]

These World Heritage designations underscored the need to conserve Rio's cultural landscapes, which continuing urbanization has long assaulted. The city reached a population of about 6.7 million in 2019, representing slightly over half of the 13.3 million residents of the metropolitan region, comprising twenty municipalities and covering 1,809 square miles (4,686 km^2).[46] With Rio's breathtaking panoramas of land and water, dense historic districts, steep residential hillsides, and towering tropical forests and mountains, it ranks among the world's most scenic places. Rio's social geographies, however, reflect entrenched socioeconomic disparities of wealth and poverty. Affluent southern districts like Copacabana and Ipanema signal relatively high social status, while informal communities of self-built housing known as *favelas*, reflect concentrated poverty and institutional marginalization (see figure 1.3). Amid the city's remarkable human diversity, the poor are predominantly people of color, and racial differences largely coincide with patterns of uneven development, employment, social status, and resident and environmental amenities. As a result, many residents live in gritty urban settings where concerns about security, public housing, and urban services persist, as reported in the news media and in popular films.

This discrepancy between the city's magnificent surroundings and its urban poverty goes back to colonial times. In *Rio in the Time of the Viceroys*, historian Luiz Edmundo lamented this disparity: "What a contrast between that old city and the natural beauty in the midst of which it stood!"[47] The contemporary city begs the question of how much has changed, since environmental degradation continues to this day. Still, Rio's past has proven a source of civic pride, heritage tourism, and cultural reinvention. The awakening of memory has served as a strategy of regeneration amid concerns about civic decline. After a prolonged dominance of modern redevelopment, the past has now become an alternative resource for urban reinvention, place memory, and contemporary identity. While Rio's heritage now constitutes

Figure 1.3. Map of metropolitan Rio de Janeiro. By the author.

cultural capital for a strategy of historic placemaking in an aspiring world city, it would be a mistake to consider only the top-down marketing perspective of urban elites: the impacts of memory have been much broader and more complex. Collective memory has served the interests of the "urban growth machine," as evidenced by heritage tourism and mega-events, but the past has also become a source of counter-memory for grassroots organizing around issues of sustainability, environmental conservation, and social justice.

The growing interest in Rio's heritage has been evident, for example, in the popular "Geographic Itineraries" (Roteiros Geográficos), open to the public, led by Professor João Baptista Ferreira de Mello of the Geography Department at the State University of Rio de Janeiro (UERJ). Offered since 2001, these free walking tours have stressed the "defense of the City of Rio de Janeiro" through programs of participatory heritage education. From my personal experience in participating in several of these walking tours, attendance

Photo 1.2. A walking tour of the Salt Point historic site, considered the birthplace of the samba, led by Professor João Baptista Ferreira de Mello of the Geography Department at the State University of Rio de Janeiro, on July 22, 2017. His free walking tours of notable districts, offered since 2001, have grown steadily in attendance and suggest an increasing interest in Rio's historic places. Photo by the author.

has always included scores of participants, primarily Cariocas interested in learning more about their city's colorful past, cultural landscapes, and diverse historic districts (see photo 1.2). Over the years, Professor Ferreira de Melo has regularly offered about a dozen daytime walks, including "Getting to Know Downtown by Foot," "Cathedrals of Rio de Janeiro," "Order and Progress in Republican Rio," "The Routes of Women in the City," and most recently "Valongo Wharf, History of Black Suffering." In 2009, the program began offering nighttime tours, both to attract working people and to counter images of nocturnal insecurity. Evening itineraries have included "Walking among the Lights of Downtown Rio," "Copacabana, Princess of the Sea," "Memory and Metamorphoses of the Downtown Hills," and "Walking the Black Geographies of Downtown Rio." As implicit exercises in the "right to the city" through active remembrance, these city walks have not experienced a single robbery or assault over the years, according to the professor, thereby demonstrating the value of public presence in the city.[48]

Such educational walks contribute to historic placemaking—a multifaceted phenomenon that may involve preservation, branding, remembrance, and reinvention. Although professionals and international agencies differentiate among types of heritage management, commonly accepted principles have been summarized by the Burra Charter, adopted by the Australian chapter of the International Council on Monuments and Sites (ICOMOS). The most encompassing term is *conservation*, defined as "all the processes of looking after a place so as to retain its cultural significance."[49] While *heritage conservation* is the preferred term in Europe, *historic preservation* prevails in the United States. Both terms refer to the renovation and adaptive reuse of heritage sites, including historic buildings, public spaces, landmarks, and other built forms. In this book, I extend this concept of historic preservation to include the defense of people, places, and environments in need of protection.

MEMORY, PRESERVATION, AND HERITAGE

"Memoria" was a classical muse who pointed to society's existence in time. Beginning in the late nineteenth century, modernist thinkers emphasized memory's importance in forging nationalism and social identity. During the contemporary "memory boom," theorists have taken on such issues as genocide, holocaust, human rights, historic preservation, and globalization. The global rise in public and academic interest in memory since the 1980s has also been explained in terms of multiculturalism, postmodernity, the fall of Communism, new information technologies, and so on.[50] Former clear boundaries between official history and subjective memory have eroded as scholars, following the seminal works of Michel Foucault, have implicated institutions of power in the construction of knowledge and thereby questioned long-standing assumptions of linear historical progress, objectivity, and truth. Furthermore, as the academic field of history has broadened its purview from official documents to other phenomena, social memory has become another form of evidence alongside more traditional sources. Jeffrey Olick and Joyce Robbins note that "memory frequently employs history in its service: professional historians have often provided political legitimation and other more reconstructive identity struggles."[51]

Historic cities embody layers of time, which often relegate relics of the past to obscurity in the changing cityscape; or, elevated by memorialization or heritage conservation, they become monuments of collective memory. Although it is obviously individuals who remember, social and spatial relations inevitably inform people's memories. French sociologist Maurice Halbwachs (1877–1945), who formulated the concept of "collective memory," rejected the individual emphases of Freudian psychology and argued that family, religion, ethnicity, class, and other group relations mold one's recollections. He maintained that "collective memory endures and draws its strength from its base in a coherent body of people." Although some critics have claimed that this perspective downplays individual variation, Halbwachs maintained that "there is no universal memory. Every collective memory requires the support of a group delimited in space and time."[52] Similarly, the word "memory" connotes collective social association with regard to remembrance. Memories persist insofar as they derive from shared traditions, images, landmarks, and places. Indeed, built environments and social spaces—the buildings and streets, public squares, and other spatial elements—provide a material continuity that promotes heritage and memory. As Halbwachs put it, "Thus, every collective memory unfolds within a spatial framework. Now space is a reality that endures: since our impressions rush by, one after another, and leave nothing behind in the mind, we can understand how we recapture the past only by understanding how it is, in effect, preserved by our physical surroundings."[53]

With the global rise of cultural tourism, controversies arise about the uses of the past: Whose heritage is to be conserved? On close inspection, this very terminology requires clarification. UNESCO defines heritage as "our legacy from the past, what we live with today, and what we pass on to future generations. . . . What makes the concept of World Heritage exceptional is its universal application."[54] While this definition captures the prevailing official attitudes toward heritage management, it tends to simplify and naturalize "our legacy from the past" as a fixed inheritance rather than recognizing the extent to which institutions continually reinvent public history and tradition to suit their purposes. As Andreas Huyssen has put it, "Inevitably, every act of memory carries with it a dimension of betrayal, forgetting, and absence."[55]

This selectivity of memory, which involves both remembrance and forgetfulness, reflects the politics of identity. Whose heritage deserves to be preserved and commemorated? Who has, or should have, the right of remembrance? Who makes the decisions about the protection of historic sites and cultural environments? Such questions point to the political dimensions of memory, which are central to the study of heritage, monuments and memorials, places of memory, cultural landscapes, and other public symbols. Since the late nineteenth century, heritage has served as a tool of nation-states. But this concept may be deployed on a variety of other scales—local, city, regional, global. Indeed, the contemporary "memory boom" has become associated with collective trauma and human rights, frequently at odds with hegemonic nationalism. Because global cities become icons of identity, their heritage conservation or destruction also reveals the dynamics of power.

With the rise of neoliberalism in the late twentieth century, public-private partnerships and business-improvement districts came into vogue and brought new possibilities for the financing and management of historic districts.

Christine Boyer argues that commercial interests and their visual marketing technologies appropriate architectural history to create a nostalgic "City of Collective Memory," which favors a historicized consumer experience that "is itself an incomplete and impoverished picture that can be sustained only by inventing traditions and narrative stories that it calls to its support." Selectively referencing landscape imagery through appropriation of historical styles and design elements, the sites fragment our sense of space and time. Historic preservation reflects a crisis of memory, she argues, reflected in "the migration of history into advertising and the nostalgia industry."[56]

While historic preservation may assume the disinterested guise of a moral crusade by enlightened citizens, the politics of heritage reveal varying degrees of concern with prestige, social status, and self-interest. In theoretical terms, this insight highlights the importance of understanding the leading preservationists and other power brokers, whose imaginaries have guided the reinvention of places. Our contemporary cultural lenses and social contexts also filter collective memory, rendering problematic common assertions of authenticity in heritage debates. As a society protects one heritage site, it ignores others. In preserving a particular built heritage, we erase other vestiges of the past: a historic district alludes primarily to a particular architectural style, social or ethnic history, or event—but not others. In fact, every cultural landscape simultaneously reveals some things while it obscures others. Indeed, collaborative partnerships often create jarring paradoxes of inclusion and exclusion in heritage sites. Authorities may celebrate a particular kind of heritage, while those excluded may contest the official boundaries of a people or place. This phenomenon helps to explain why urban revitalization remains so uneven, and heritage tourism has not yet succeeded in broadening the economic base sufficiently to benefit much of the population.

Contemporary scholars have shown how historic preservation essentially constitutes a negotiation among stakeholders about the meanings and uses of heritage in particular sites. Despite the frequent invocation of historical "accuracy," powerful individuals, social forces, and institutions "author" preserved places, landscapes, and built heritage. The search for the "authentic" past proves ultimately fruitless: institutionalization of heritage inevitably involves subjective interpretation, cultural perception, and political power. As Diane Barthel has noted, collective memory "does not emerge simply, naturally, from history. Rather it is shaped by status groups who become society's preservationists and whose efforts to save heritage sites or artifacts often assume the character of symbolic crusades."[57] Through historic preservation, these "symbolic bankers" work to harness, perpetuate, and manipulate the cultural capital of favored times and places. By promoting selected narratives, memory brokers may hope to enhance their social or financial status.

These memory brokers benefit from heritage promotion in various ways—altruism may be evident, but the enhancement of group status and material benefit cannot be ignored. Since the creation of heritage also implies the erasure of unwanted elements of the past, social competition highlights underlying motivations of prestige and material benefit. Understanding group self-interest and perception also helps to explain what periods and styles are deemed worthy of preserving. But we must also consider urban political economy to understand the uses of collective memory. Grassroots citizen groups may begin campaigns to preserve landmarks and historic districts; heritage-based programs have become attractive development strategies in contemporary entrepreneurial cities. Pro-growth coalitions may even form around historic preservation to create veritable "heritage machines," leading to commodification of venerable architectures, landmarks, and districts. Nostalgic images of a city's past often become centerpieces of campaigns for urban renaissance, focused on the potential for architectural renovation, adaptive reuse, and profit of long-declining districts.

Such nostalgic memory is often more than mere sentimentality: it becomes a critique of the present and a tool to shape the future. Literary theorist Svetlana Boym suggests that nostalgia is not just retrospective mourning for a lost past, but also becomes prospective about future possibilities. "The fantasies of the past, determined by the needs of the present, have a direct impact on the realities of the future," she suggests. "The consideration of the future makes us take responsibility for our nostalgic tales." Boym proposes two alternative general types of nostalgia. Restorative nostalgia attempts a return to a lost home, a place of truth and tradition, corrupted by the onset of modernity. Restorative narratives, therefore, involve "the return to origins and the conspiracy," which become fodder for national, ethnic, and religious revivals and even xenophobic persecution of those considered outsiders. Boym characterizes reflective nostalgia, in contrast, as broadminded, pluralistic, and curious about "the ambivalences of human belonging," and refusing to "shy away from the contradictions of Modernity."[58] Rather than bemoan social change and escape into restorative fantasies, a reflective approach explores times and places with curiosity, equanimity, and open-mindedness.

The creation of cultural heritage cannot be reduced to the simple rediscovery of a primordial past: it inevitably involves political debate, negotiation, and accommodation. Rival claims tend to be couched in terms of various narratives of the past—with alternative beginnings, chronological storylines, definitive endings, and moral conclusions. This perspective usefully broadens the understanding of heritage by highlighting how various stories compete in the formulation of historical narratives of place. The politics of place ultimately affects which historic tableau is commemorated, taught in schools, and accorded widespread visual representation in photography, television and film, museum exhibitions, and other arts and design. Places are seldom designed in the first instance as memorials, but over time they may become important places of collective memory. Through their preservation, these historic centers become visual monuments of the past and important sources of national, regional, ethnic, and other sources of identity. The process of heritage conservation thus provides a window on cultural politics and governance.

APPROACHING PLACE MEMORY AND IDENTITY

From a critical perspective on cultural and historical geography, I suggest that collective memory serves present-day purposes: heritage programs alternately maintain or contest the status quo, depending on their respective social standings and political alliances. Readings on historic preservation emphasize the roles of influential leaders, architects, and stakeholders in reclaiming an "authentic" built heritage, but this search usually proves very subjective. Far better, in my opinion, is an emphasis on power relations and social statuses, which help to explain the proliferation, differentiation, and appropriation of the city's imaginaries. After all, diverse narratives have continually reinvented Rio de Janeiro over the centuries, generally promoted by representatives of elite society and supported by the state apparatus, while counter-memories increasingly voice calls for social change and environmental conservation. The city vividly illustrates the interplay of historical, cultural, and environmental heritages.

This project springs from the academic fields of cultural and historical geography, buttressed by interdisciplinary links to history, memory studies, political economy, and urban studies. The study is "critical" in that it interprets historic preservation not simply in aesthetic or cultural terms, but with regard to political-economic power and social status. In terms of its intellectual history, cultural-historical geography initially arose with a focus on human-environmental impacts; origins and diffusion of plants, animals, and human artifacts; and the historical geography of places and regions. As exemplified by the influential work of Carl O. Sauer, early study sites were largely rural and relatively isolated in Latin America or the US West.[59] But as societies become more urbanized and heterogeneous, geographers began to grapple with issues of social diversity, multiculturalism, and class conflict. Historical and theoretical debates on cultural geography have at times become quite heated.[60] Beginning in the 1980s, a wave of young scholars fashioned a "new cultural geography." Rather than focusing so intently on visible material cultures, the new approach incorporated symbolic dimensions, contested meanings, multiple cultures, and questions of agency and causation. In 2000, Don Mitchell criticized Sauerian geography for using "culture" as a "thing," rather than as a contested process of signification and political debate, which thus obfuscated "how cultural geographies were really made in the struggles of everyday life."[61] Accordingly, geographers and related scholars have come to regard cultures as complex and charged with multiple meanings, both overt and latent. A rising tide of multiculturalism also encouraged geographical inquiry into nationalism, class, gender, sexuality, race, and ethnicity.

This critical cultural-historical geography, carefully contextualized, serves as my framework to study historic placemaking as an arena of representation and debate in Rio. Although official preservation began in early twentieth-century Brazil, contemporary "branding" campaigns now market iconic images at various geographic scales—districts, cities, states, regions, and so on. Under neoliberalism, contemporary historic sites have been redeveloped and rebranded for heritage tourism, consumption, and cultural capital. As Miriam Greenberg has documented for New York City, the use of branding campaigns often reflects a sense of urban decline and a willingness to promote new slogans, catchy logos, and slick advertising campaigns—all designed to create new place narratives, remedy negative perceptions, and promote urban revitalization.[62] In contemporary neoliberal cities more concerned with attracting investment and fostering economic growth than with providing for public health and welfare, authorities have often planned and administered their historic centers in concert with private capital. In a study of nine Latin American *centros históricos*, Joseph Scarpaci found that only one—Trinidad, in socialist Cuba—invested significantly in affordable housing. Instead, governments have favored historic preservation and commercial development oriented to heritage tourism, thereby excluding many residents from the benefits.[63]

Commentators have puzzled over the paradox of cultural differentiation amid economic globalization: Why do place-based identities so often seem more, rather than less, important in an era of diminishing spatial barriers to human communication, movement, and trade? The causes no doubt reflect transnational economies that encourage place branding, as heritage programs serve to foment cultural difference for purposes of tourism, the arts, and real-estate development. Thus, global markets and spatial mobilities encourage a quest for places of "authenticity." Still, outcomes vary with different policies: heritage programs may enshrine nostalgic images or keep historic sites accessible through democratic planning and education. As Doreen Massey eloquently suggests, "Instead of looking back with nostalgia to some identity of place which it is assumed already exists, the past has to be constructed."[64]

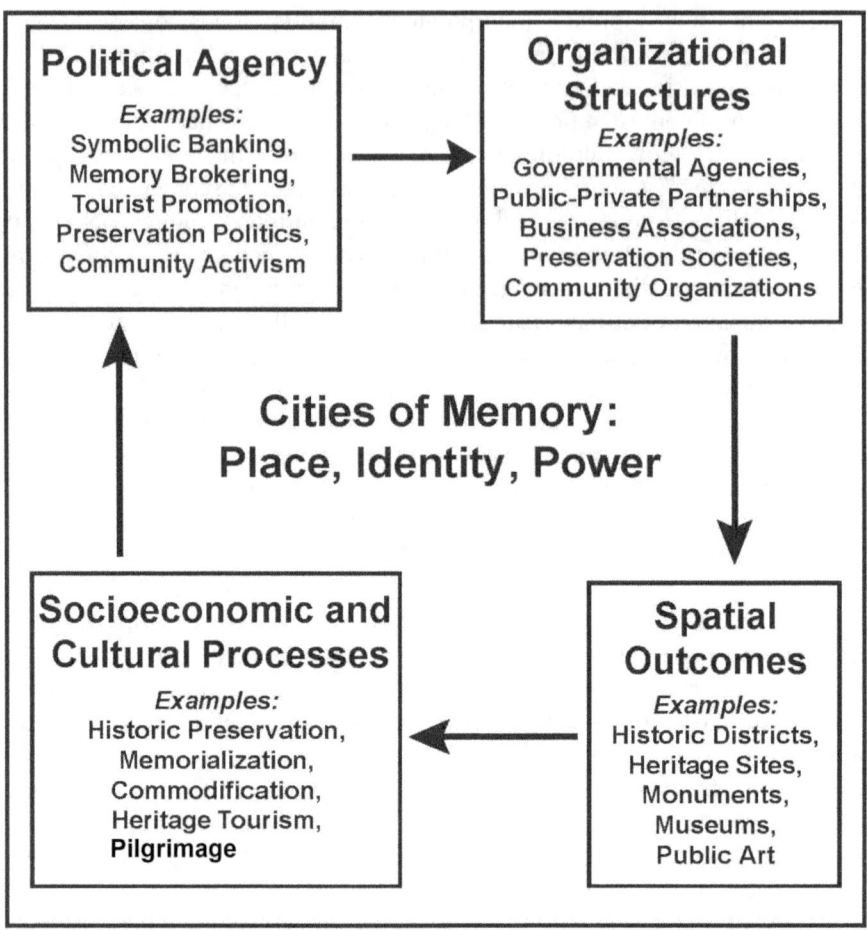

Figure 1.4. Historic placemaking in the city. By the author.

Along these lines, this project examines how heritage sites are named, renovated, represented, and institutionalized. Placemaking involves the active creation of a sense of place through the preferred designs, political-economic processes, and narratives of a site, rather than just the rediscovery of a hidden past. Figure 1.4 stresses political agency, organizational structures, spatial outcomes, and socioeconomic and cultural processes of placemaking. By examining the continuities and ruptures of urban memory, we see how processes of remembrance (and forgetting) affect society, space, and identity.

Study of historic placemaking illuminates how symbolic bankers have reinvented Rio de Janeiro. According to Ruy Castro, the city has successively been imagined during its five centuries as "an Eden dreamt of by utopians;

the failed Antarctic France; a port for pirates and corsairs; a market for gold and slaves; the capital of a Portuguese empire; the court out of an operetta; the Marvelous City; the land of Carnival; and always, even if on the quiet, a kind of sexual Mecca."[65] In addition, one could add several other contemporary imaginaries: a site of modernist architecture; a beach resort and tourist destination; a dangerous city, plagued by crime and violence; a favored site for celebratory mega-events; and most important for our purposes, a city of memory, which may incorporate all of these perspectives. This work unpacks such representations through analysis of the origins and evolution of selected heritage sites, historic districts, and conservation areas. Primary materials from archival sources and personal interviews provide insight into the patterns of remembrance, erasure, exclusion, and branding. In addition, I gather diverse perspectives on place memory from chronicles of discovery, travelers' guides and memoirs, and scholarly and journalistic accounts.

Chapter 2 examines ongoing debates over urban planning, design, and preservation in Rio. These contested memories echoed through the first republican period (1889–1930), before the first regime of Getúlio Vargas (1930–1945) institutionalized national memory through new patrimonial institutions. UNESCO World Heritage and locally inspired programs, beginning in the 1970s, further expanded the collective memories of Brazilian cities. Rio's Cultural Corridor program, the most famous of the country's municipal preservation, reflected a neoliberal shift to entrepreneurial urban regimes. The city selected "imperial" and "old republican" period styles to historicize the city center in an innovative, if top-down fashion: while property owners and commercial interests financed the historically themed building renovation (largely reimbursed by tax abatements), behind the refurbished built heritage lies a public-private revitalization program, designed to revive the business sector and social status of the city center.

Chapter 3 turns to contemporary "counter-memory," which presumes an oppositional stance toward the political status quo and conventional readings of history. Although not immune to institutionalization, counter-narratives build a sense of place through the cultural politics of alternative identity, resistance, and social justice. The recent rediscoveries of long-buried sites of the transatlantic slave trade have belatedly given rise to a series of heritage sites related to Afro-Brazilian history and culture in Rio, branded the "African Heritage Circuit." The intersections of race, class, space, and heritage have created a lively milieu for cultural politics and place identity, one widely debated in terms of the implications for contemporary Brazilian "racial democracy." While the cultural reinvention of "Little Africa" has affirmed Afro-descendant identities, I suggest that place branding in this case constitutes less of a transformative rupture in favor of civil rights than an accommodation to prevailing neoliberal policies of urban revitalization, heritage tourism, and multiculturalism.

Chapter 4 explores the rise of counter-memory and heritage in Rio's favelas. Instead of a conventional celebration of architectural monuments and landmarked buildings, *historic preservation* here refers primarily to the defense of people and place. Beginning with Providence Hill (Morro da Providência) at the turn of the twentieth century, narratives of community struggle and marginalization have served to resist displacement, lessen place stigma, and raise community visibility. Inhabited largely by low-income people of color, local nongovernmental organizations (NGOs) have celebrated the history and traditions of favelas. Long derided as violent, marginal, and unsightly, these districts began as squatter settlements but have often evolved into neighborhoods with their own distinctive forms of music, dance, and culture. The collective memory and built heritage of favelas also commonly display highly beneficial, if overlooked, aspects of sustainable and resilient urbanism. The entrepreneurial potential of "favela chic" even raises issues of cultural commodification. Well-situated favelas have experienced such significant improvements in housing, services, and infrastructure, along with middle-class upgrading and gentrification.

Chapter 5 further extends the study of memory to include environmental heritage. Although heritage sites downtown have been preserved since the 1930s, only in the late twentieth century did the city's natural heritage and scenic landmarks gain protection, as a result of mounting public pressure. The federal landmarking of Tijuca Forest and National Park in 1967 provided the impetus for an incipient local environmentalism, followed by efforts to protect historic hills and mountains. In 2012 this process culminated in approval of the UNESCO World Heritage site Carioca Landscapes between the Mountain and the Sea. After reviewing the status of this World Heritage site, the chapter examines historic placemaking on Rio's southern seaside, including Copacabana Beach and Fort Copacabana. Rio's beaches are complicated public spaces: at the seashore, egalitarian aspirations confront social privileges.

Chapter 6 concludes the book with a review of trends in Rio's historic placemaking. The chapter reiterates the argument that historic preservation and heritage conservation always involve some degree of cultural reinvention, which responds to the needs of the times, as interpreted by active memory brokers. The book maintains that official, state-sponsored preservation first arose in the early twentieth century as a patrimonial project to centralize federal power and build nationalism, while subsequent pressures to broaden political participation and promote economic development have gradually incorporated more diverse regional, social, and ethnic heritages. The city's collective memory has become a contemporary site of debate and struggle, subject to diverse grassroots and official efforts to reshape the narratives and reinvent the fortunes of Rio de Janeiro.

NOTES

1. This and all other Portuguese-language materials are translated into English by the book's author, unless otherwise noted.
2. José Luis Cardoso, "The Transfer of the Court to Brazil, 200 Years Afterwards," *E-Journal of Portuguese History* 7, 1 (Summer 2009), https://www.brown.edu/Departments/Portuguese_Brazilian_Studies/ejph/html/issue13/html/jcardoso.html.
3. M. Christine Boyer, *The City of Collective Memory: Its Historical Imagery and Architectural Entertainments* (MIT Press, 1994), 6.
4. Brian Graham, G. J. Ashworth, and J. E. Tunbridge, *A Geography of Heritage: Power, Culture, and Economy* (Arnold/Oxford University Press, 2000), 2.
5. Eric Hobsbawm, "Introduction: Inventing Traditions," in *The Invention of Tradition*, ed. E. Hobsbawn and Terrence Ranger (Cambridge University Press, 1983), 1–14.
6. David Harvey, "The Right to the City," *International Journal of Urban and Regional Research* 27, 4 (2003), 939.
7. D. Harvey, "The Right to the City," *New Left Review* 53 (Sept.–Oct. 2008), 23–40; and Kafui A. Attoh, "What Kind of Right Is the Right to the City?" *Progress in Human Geography* 35, 5 (2011): 669–85.
8. Gabi Dolff-Bonekamper, "Cultural Heritage and Conflict: The View from Europe," *Museum International* 62, 1–2 (2010): 14–19.
9. IPHAN, *Bens móveis e imóveis inscritos nos Livros do Tombo do Instituto do Patrimônio Histórico e Artístico Nacional, 1938–2009* (Rio de Janeiro: IPHAN/COPEDOC, 2009).
10. Michael Curry, *The Work in the World: Geographical Practice and the Written Word* (Minneapolis: University of Minnesota, 1996); and Benedict R. Anderson, *Imagined Communities: Reflections on the Origin and Spread of Nationalism* (London and New York: Verso, 2006).
11. Eduardo Bueno, *Náufragos, Traficantes e Degredados: As Primeiras Expedições ao Brasil, 1500–1531* (Editora Objetiva, 1998).
12. Pero Vaz de Caminha, "Letter to King Manuel," in *The Voyage of Pedro Alves Cabral to Brazil and India*, ed. William B. Granlee (London: Hakluyt Society, 1938), 3–33.
13. Bueno, *Náufragos, Traficantes e Degredados*.
14. John J. King, *Magical Reels: A History of Cinema in Latin America* (London and New York: Verso, 1990).
15. Abreu, *Geografia Histórica do Rio de Janeiro (1502–1700)*, II: 248–51; and Brian J. Godfrey, "Spanish and Portuguese Colonial Cities in the Americas: A Historical-Geographical Approach to Urban Morphology," in *Cities and Urban*

Geography in Latin America, ed. Vicent Ortells Chabrara, Robert B. Kent, and Javier Soriano Marti (Barcelona: Publicacions de la Universitat Jaime I), 8–29.

16. Robert C. Smith, "The Seventeenth- and Eighteenth-Century Architecture of Brazil," in *Proceedings of the International Colloquium of Luso-Brazilian Studies* (Vanderbilt University Press, 1953), 109.

17. Sérgio Buarque de Holanda, *Raizes do Brasil* (J. Olympio, 1936).

18. Nestor G. Reis Filho, *Contribuição ao Estudo da Evolução Urbana do Brasil* (Ed. da Univ. de São Paulo, 1968); and Murillo Marx, *Cidade Braslieira* (Ed. da Univ. de São Paulo, 1980).

19. Lieutenant Henry Chamberlain, *Vistas e Costumes da Cidade e Arredores do Rio de Janeiro em 1819–1820* (Rio de Janeiro and São Paulo: Livraria Kosmos Editora, 1943, originally published by Columbian Press, London, 1822), 195.

20. Preston E. James, "Rio de Janiero and São Paulo," *Geographical Review* 23, 2 (1933): 274.

21. Patrick Wilcken, *Empire Adrift: The Portuguese Court in Rio de Janeiro, 1808–1821* (Bloomsbury, 2004), 96.

22. Maria Dundas Graham, *Journal of a Voyage to Brazil* (London, 1824, quoted from the edition of Praeger Publishers, 1969), 189.

23. Luciana L. Martins and Maurício de Almeida Abreu, "Paradoxes of Modernity: Imperial Rio de Janeiro, 1808–1821," *Geoforum* 32, 4 (2001): 542.

24. Nireu Cavalcanti, *O Rio de Janeiro Setecentista: A Vida e a Construcção da Cidade, da Invasão Francesa até a Chegada da Corte* (Rio de Janeiro: Jorge Zahar Editores, 2004), 284.

25. Kirsten Schultz, *Tropical Versailles: Empire, Monarchy, and the Portuguese Royal Court in Rio de Janeiro, 1808–1821* (Routledge, 2001), 151–88.

26. Lieutenant Chamberlain, *Views and Costumes of the City and Neighbourhood of Rio de Janiero, Brasil* (Thomas McLean, 1822), 234.

27. Luiz Edmundo, *Rio in the Time of the Viceroys* (Rio de Janeiro: J.R. Oliveira, 1936), 12.

28. Johann Moritz Rugendas, *Viagem Pitoresca através do Brasil*, 19–20.

29. Jean-Baptiste Debret, *Voyage Pittoresque et Historique au Brésil* (Paris, 1834; reprinted in Aries: Actes Sud, 2014), "Vue de la Place du Palais, Le Jour de l'Acclamation de Dom Jean VI," Planche 137, 526.

30. Debret, *Voyage Pittoresque et Historique au Brésil*, Planche 145, "Départ de la Reine pour le Portugal," 549.

31. Quoted in E. Bradford Burns, *A History of Brazil*, 3rd ed. (New York: Columbia University Press, 1993), 117.

32. Edmundo, *Rio in the Time of the Viceroys*, 11–12.

33. Maria Dundas Graham, *Journal of a voyage to Brazil and residence there, during part of the years 1821, 1822, 1823* (London, 1824; reprinted in New York and London: Praeger Publishers, 1969), 169.

34. Johann Moritz Rugendas, *Viagem Pitoresca através do Brasil*, 19–20.

35. David Underwood, *Oscar Niemeyer and Brazilian Free-Form Modernism* (George Braziller, 1994).

36. Stefan Zweig, *Brazil: A Land of the Future* (Riverside, CA: Adriadne Press, 2000).

37. Zweig, *Brazil: A Land of the Future*, 7–9.

38. John P. Dickenson, "The Future of the Past in the Latin American City: The Case of Brazil," *Bulletin of Latin American Research* 13, 1 (1994): 13–25.

39. Alexei Bueno, Augusto da Silva Teles, and Lauro Calvacanti, *O Patrimonio Construído: As 100 Mais Belas Edificações do Brasil* (Editora Capivara, 2002); José Pessôa and Giorgio Piccinato (eds.), *Atlas de Centros Históricos do Brasil* (Casa da Palavra, 2007); Augusto Carlos da Silva Teles, *Atlas dos Monumentos Históricos e Artísticos do Brasil* (IPHAN/Programa Monumenta, 2008).

40. Mauricio de Almeida Abreu, "Sobre a memória das cidades," *Revista da Facultade De Letras-Geografia* XIV, 1 (1998): 77.

41. Ruy Castro, *Rio de Janeiro: Carnival under Fire* (New York: Bloomsbury, 2003), 157–59.

42. Michael Kimmelman, "What Is Lost When a Museum Vanishes? In Brazil, a Nation's Story," *New York Times*, Sept. 16, 2018; and Alejandro Chacoff, "Brazil Lost More Than the Past in the National Museum Fire," *New Yorker*, Sept. 16, 2018.

43. Arquivo da Cidade, *Memória da Destruição (Rio—Uma História que se perdeu, 1889–1965)* (Prefeitura da Cidade do Rio de Janeiro, 2002).

44. UNESCO, "The Evaluations of Nominations of Cultural and Mixed Properties of the World Heritage List," 36th session of the World Heritage Committee in Saint Petersburg, Russian Federation, June–July, 2012, 378–79, http://whc.unesco.org/en/sessions/36COM/.

45. UNESCO, World Heritage Center, "Valongo Wharf and Archeological Site," 2017, http://whc.unesco.org/en/list/1548/.

46. Instituto Brasileiro de Geografia e Estatística (IBGE), "Cidades e Estados," https://www.ibge.gov.br/cidades-e-estados, retrieved May 21, 2020.

47. Edmundo, *Rio in the Time of the Viceroys*, 12.

48. João Baptista Ferreira de Mello, "Roteiros Geográficas: Roteiros gratuitos em defesa da cidade do Rio de Janeiro," https://roteirosgeorio.wordpress.com/nossos-roteiros/roteiros-diurnos/, accessed May 25, 2020.

49. ICOMOS, "The Burra Charter: The Australia ICOMOS Charter for the Conservation of Places of Cultural Significance." Last modified 2008. http://www.icomos.org/australia/burra.html.2008, accessed August 15, 2012. Secretariat, "The Burra Charter," http://australia.icomos.org/publications/charters/, accessed May 25, 2020.

50. Jeffrey K. Olick, V. Vinitzky-Seroussi, and D. Levy, "Introduction," in *The Collective Memory Reader* (Oxford University Press, 2011), 3–62.

51. Jeffrey K. Olick and Joyce Robbins, "Social Memory Studies: From 'Collective Memory' to the Historical Sociology of Mnemonic Practices," *Annual Review of Sociology* 24, 1 (1998): 110.

52. M. Halbwachs, "From *The Collective Memory*," quoted in *The Collective Memory Reader* 142–45; and M. Halbwachs, *On Collective Memory* (University of Chicago Press, 1992), 52–53.

53. M. Halbwachs, *The Collective Memory* (New York: Harper and Row, 1980), 140.

54. UNESCO World Heritage Program, http://whc.unesco.org/en/about/, accessed May 25, 2020.

55. Andreas Huyssen, *Present Pasts: Urban Palimpsests and the Politics of Memory* (Stanford University Press, 2003), 4.

56. Boyer, *City of Collective Memory*, 131.

57. Diane Barthel, *Historic Preservation: Collective Memory and Historic Identity* (Rutgers University Press, 1996), 152.

58. Svetlana Boym, "Nostalgia and Its Discontents," in *The Collective Memory Reader*, ed. Jeffrey K. Olick et al. (Oxford University Press, 2011), 452–57.

59. Carl Sauer, "Morphology of Landscape," 1925, reprinted in John Leighly (ed.), *Land and Life: A Selection of the Writings of Carl Ortwin Sauer* (Berkeley and Los Angeles: University of California Press, 1963), 315–50.

60. James Duncan, "The Superorganic in American Cultural Geography," *Annals of the Association of American Geographers* 70 (1980): 181–94; and Marie Price and Martin Lewis, "Reinventing Cultural Geography," *Annals of the Association of American* Geographers 83 (1993): 1–17.

61. Don Mitchell, *Cultural Geography: A Critical Introduction* (Blackwell, 2000), 34.

62. Miriam Greenberg. *Branding New York* (Routledge, 2008).

63. Joseph Scarpaci, *Plazas and Barrios: Heritage Tourism and Globalization in the Latin American Centro Histórico* (Tucson: University of Arizona Press, 2005).

64. Doreen Massey, "Power-Geometry and a Progressive Sense of Place," in *Mapping the Futures: Local Cultures, Global Change*, ed. J. Bird, B. Curtis, T. Putnam, G. Robertson, and L. Tickner (Routledge, 1993), 171.

65. Ruy Castro, *Rio de Janeiro: Carnival under Fire*, 10.

Chapter 2

Preservation Politics
Narrating a City and a Nation

> I consider the central area of November 15th Square and its surroundings to have been our city's "living room" for three centuries, and retrospectively it is possible to review our nation's history there.
>
> —Gilberto Ferrez, 1990[1]

Long the national center of political-economic power, Rio de Janeiro remains a visual archive of Brazilian history, culture, and identity. The observer inclined to explore the landscape encounters much to contemplate, given the many historic landmarks, cultural landscapes, and public spaces accumulated over two centuries, when the city served as the colonial, imperial, and republican capitals (1763–1960). Even after losing the political capital to Brasília and the economic capital to São Paulo, Rio remains the country's premiere picture postcard and contains by far the largest concentration of national historic sites. The built heritage continues to evoke the past and to serve the present: preservation politics have sculpted much of the city. Rio, above all cities of Brazil, still arguably best reflects the nation's historical formation.[2] As historian Gilberto Ferrez notes above, Rio's historic center near November 15th Square—including the former Imperial Palace and National Cathedral, colonial-era churches and commercial arcades, and the early waterfront—narrates histories of both the city and the nation.

Since place memory arises largely from narratives articulated by a society's strongest voices, this chapter examines how power brokers have shaped the city center's forms and meanings. Symbolic bankers of memory have not acted entirely freely or arbitrarily: power relations alternately enabled and constrained them, since historic placemaking follows the vicissitudes of politics and policy, culture and fashion, and pride and prejudice. Thus, heritage designation and representation have taken various forms, depending on political-economic contexts and social agendas. To illustrate how preservation and planning have changed, let us turn briefly to a project from an earlier era: President Vargas Boulevard, which tore through the dense urban fabric from 1942 to 1944. This case illustrates a legacy of autocratic decision making, which contrasts with the flexible public-private partnerships and entrepreneurial projects of the contemporary city.

As Brazil's charismatic president from 1930 to 1945, Getúlio Vargas centralized power in Rio, then the Federal District. Scholars have traced to this first Vargas regime (he served as president again in 1951–1954) the creation of an enduring "patrimonial state," dominated by powerful bureaucracies at the service of national elites.[3] One enduring federal program began in 1937 with creation of the National Historic and Artistic Heritage Service, which would preserve "all movable and immovable property" in the public interest "because of connection with memorable events in the history of Brazil or exceptional archaeological, ethnographic, bibliographic or artistic value."[4] The new national-heritage agency rapidly inscribed some eighty properties in Rio during one year, 1938–1939. These early listings occurred quickly with virtually no public participation: national heritage arose dictatorially as the Vargas administration determined what should be preserved for the future and what should not.

One historic site listed in 1938 was the Campo de Santana, a public park and parade ground dating from colonial times, also known as Republic Square after 1889. A few years after this protective measure, however, the Vargas administration planned a broad boulevard that would pass through the park. By a decree of November 29, 1941, the president removed the Campo de Santana from the National Registers (Livros do Tombo). The new arterial appropriated a broad swath of the site, besides destroying 525 buildings dating from the eighteenth century, including four historic churches. The district also lost June 11th Square (Praça Onze), where early samba song and dance arose, along with the first organized carnival parades.[5] The boulevard displaced nearby ethnic communities of Afro-Brazilians from Bahia, Jewish immigrants, and Portuguese expatriates. Despite their resistance to the roadway, expressed in widespread grumbling and *samba* protest songs, residents had little political clout to wield. While such arterials improved the city's transportation efficiency in the short run, they ultimately weakened the city's social cohesion and sense of place. The growing network of traffic corridors ruptured the local street patterns and intensified segregation by class and race.

Fast-forward to 1979–1984: as Rio struggled with economic stagnation, insecurity, and other urban problems, the planning department implemented a novel program of heritage-based rebranding in the city center. Rather than to prioritize traffic corridors, the "Cultural Corridor" stressed historic preservation, creative placemaking, quality of life, culture and the arts, and commercial ventures. Unlike the authoritarian regime that had imposed President Vargas Boulevard, the Cultural Corridor program coincided with the global ascent of neoliberalism during the 1980s, which in turn gave rise to what David Harvey has called the "entrepreneurial city." More concerned with investment, profit, and growth than with urban service provision as in earlier "managerial" eras, neoliberalism led to greater socioeconomic inequality in cities.[6] Public-private alliances and business improvement districts, for example, have often improved the quality of life for upscale enterprises and affluent populations, while displacing the poor and the homeless. Indeed, a major focus of inquiry in Latin American cities has been how revitalization and beautification programs have excluded informal street venders, small-business people, and low-income residents, thereby provoking local resistance and struggle over space in contemporary entrepreneurial cities.[7]

In Brazil, democratization since the 1980s permitted electoral politics, local activism, commercial initiative, and a proliferation of heritage sites and historic districts in what I call "entrepreneurial preservation." After two decades of military rule, the change from centralized autocracy to flexible neoliberal regimes opened new possibilities for social change. Thus, Rio's public-private collaboration in the Cultural Corridor, so different in style and rhetoric from the authoritarian planning previously dominant, proved popular and encouraged other Brazilian cities to follow suit by renovating their historic centers in similar fashion. The news media greeted the Cultural Corridor program with great acclaim, while academic observers applauded the use of historic preservation to revitalize downtown Rio. Even if there is much to praise, however, one wonders how fully the program represented Rio's multicultural kaleidoscope in the historic center's renovation. Four decades after the Cultural Corridor's implementation, now is an opportune moment to reconsider the effusive praise received. In fact, such celebratory discourse is part of the story and becomes important to interrogate in a critique of urban policy.

This chapter examines historic placemaking in the context of urban renewal and redevelopment in the city center. From a critical preservationist perspective, I trace the historical shift from centralized autocratic planning to more flexible entrepreneurial approaches. In my view, the Cultural Corridor program signaled a turn to neoliberal urbanism, which rebranded the central city through historic districts for heritage tourism, the arts and cultural centers, and upscale businesses of consumption—in other words, as places of memory for the accumulation of cultural as well as financial capital. While local innovation and adaptation may benefit from this collaborative public-private model, I suggest that entrepreneurial urbanism has shortcomings evident in a lack of significant citizen participation, cultural variety, and socioeconomic equity. While largely successful in conventional socioeconomic terms, the Cultural Corridor depicts a decidedly selective and glorious version of public history. Given the emphasis on great leaders and important institutions, where is the diversity of class, race and ethnicity, and gender in Rio's historic center? These issues raise questions to explore here: Have power brokers used memory to rationalize entrepreneurial preservation, thereby preserving elite authority in "democratic" trappings? If so, how does this "pluralistic" discourse mobilize collective memory in legitimizing a flexible neoliberal regime?

POSTCOLONIAL URBANISM IN RIO DE JANEIRO

The search for a usable past depends in the first instance on the survival of a built heritage. Rio remained the political-economic hub of an independent empire after 1822 and thereby provided continuity with the colonial regime. After the monarchy's fall in 1889, however, leaders of the "Old Republic" (1889–1930) sought to eliminate symbols, monuments and palaces, and other vestiges of imperial Brazil. Furthermore, in the historic centers of Rio and other major cities, the presence of old dilapidated buildings, set along narrow colonial streets, appeared to hinder capitalist development. Modern urban planning and renewal began with the extensive "urban reforms" of 1902–1906, which demolished and rebuilt much of the Federal District's core. Before discussing the contemporary entrepreneurial city, it is important to review the autocratic legacy of urban planning and preservation in Rio.

As the largest city, national capital, main port, and commercial and cultural center, Rio long experienced greater growth than did provincial nineteenth-century cities. Brazil became a major exporter of coffee and other primary commodities, which pressed port and transportation facilities to circulate goods more efficiently. With steady regional in-migration, the city's population also grew steadily. Despite the veneer of aristocratic life, Afro-Brazilian slaves and freepersons, along with Portuguese and other European working-class immigrants, bore the brunt of urban problems. Rio remained subject to tropical disease, deficient sanitation, and widespread poverty. With the rapid urbanization, authorities used hygienic rationales to separate African slaves and the poor generally, as a spatial strategy of social stability. The first national census in 1872 showed Rio with a population of 274,972, compared with 31,385 in São Paulo.[8]

Before the modern proliferation of favelas during the twentieth century, much of the city's working class crowded into tenements known as *cortiços* (literally "beehives") and, less commonly, *casas de dormidas* (lodging houses). Historians estimate that some 20 percent of the city's population resided in these dwelling units in 1888. Dilapidated buildings were subdivided into rooms for rent, which allowed little privacy and required the use of shared bathrooms and kitchens. Fresh water was often scarce, while sanitation was inadequate. With a density rate of 2.6 people per room in 1888, such crowding made living conditions difficult. Frequently lacking sunlight and ventilation, apartments depended on kerosene lamps for illumination, which raised dangers of gas fumes and fires. The cramped housing conditions raised concerns for public-health problems, which authorities attributed to overcrowding, poor hygiene, and lack of education. Indeed, health inspectors found high rates of yellow fever, tuberculosis, and other infectious diseases in tenements.[9] Still, for impoverished migrants from the countryside, even the crowded *cortiços*—and later the favelas—provided access to job opportunities.

Tenement residents ran the gamut of low-wage workers, including day laborers and construction workers, domestic servants, washerwomen, peddlers, and of course those in illicit activities, such as sex workers, pickpockets, and scam artists of various kinds. Indeed, moral reform of the working classes became an issue among elites. During the late nineteenth century, for example, Tirandentes Square became the city's "Crossroads of Sin," due to the popular theaters, hotels, bars, prostitution, and homosexual encounters.[10] Aluísio Azevedo's critically acclaimed novel *O Cortiço*, first published in 1890—and later translated into English as *The Brazilian Tenement* (1926) and more recently as *The Slum* (2000)—vividly depicts the crowding, poverty, crime, sex, and ethnic tensions among hard-driving Portuguese immigrants and the more laidback Brazilians. Even allowing for artistic license, life was difficult in such collective housing, where a large proportion of Rio's population lived. In 1858, the city contained 842 tenements and buildings with rented rooms; in 1920, there were 2,661 of them, concentrated in central working-class districts, where as much as a third of the population resided. Geospatial analysis of the 1870s and 1880s indicate that Rio's tenements clustered in neighborhoods around downtown, which provided consistently high profits for landlords. In 1888, nearly 12 percent of the city's population lived in tenements; in 1890, an estimated 100,000 people found residence in tenement housing, which provided a means for landlords "to turn cheap real estate into gold."[11]

The late-nineteenth-century proliferation of tenements in the central (and most valuable) parts of the Federal District alarmed the local and national governments. Public-health authorities repeatedly filed alarmist reports, such as one in 1886, which "deplored the conditions of the *cortiços* and agreed that the dwellings were 'hygienically dangerous' and that the residents should be removed." Such reports pressured the government to expropriate the tenements, demolish them, and build individual houses for the poor. Successive administrations followed these recommendations, particularly in the expropriation by eminent domain and destruction of the *cortiços*. The administration of Mayor Barata Ribeiro virtually declared war on the slums, resulting in the destruction of the infamous "Pig's Head" tenement (Cabeça de Porco), which served as a model for Aluísio Azevedo's novel *O Cortiço*. Requiring a full police and military action to carry out the demolition, given popular indignation, this episode served to intensify the state's direct intervention in redeveloping the central city.[12]

The city's population grew by nearly 7 percent annually from 1872 to 1900 to reach 811,443 by the turn of the century.[13] Central areas were increasingly congested, the outmoded old port delayed shipping, and outbreaks of yellow fever, malaria, smallpox, and even bubonic plague prompted intermittent international quarantines. Fin de siècle leaders viewed the city's infrastructure as obsolete and a hindrance to capitalist development, while planners regarded Rio's narrow streets, dating from colonial days, as antiquated, unsightly, and dangerous. The Carioca press compared Rio unfavorably with its Argentine rival, Buenos Aires. The visual logic of modern photography and urbanism encouraged the spatial ordering of cities—in Foucault's terms, the disciplining of space. Observers have often seen spatial irregularity as a major shortcoming. Historian Murillo Marx has summarized this position: "In general, the Brazilian city is irregular, tending to be linear and polynuclear with an undefined periphery. Contemporary urban form—or its lack—reflects, vividly and clearly, an undisciplined and condescending way of life forged in colonial times." As elsewhere in Latin America, dominant ideologies stressed the need to "civilize" the city by eliminating "colonial" characteristics and creating an orderly "modern" appearance.[14]

Rio's first massive program of urban renewal began in 1902, after the new president Francisco Rodriguez Alves announced ambitious "urban reforms" and public-health measures. Francisco Pereira Passos, the appointed mayor of the Federal District, acquired powers of eminent domain to rebuild the city center through expropriation and demolition, leaving property owners without recourse to judicial review. Pereira Passos had studied engineering in Paris, where he admired the work of Baron George-Eugene Haussmann in transforming the French capital. Emperor Napoleon III had commissioned Haussmann to redevelop the old city with its narrow medieval streets and to construct broad boulevards and upscale buildings in the urban core. Similarly, the mayor and his backers in the Engineering Club, a group of reformist boosters and entrepreneurs, aspired to transform Rio into their own "tropical Paris." Given their hygienic bent, the reformers justified urban renewal largely in terms of sanitizing the city, ordering and ventilating the built form, and improving public health.[15]

Rio's radical surgery between 1902 and 1906 replaced narrow colonial streets with broad avenues and monumental views. Traditional two- and three-floor townhouses (*sobrados*) and tenements (*cortiços*) gave way to higher-density buildings. Despite popular discontent, the government rapidly demolished 1,600 *cortiços* and other aged structures to tear the new Central Avenue through the city center. New buildings arose in Beaux Arts style, including the School of Fine Arts, the National Library, the Supreme Court, and the Municipal Theater. Along with this redevelopment came a shift in the focus of republican modernity from the historic area near the Imperial Palace and to the Avenida Central (later renamed the Avenida Rio Branco). To improve trade and transportation, the port was moved away from the central square to new facilities on the northern waterfront, where railroads connected with the ships, products, and people. Extending Seaside Avenue (Avenida Beira-Mar) from downtown to Botofogo further encouraged movement of the affluent classes to the southern zone. Meanwhile, the working poor moved to less scenic locations. Much of the population displaced from tenements moved to squat on the surrounding hills—most notably Providência, the first informal settlement to be called a "favela." In short, Rio became increasingly divided by race, class, and space.[16]

The city also began an aggressive public-health campaign. A program of mandatory smallpox vaccination, announced in 1904, alarmed the suspicious populace, tabloid newspapers, labor unions, and rival politicians. Given widespread mistrust of the authorities, protests turned violent and escalated into a week of looting, burning, and fighting during the "Revolt of the Vaccine" during November 10–16, 1904. Organized largely by Afro-Brazilian working classes of the northern Gamboa and Saúde districts, rebels set up barricades to fight the republican police and military, as discussed more fully in chapter 3. The popular revolt soon withered away, although counter-memory of popular resistance remained for future reference. Still, the urban renewal program established a precedent for aggressive redevelopment of areas that betrayed timeworn, deteriorated, and unfashionable aspects. The resulting real-estate speculation generated profits for developers, in addition to embellishing and verticalizing the urban core, while largely ignoring the needs of low-income districts.

Rio suffered notable losses of historic places during the early twentieth century. To expand the city's irregular physical site, cramped between mountains and the sea, public-works projects demolished hills and their buildings and disposed of the resulting landfill along the expanding shoreline. Castle Hill (Morro do Castelo)—the city's main site of early settlement, fortification, and religious orders—became a victim of redevelopment. Long a looming presence over downtown, Castle Hill once rose 206 feet (63 meters) high and covered an area of 45 acres (184 m^2). The destruction of the hill and its built heritage occurred in stages. The construction of Central Avenue, from 1902 to 1906, first required the flattening of the hill's western side, behind the new National Library. In 1921, the rest of the hill virtually disappeared to create level terrain for the city's first international mega-event: Independence Centenary International Exposition, the World's Fair held from September 7, 1922, to March 23, 1923. Commemorating the centennial of Brazilian independence, the event also aimed to display the country's progress under the republican regime. Over three million visitors attended the exposition, which featured exhibits by fourteen countries from three continents.[17]

While authorities considered the World's Fair a great success, the demolition of Castle Hill destroyed historic churches, schools, and businesses, along with the modest hillside homes of about four thousand residents "in the interests of ventilation and hygiene."[18] There were also persistent rumors that a treasure trove of gold remained buried in the hills, left behind by Jesuits hurriedly expelled in 1759 by orders of the Portuguese crown. While the golden treasure never surfaced, the legend of its existence added an element of excitement to the demolition. Mayor Carlos Sampaio argued that the modest housing atop the hill blocked air circulation and therefore threatened public health. Still, the assault on the city's birthplace provoked significant opposition. Notable intellectuals opposed the clearing of the hill. José Bento Monteiro Lobato protested: "The Hill we know is condemned. . . . How can it resist the commercial tide, if its credentials—ancient, beautiful, picturesque, historical—are not the values priced on the stock exchange?"[19] Similarly, critic Afonso Henriques de Lima Barreto sarcastically observed: "There are not enough houses, so we want to demolish Castle Hill, removing the housing of thousands of people. As administrative logic, there could be nothing more perfect!"[20]

After the World's Fair ended in 1923, the flattened Castelo esplanade became available for redevelopment. Debris from the hill resulted in landfill to construct Santos Dumont Airport. Urban planners and architects, inspired by the Radiant City of modernist master Le Corbusier, then proposed leveling even larger areas to make way for new traffic arteries and high-rise buildings. The Agache Plan, proposed by French architect Donat-Alfred Agache from 1926 to 1930, envisioned further rebuilding of central areas, eradication of favelas, and reorganization of land uses. The inspiration for President Vargas Boulevard, for example, can be traced to the Agache Plan. For the most part, however, the plan was not implemented after the Revolution of 1930: the first Vargas regime generally left the favelas intact, given its populist-authoritarian leanings. The Castle Hill district became home for many Art Deco buildings, including new office towers. The most famous high-rise modernist structure there is the Gustavo Capanema Palace, first known as the Ministry of Education and Health Building, built between 1936 and 1945. Designed by Le Corbusier in collaboration with a Brazilian team that included architects Lúcio Costa and Oscar Niemeyer, and landscape architect Roberto Burle Marx, the sleek fifteen-story structure became an early icon of Brazilian modernism.

Yearning for heritage conservation mounted along with Brazil's rapid urbanization. Although the past had seemed to constitute a heavy burden of backwardness for early republican regimes, modernist trends of the 1920s paradoxically stimulated the stirrings of historic preservation. National museums had been established, but no federal legislation protected the country's cultural artifacts, historic sites, and monuments of importance. Artists, architects, and intellectuals began to agitate for cultural heritage. As opposed to Europe and North America, where modernism often discarded historical forms in promoting a more egalitarian world, progressive modernists in Brazil favored an integration of avant-garde movements with popular culture and built heritage. During the Modern Art Week of 1922, held in São Paulo, artists like Tarsila do Amaral shifted the subject matter away from elite portraits to include people of color, plantation agriculture, and urban landscapes. Similarly, rather than replicating traditional styles, modern structures could coexist with historical buildings, especially those of the late-colonial baroque style, as varied examples of good architecture. As Leonardo Castriota has noted, "Brazilian modernists developed a peculiar relationship with tradition, refusing the idea of a radical rupture with the past."[21]

Enduring national institutions of cultural heritage arose during the first Vargas regime. The Ministry of Education and Public Health, directed by Gustavo Capanema, whose chief of staff was poet Carlos Drummond de Andrade, coordinated heritage policies. Since the Constitution of 1934 committed to protect the country's national historic and artistic patrimony, Capanema proposed the creation of a "patrimonial service." Federal Decree-Law n° 25 of November 30, 1937, created the National Historic and Artistic Heritage Service (SPHAN, now IPHAN), initially considered a mere "service," but now as a more prestigious "institute" within the Ministry of Culture. Charged with the definition and preservation of national heritage, this agency became the official guardian of memory. The original legislation, still in effect, created four national registers of historic and artistic heritage, known as the "Livros do Tombo." Brazilian historic preservation has emphasized material culture and built heritage, similar to the listing of sites on the U.S. National Register of Historic Places. The IPHAN central archives—the

Arquivo Noronha Santos in Rio de Janeiro—now include information on 1,362 listings in one or more of the four registry books, but consolidation of multiple inscriptions results in a total of 1,047 different properties:

Book 1: Archeological, Ethnographic, and Landscape Register (*Livro do Tombo Arqueológico, Etnográfico, Paisagístico*), 119 items;
Book 2: Historic Register (*Livro do Tombo Histórico*), 557 items;
Book 3: Fine Arts Register (*Livro do Tombo de Belas Artes*), 682 items;
Book 4: Applied Arts Register (*Livro do Tombo de Artes Aplicadas*), 4 items.[22]

Analysis of the listings in the IPHAN central archives in Rio suggests the general contours of historic preservation in Brazil. For the purposes of national heritage, the most important cities arose as colonial and nineteenth-century metropolises. Rio de Janeiro, long the country's capital (1769–1960) and main port of entry, contains by far the largest concentration of historic landmarks in the country—as of 2009, the city contained 147 IPHAN listings in one or more of the registry books, for 14.0 percent of the national total. The second most important center of national heritage is Salvador da Bahia, the first colonial capital (1549–1769), which represents 102 sites, or 9.7 percent of the IPHAN listings in a recent inventory. A third major cluster of 113 national landmarks may be found in the historic mining cities of Minas Gerais—Ouro Preto, Mariana, Sabará, Diamantina, Tiradentes—which together represent more than 10 percent of the national total.[23]

Historic and artistic listings are overwhelmingly urban properties. *Religious structures*—churches, convents, monasteries, chapels, and so on—make up the largest single group, more than a third of all items in the four registers. *Residential dwellings*—primarily the grand mansions, estate houses, and ordinary city houses—account for nearly a fifth of the sites. *Public buildings and works*, which account for about 15 percent of the listings, include schools, hospitals, theaters, asylums, botanical gardens and parks, city markets, museums, city halls and jails, fountains, and customs houses. Other types of preserved sites altogether make up fewer of the total IPHAN listings. *Military fortifications* overwhelmingly date from the colonial period, when the Portuguese authorities desperately tried to protect against incursions by French, Dutch, and other European interlopers. *Agricultural and rural sites* include sugar mills, coffee plantations, and cattle ranches. *Collections of artifacts*, *visual arts*, and *performing arts* are scattered throughout the country. *Miscellaneous commercial buildings* (factories, hotels, office buildings, and so on) make up a small group of IPHAN items. *Archaeological sites*, *indigenous places*, and *colonial ruins* make up only a handful of sites on the list. Likewise, *natural landscapes*—mountains, hills, forests, mounds, and caves—also represent a surprisingly small number of listings. Overall, the IPHAN registers reflect the urban and historical emphases of the preservation agencies and Brazilian cultural agencies. Altogether, the nonurban sites (agricultural and rural; archeological, indigenous, and colonial ruins; and natural landscapes) account for only about 7 percent of the preserved national landmarks in Brazil.[24]

Not surprisingly, historic preservation has often involved political controversy. Brazilian Decree-Law n° 25 created enforcement measures to protect the national heritage, including steep fines against those who disobeyed the preservation regulations. According to the law's article 17: "Under no circumstances may registered property be destroyed, demolished or disfigured, nor may it be repaired, painted or restored, without the special prior authorization of the IPHAN. Violations shall be punishable by a fine equal to 50 percent of the value of the damage caused."[25] During the early 1940s, however, the Vargas administration passed legislation to allow for the removal of heritage properties from federal protection "in the public interest," such as for construction of President Vargas Boulevard.

In another case, demolition of Rio's Monroe Palace in 1976 became a cause célèbre for preservationists. Originally designed for the Brazilian exhibition at the 1904 World's Fair in St. Louis, Missouri, and subsequently reconstructed in Rio, the eclectic neoclassical building hosted the third Pan American Conference in 1906, served as the country's Chamber of Deputies from 1914 to 1922, and thereafter functioned intermittently as the Federal Senate and other political and judicial functions. Brazil's military dictatorship demolished this civic landmark in 1976, supposedly to facilitate construction of an underground Metro transit line, despite widespread protests by professional organizations and the public generally. Like the widely lamented demolition of New York City's Pennsylvania Station in 1964, which prompted the creation of the Landmarks Preservation Commission, the loss of the Monroe Palace stimulated a movement to conserve and, if necessary, repurpose the remaining historic structures. In the historical arc of urban redevelopment, a series of interventions transformed Rio and increasingly provoked public responses during the twentieth century (see table 2.1).

Although it is common in preservationist quarters to interpret heritage conservation solely in terms of enlightened governance, cultural politics are more complicated. Institutionalization of heritage became subject to the modern state's promotion of nationalism, economic development, and its own legitimacy. In addition, Brazilian heritage legislation initially concerned itself primarily with the designation, rather than the protection and conservation, of historic sites. National policies understandably prioritized infrastructural development and economic growth to address widespread problems of poverty, public health, and so on. Only in the late twentieth century did heritage

Table 2.1. Major Periods of Urban Transformation in Rio de Janeiro

Period	Interventions	Objectives	Consequences
17th–19th centuries	Demolition of hills, filling of wetlands, waterfront development	Occupation of irregular site, defense, commerce, political centralization	Urban expansion, port development, environmental degradation, tropical disease
1900–1910	Urban renewal, new boulevards, transfer and port modernization	Sanitation, public health, beautification, functional efficiency	Transport and port efficiencies, tenement removal, favela growth, loss of historic sites
1920s–1940s	Castle Hill leveled, Consumer business district (CBD) expansion, opening of Avenida Presidente Vargas	Urban expansion, high-rise commercial and real-estate development, new transportation arterials	Destruction of Rio's colonial historic patrimony, social displacement, verticalization of CBD
1950s–1960s	Santo Antônio Hill razed, diverse traffic arterials, Flamengo Park landscaped	CBD modernization, vehicular circulation, public recreation, real-estate development	New high-rises and parks, bay pollution, shoreline expansion, affluent move to Zona Sul, removal of selected favelas
1970s	Construction of Rio-Niterói Bridge, opening of Metro (subway) system	Mass transport, metropolitan integration, suburbanization, multiple urban nuclei	Destruction of historic structures, formation of open spaces, bay pollution, further urban decentralization
1980s	CBD Cultural Corridor, renovation of historic squares and buildings, tenements (cortiços)	Historic preservation, urban revitalization	Preservation of built heritage, commercial displacement of central housing by the Decree 322/76
1990s	Guanabara Bay cleanup program, Rio Orla waterfront renewal, cultural projects	Environmental cleanup, urban revitalization, renewed urban centrality	Cultural renewal of CBD, restoration waterfront linkages, urban in-fill and occupation of open spaces
2000–present	Mega-event planning, "Wonderful Port" program, "Shock of Order," Pacifying Police Units (UPPs)	Modern athletic and convention facilities, waterfront redesign, security, "pacification" of favelas	Increased real-estate values, redevelopment of port district, expansion of security forces, and displacement of low-income communities

programs attract significant governmental funding, corporate sponsorship, and public support. Cultural heritage focused on tourism after 1968, as the Brazilian military regime began to fund heritage programs according to the potential for tourist development. With the establishment of the national Historic Cities program in 1973, the federal government committed to funding up to 80 percent of the restoration for landmarked buildings.[26]

The rise of UNESCO's World Heritage program reinforced the trend toward cultural tourism in Brazil. Beginning with the historic town of Ouro Preto in 1980, UNESCO has listed twenty-two World Heritage sites in the country—second only to Mexico's thirty-five listings—in all of Latin America and the Caribbean (as of May 2020). In Brazil as in the larger region, most of the places are "cultural" as opposed to "natural" heritage designations. Referring to "monuments, groups of buildings and sites with historic, aesthetic, archaeological, scientific, ethnological or anthropological value," twelve of the country's fourteen "cultural" sites represent historic towns and cities, while the seven "natural" sites and one "mixed" site tend to be national parks and ecological reserves. While Brazil's early World Heritage cities featured cohesive centers, Rio de Janeiro presented the challenge of historic placemaking in a larger, more socially diverse, and architecturally eclectic center. Only during the last decade has the city acquired two highly distinctive listings: "Rio de Janeiro: Carioca Landscapes between the Mountain and the Sea" in 2012 and the "Valongo Wharf Archaeological Site" in 2017.[27] As in the rest of Latin America, world heritage has become a strategy of urban and regional development in Brazil. No doubt the UNESCO program has popularized historic preservation: heritage conservation became pervasive as it became commercially lucrative for tourism.

ENTREPRENEURIAL PRESERVATION

After losing the federal capital to Brasília, a sense of decline gradually descended on Rio's downtown, given the loss of federal patronage, the exodus of residents to outlying districts, and the visual blight of traffic arterials and elevated freeways. The expansion of shopping malls in outlying districts also detracted from downtown commerce. With the rise of the automotive industry in Brazil and the car's popular allure, urban planning focused increasingly on the construction of expressways, tunnels through Rio's hills and mountains, and high-rise buildings throughout the city. Streetcar lines, which had extended over 450 kilometers, were deactivated in 1964. Rio's beloved *bonde* trolleys, beautifully captured in the 1959 film *Black Orpheus*, disappeared amid buses and automobiles, except in the picturesque Santa Teresa district overlooking downtown. Augusto Pinheiro refers to the 1970s and 1980s as the city's "years of decadence," characterized by a weakened urban economy, a socioeconomic dispersal to outlying districts, and a prevailing image of a deteriorating central city. Urbanists worried that their city, once known as a fin de siècle "tropical Paris," was becoming a mere seaside resort or, in the words of Carlos Lessa, "the Miami of South America."[28]

Rio's central business district remained busy and often congested with traffic, but there was a growing fear that it was losing both status and business during the 1970s. The flight of high-end commerce and affluent residents was a familiar phenomenon in North America and Europe, but historic districts there were becoming popular precursors to renovation and gentrification. Augusto Pinheiro, a local architect and planner, admired this coexistence of historic preservation and redevelopment—a model he proposed for Rio. His travels abroad suggested that it was feasible to carry out successful preservation programs. He has noted, "Rio was not, from the architectural point of view, an ancient city, but there were interesting places that deserved to be preserved."[29] While the federal heritage agency initially privileged the protection of individual structures over historic districts, Pinheiro argued that historic preservation should take place more broadly. Federally protected "architectural, urbanistic, and landscape complexes" do go back to the original legislation of 1937, but the number of such historic districts has increased markedly during the 1970s. There are now 140 such complexes listed in the National Registers, including one that, since 1990, has encompassed November 15th Square and its surroundings in Rio's central area.[30]

Besides the growing interest in urban heritage during the 1970s, there was a growing interest in urban rebranding and theme parks. New York City launched its influential "I ♥ New York" campaign to revive the city's devalued "brand" and encourage investment after its brush with bankruptcy in 1975. Similarly, the civic authorities proposed to rebrand Rio: in conjunction with state and federal authorities, and in partnership with the private sector, the city turned to urban heritage. Rio's leaders devised a neoliberal strategy of cultural reinvention and image enhancement. Given the rising interest in historic preservation, planners and policy makers astutely recognized the cultural capital awaiting valorization in the city center. Thus, city leaders proposed new programs to revive the economy and to renew the civic pride of place. In 1977, Rio adopted the Basic Urbanist Plan (Plano Urbanístico Básico), with an explicit "environmentalist vision," notable for an official emphasis on historic preservation and environmental conservation. The Planning Department created a policy framework of special districts, known as Cultural Environment Protection Areas (APACS), which invoked the cultural identity and memory of city neighborhoods to regulate land use.

The Cultural Corridor Special District, the first of the APACS, began to be implemented between 1979 and 1984. Given the importance of naming, the evocative designation "cultural corridor" proved to be branding genius. As an alternative to the "traffic corridors" that had so eviscerated the city center, planning director Armando Mendes asked why the city could not have a "cultural corridor." He proposed to create a series of historic districts downtown through entrepreneurial promotion, building renovation and adaptive reuse, and heritage programs. While valorizing downtown's cultural and architectural history, this rebranding campaign also represented an effort to overcome economic stagnation and security concerns. The program initially faced opposition inside city government from the Construction Department, which defended the demolition of old buildings, widening of streets, and expansion of expressways. For its part, the Planning Department traditionally favored high-rise redevelopment over preservation. Yet city mayors of the era supported the Cultural Corridor, helping the pro-preservation forces overcome the opposition. Local community groups concerned about further urban renewal and demolition also favored historic preservation.[31]

Officially approved by municipal legislation on January 17, 1984, the "Cultural Corridor Law"—officially, "Preservation of the Landscape and Ambiance of Rio de Janeiro's Downtown," Law 506—constituted the first local legislation to preserve a major historic center of Brazil. A working group within the Planning Department delimited the program's historic districts, preservation instruments, and land-use legislation. The new legislation focused particularly on the historic preservation of façades and roofs to maintain the original decorative elements and to eliminate any clashing contemporary signage; regulations specified billboard dimensions and locations on the building façades. The interiors, on the other hand, could be extensively renovated according to their new purposes. Buildings were not to be repurposed as parking garages, given the emphasis on the historical pedestrian scale. To oversee the building renovations, Law 1139 created the Cultural Corridor Technical Office and provided other administrative adjustments on December 16, 1987.[32]

Property owners were wary of the Cultural Corridor at first, but despite some initial resistance, businesses generally came to accept the program's goals and stylistic guidelines, as the results generally proved good for commerce.[33] In return for following approved guidelines, property tax abatements could finance building renovations in as little as three years. Although the Cultural Corridor's appeal initially proved more socioeconomic than architectural or cultural, local organizations tended to support historic preservation as a means of survival. In the context of Brazil's political opening during the early 1980s, as the military regime allowed increasing democratization, social movements and neighborhood associations gained strength. In fact, many small businesses feared displacement by urban redevelopment and the expansion of large educational and religious institutions, prompting local civic and business associations to lobby for preservation. Among the more influential local district groups, the Society of Friends of Alfândega Street and Vicinity (SAARA) and the Society of the Friends of Carioca Street (SARCA) supported the Cultural Corridor as both a protection against urban renewal and a strategy of economic reinvention.[34]

As a result, the Cultural Corridor program created several distinct historic districts downtown through entrepreneurial promotion, building renovation and adaptive reuse, and cultural heritage programs (see figure 2.1). The municipal government invested in infrastructure and public spaces, while the Technical Office promoted consistent styles of restoration, mainly from the "imperial" (1808–1889) and "old republican" (1889–1930) periods, to historicize the city center. By targeting several swaths of downtown, rather than individual structures, while harnessing private capital through tax incentives, the Cultural Corridor attracted new businesses, visitors, and public events.

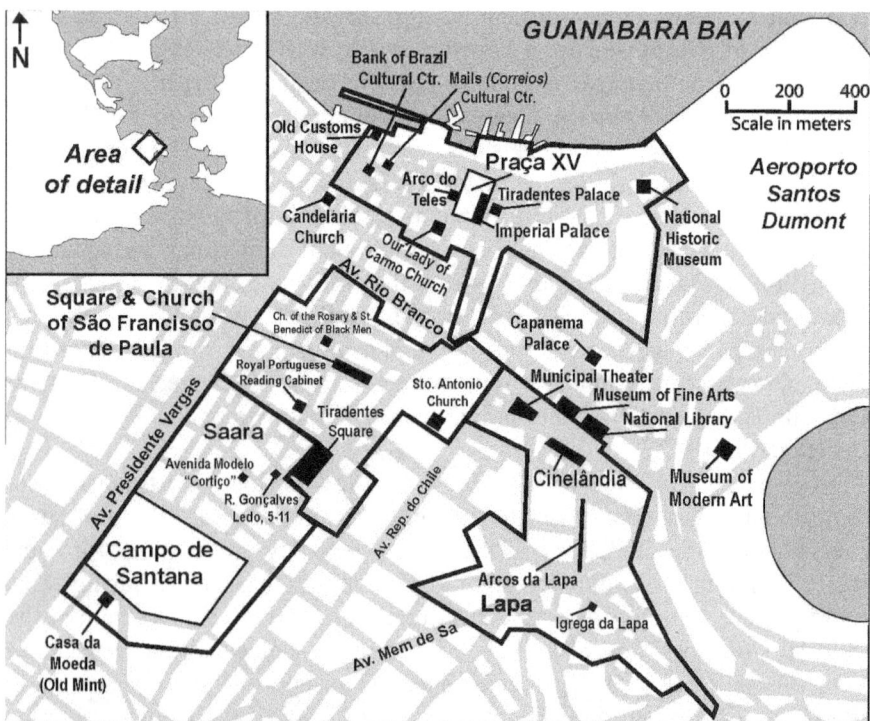

Figure 2.1. Map of the four historic districts in Rio's "Cultural Corridor." By the author.

This vision of revitalization attempted to reverse the central area's perceived decline by renovating deteriorated buildings, rebranding the cultural identity, and reinventing the economy.

Each district emphasizes its own particular history and sense of place. In terms of historic placemaking, the oldest and once most prestigious district centers on November 15th Square, which reflected a late colonial and imperial imaginary that spanned the seventeenth through nineteenth centuries. As the city's early zone of inception, this area remained the main center of power, commerce, and society until the waning years of the monarchy. Twenty sites in this district have been listed on the National Historic Register, probably the largest local concentration of national landmarks in the country. As can be seen in table 2.2, half of these listings are colonial religious buildings, including ten churches, convents, and monasteries. Five historic public buildings can also be found here, including the Old Customs House, a colonial hospital, the Imperial Palace, the Palace of Tirandentes, and collections of the National History Museum. The Arch of Teles (Arco de Teles) and two component buildings can be considered public monuments, along with November 15th Square and the Master Valentim Fountain. Many of these historic buildings have been repurposed into cultural centers and museums, such as the Imperial Palace and National History Museum. As a result, heritage tourism, office employment, governmental work, and other enterprises stimulate the restaurants, cafés, bars, and other businesses nearby. Given the massive public and private investments in historic preservation, this district has been revitalized, even commercially gentrified, in recent decades. Although popular perception often equates the entire Cultural Corridor with November 15th Square and its surroundings, in fact there are several other historic districts with their own cultural identities.

Cinelândia, which features Beaux Arts, Art Deco, and modern sensibilities, includes eight listings on the National Historic Register. The district lies along busy Rio Branco Avenue, an important commercial, cultural, and administrative area since the urban renewal of 1904–1906. With the subsequent demolition of the Ajuda Convent near the Municipal Theater in 1911, this district arose with new high-rise buildings. New institutions lined the Rio Branco Avenue: the Municipal Theater, the National Library, the Museum of Fine Art, and others. But the district gained its popular identity in the 1920s, nicknamed for its many grand movie houses and theaters, through the efforts of Francisco Serrador and other entrepreneurs of the period. In its heyday, Cinelândia theaters included the Glória, Regina, Municipal, and Mezbla; movie houses included the Plaza, Metro Passeio, Palácio, Vitória, Odeon, Patheon, Capitôlio, Império, Orly, and Rex. After World War II, Cinelândia began to lose its allure to attractions of the southern neighborhoods.

Table 2.2. Listings in the National Historic Registers, November 15th Square Historic District

CULTURAL CORRIDOR—Nov. 15th Square Historic District (20 listings)				
Bens Tombados (Registered Properties)	Registry Book(s)	Listing Number	Year Listed	Formative Period
Alfândega: Prédio/Old Customs House: Building	2 3	036 075	1938	1800–1850
Arco de Teles/Arch of Telles	3 2	158 064	1938	1750–1800
Arco e Oratório de N. Sna. da Boa Esperança/Arch & Oratory of Our Lady of Good Hope	3	455	1960	1750–1800
Casa à Praça 15 de Nov., 32 (Arco de Teles)/House on Nov. 15th Square, 32 (Arch of Teles)	2 3	084 177	1938	1750–1800
Casa à Praça 15 de Nov., 34 (Arco de Teles)/House on Nov. 15th Square, 34 (Arch of Teles)	2 3	099 206	1938	1750–1800
Chafariz do Mestre Valentim/Fountain of Master Valentim	2 3	025 058	1938	1750–1800
Convento do Carmo/Convent of Carmo	2	375	1964	1550–1600
Hospital da Santa Casa de Misericórdia: Prédio/Hospital of the Holy House of Mercy: Building	3	174	1938	1550–1600
Igreja da Candelaria/Church of Candelaria	3 2	026 012	1938	1750–1800
Igreja da Nossa Sra. da Lapa dos Mercadores/Church of Our Lady of Lapa of Merchandise	2 3	014 031	1938	1700–1750
Igreja de Nossa Senhora do Bom Sucesso/Church of Our Lady of Good Fortune	3	173	1938	1700–1750
Igreja de Nossa Senhora do Carmo/Church of Our Lady of Carmo	2 3	186 253-A	1942	1750–1800
Igreja da Ordem Terceira de N. Sra. do Carmo/Church of Third Order of Our Lady of Carmo	2 3	013 028	1938	1750–1800
Igreja de Santa Cruz dos Militares/Church of the Holy Cruz of the Military	2 3	089 192	1938	1750–1800

Bens Tombados (Registered Properties)	Registry Book(s)	Listing Number	Year Listed	Formative Period
Igreja de Santa Luzia/Church of Saint Luzia	3	180	1938	1750–1800
Igreja de São José/Church of Saint Joseph	2 3	081 167	1938	1800–1850
Museu Histórico Nacional: Acervos/National History Museum: Collections	2	598	2009	1900–1950
Paço Imperial/Imperial Palace	2 3	009 023	1938	1750–1800
Palácio Tiradentes/Tiradentes Palace	2 3	533 602	1993	1900–1950
Praça Quinze de Novembro/Nov. 15th Square	1 2 3	106 531 598	1990	1850–1900

Sources: IPHAN, *Bens móveis e imóveis inscritos nos Livros do Tombo do Instituto do Patrimônio Histórico e Artístico Nacional* (RJ: IPHAN/COPEDOC, 2009); and http://www.iphan.gov.br/.

Demolition of the grand Monroe Palace in 1976 and the closing of the Plaza Cinema in 1980 were signs of the district's decline. Although most of the cinemas have now closed and been converted to other uses, the district remains a vibrant transit hub and commercial center.[35]

The adjacent Lapa district is another notable part of the Cultural Corridor. Located around the picturesque Arches of Lapa, once the city aqueduct, this famous monument later became a bridge for streetcars to the Santa Teresa district. Lapa was long a notorious vice district of bars and brothels, but in recent years it has flourished as a center of nightlife, with its many nightclubs, bars, and restaurants. Lavradio Street, long known for its antique stores, has featured street fairs, festivals, and open houses to attract customers to public spaces improved by the city. Contemporary revitalization began in the early 1980s with the efforts to save an abandoned factory, the Progresso Foundry, which closed in 1976. In 1982, a group of artists and cultural figures occupied the huge building to prevent its demolition; with support from the National Development Bank, the building was preserved and repurposed into a cultural center with capacity for five thousand people. Lapa became another pole of revitalization in central Rio, but with a more youthful, artistic, and bohemian character, as opposed to the more conventional, upscale, and elitist orientations found in the Praça XV and Cinelândia districts.[36]

The other two historic districts of São Francisco and SAARA struggle economically, face problems of building maintenance, and remain the most ethnic in composition. The former, which includes seven historic listings on the National Historic Register, centers on the grand colonial church of São Francisco de Paula, near the Church of the Rosary and the St. Benedict of Black People—the historically Afro-Brazilian church downtown, which now features the Black Museum. Theater and live entertainment still thrive near Tiradentes Square at the intersection of these two districts, along with low-end commerce, street vending, and "motels" that rent rooms by the hour. SAARA, which includes historic listings, also remains a distinctive ethnic quarter: Portuguese merchants once predominated, followed by Lebanese and other Arab merchants, European Jews, and now increasingly Chinese business people as well. Despite the diversity of ethnic groups, there appears to be little conflict—the district's merchants are said to speak the "language of commerce." The district's identity dates from 1962, when a local SAARA business association formed to oppose the construction of a diagonal avenue between the Lapa district and President Vargas Boulevard. After escaping a disruptive urban renewal program, the area recognized the need for physical renovation.[37] Although these districts have so far shown only a few signs of commercial upgrading, they are vibrant areas of popular and informal commerce.

Protected sites have long favored the upper classes, leaving very few examples of working-class heritage. Of the many cheap hotels and boarding houses in central Rio, I found that only one has been subject to historic preservation by IPHAN. The three-story interconnected buildings on Conçalves Ledo Street (numbers 5–11), in the SAARA district, still advertise "Ledo Lodging" with "furnished rooms for bachelors" (see photo 2.1). Lúcio Costa considered these buildings, listed in 1980, as "the last urban complex, nearly intact, from the first half of the 19th century." Writing in 1978, Costa lamented the ground floor's "vulgar business"—an eatery featuring roasted chicken—but noted that the structure remained intact, if worn from age, and deserved preservation.[38] This complex still includes a modest restaurant, a cobbler, a residential hotel, and cheap apartments. While showing signs of physical deterioration, the buildings appear actively used and fully occupied. Employees of businesses with whom I spoke on several occasions were unaware of the historic status, and I saw no commemorative plaque indicating its landmark protection.

Former Mayor César Maia called the Cultural Corridor "a project that revolutionized the vision and treatment of historic preservation in the country."[39] It is true that, as opposed to the direct governmental intervention of earlier urban reforms, the Cultural Corridor represented a more localized and flexible form of historic placemaking, undertaken by urban planners in concert with the private sector. While the city and state invested in infrastructure, created policy frameworks, and encouraged public-private partnerships to reinvent

Photo 2.1. The five interconnected buildings on Conçalves Ledo Street, located in the SAARA district of the Cultural Corridor, illustrate the preservation of working-class housing and commerce. Listed on the national register in 1980 at the request of Lúcio Costa, the buildings are "the last urban complex, nearly intact, from the first half of the 19th century." Photo by the author.

the historic center, the government did not intervene as heavy-handedly as it had in prior urban renewal programs. But not all of downtown benefited from a boost in fortunes. Well-capitalized businesses could afford building renovation to meet historic guidelines, while capturing a higher-end clientele to patronize more expensive restaurants, upscale stores, and stylish bars and coffee houses. Smaller businesses with lower-end customers had more difficulty surviving the urban revitalization. Yet there was surprisingly little overt opposition to the Cultural Corridor. The Cultural Corridor program wielded its power extensively, but without resorting to the state's full political, economic, and police force. While appealing to local cultural identity and collective memory, the Planning Department also regulated public space, granted tax incentives, promoted real-estate values, branded the central historic districts, and set design standards.[40]

This paradox stems from the deceptive nature of entrepreneurial preservation, which involves a heady mixture of promotional branding, nostalgic memory, and historic placemaking. In the Cultural Corridor, celebratory discourse served to enhance the historic center's public appeal and private profitability in the aftermath of an autocratic military regime, whose demise in the early 1980s, interestingly, coincided with the preservation program's implementation. Downtown had suffered a relative decline in its fortunes, just as neoliberal agendas of public-private partnerships came into vogue. Some commentators, however, diverted their attention from political-economic power and governmental coercion to focus on a localized, voluntaristic conception of urban change. Vicente del Rio, for example, has argued for the "possibilities of more pluralistic and democratic urban design" in the Cultural Corridor. He has repeatedly enthused along these lines: "From the social point of view, the project has been sensitive to the needs of community groups, having involved them in the decision-making process."[41] Even though historic placemaking and preservation prevailed, it cannot be regarded as voluntary on the part of property owners, and certainly not for the residents and workers. Such an interpretation ignores the power of the state's incentives and penalties.

By emphasizing some vague community participation in the downtown program of historic preservation, commentators conceal the sources of political-economic influence. Such boosterish appraisals reflect the seductive charm of entrepreneurial preservation, which downplays uneven development, private-market coercion by the state, and urban rebranding by the authorities. Along with an increasing reliance on private capital to fund infrastructure and development projects since the 1980s, governmental bureaucracy has remained powerful at federal, state, and local levels. As Roberta Guimarães has noted, the rhetorical reliance on cultural and historic districts served as a municipal tool to create "zones of touristic interest and incentives or constraints to the real estate market and becoming a powerful regional management strategy."[42] The neoliberal regime created opportunities and distributed benefits unevenly over the city, depending on the status accorded to the special districts. Thus, the celebratory reviews have served to mystify the partnership of governmental and private power.

As a result of these preservationist initiatives, Rio became a leading example of neoliberal inner-city revitalization in Brazil. Municipal, state, and federal authorities coordinated policies—including land-use, transportation, infrastructure, and preservation policies—while encouraging public-private partnerships and property-tax incentives for building renovation and economic development. The federal government refurbished national monuments and protected historic districts, the state of Rio renovated streetscapes and public infrastructures, and the city encouraged the private sector to renovate historic buildings according to consistent style guidelines by providing property-tax incentives. This collaborative approach revalorized the historic monuments and public spaces, thereby reinventing the city center's meaning and in large part reversing its general decline. Still, not all stakeholders and districts benefited. Frequent battles occur between police and informal street venders in more upscale parts of the Cultural Corridor, where established businesses resent the informal trade and congestion of sidewalks. On several occasions, I have witnessed street merchants pack up their merchandise and fold up their tables in an instant to avoid imminent police action. This issue has been partially addressed by the city's provision of authorized stands to informal venders in squares and streets of high pedestrian flow, such as near the Uruguaiana Metro station in the São Francisco district, where a vibrant popular market features inexpensive, at times counterfeit, merchandise. Still, there is a popular enthusiasm for life here that one would seldom find elsewhere in the historic center. Indeed, the social inclusion of street venders and low-income residents, provision of public safety, conservation of dilapidated buildings, and economic profitability remain highly uneven in much of the Cultural Corridor.

Despite such shortcomings, Rio's Cultural Corridor has widely influenced other cities of Brazil. It is now difficult to find a Brazilian city of significant size and history that does not boast central historic districts with upscale pretensions. While entrepreneurial preservation has become a widespread strategy of urban revitalization, many commentators have obscured the dynamics of public-private power in their emphasis on "pluralistic and democratic urban design." The city's machinations, while seemingly democratic, were in fact imposed top down, dictated by planners, and benefiting the property owners. The city deployed preservation in a flexible but determined fashion: while commercial interests financed the historically themed building renovation (subsidized by tax incentives), behind the refurbished built heritage was a public-private partnership, designed to revive the business sector and social status of the city center. As a historic preservation program begun during the early 1980s, the Cultural Corridor reflected a neoliberal shift from a managerial to an entrepreneurial urban regime, which rebranded the city center as a place of heritage tourism, the arts, and cultural capital. The complex relationship between public and private stakeholders became particularly apparent in the case of the historic district centered on November 15th Square, the quintessential Imperial Capital.

NOVEMBER 15TH SQUARE:
PLACEMAKING ON THE PRAÇA

After the official inauguration of the Cultural Corridor program in 1984, the historic district to gain most visibility was November 15th Square. This area epitomized "the only imperial capital in the Americas," as marketed in the 2008 bicentennial celebration. In a supportive move, the federal heritage agency IPHAN subsequently listed this area as a national historic district in 1990.[43] Nicknamed the "polygon of historic monuments," the federally protected area stretches from November 15th Square to Candelária Church, and between March 1 Street and the waterfront. (The demarcations of city and federal historic districts do not exactly coincide, but they overlap extensively.) Encompassing 150 venerable buildings from the colonial and early-national periods, including twenty listed on the National Historic Register, this historic district long served as Rio's institutional nucleus. Events here reverberated throughout Brazil. The square itself went by a variety of names, including Carmel Square (Praça do Carmo, 1600–1743), Palace Square (Praça do Paço, 1743–1870), and Pedro II Square (Praça Dom Pedro II, 1870–1890) before being renamed November 15th Square (Praça XV) in 1889 to honor the proclaiming of the republic on that date. In addition to being a stage for historical events of great importance to both the city and the nation, the striking image of the Imperial Palace provided potent cultural capital for urban rebranding and revitalization. The contemporary district also reveals public-private partnerships, including the Imperial Palace and other cultural centers.

Rio's colonial public spaces arose around squares with prominent public buildings, schools, and institutions of Roman Catholic religious orders—the Jesuits, Benedictines, Carmelites, and Franciscans each had areas of influence. Castle Hill became the site of military fortifications, along with Jesuit churches, monasteries, and schools. The Benedictine order built a church and monastery on Saint Benedict (São Bento) Hill. Between them, the Carmelite order built a church and convent, begun in 1590, fronting a vacant area by the waterfront. In 1683, Carmelites requested that authorities preserve the open space as a "commons" (*rossio*), which later became the square. By 1761, construction of the current Church of Our Lady of Mount Carmel, the Old Cathedral, along with the Church of the Carmelite Third Order, solidified one side of Carmel Square. Luiz Edmundo, writing in the early twentieth century, noted the late-colonial presence of "the melancholy pile of the Convent and Church of Carmel, a characterless building, its little tower silhouetted against the blue sky."[44] But the religious complex gained stature with the royal family's arrival. The Carmelite Convent housed Queen Mother Maria I of Portugal—also called "Mad Maria" due to her mental instability—while the Carmelite Church became the Royal Chapel.

Adjacent to the Carmel complex, the colonial administrative center arose during the eighteenth century. Given Rio's rising importance, authorities contracted with Portuguese military engineer José Fernandes Alpoim to integrate the Royal Mint and Warehouses into the new Governor's Palace (later the Vice-Regal and Imperial Palace), begun in 1743. Alpoim also designed a commercial and residential complex for the wealthy Teles de Menezes family directly across the palace square from the palace. To provide an entrance to adjacent streets, Alpoim added an arch to the complex—to be known as the Arch of Teles—that completed the square's symmetry with its adjacent religious, government, commercial, and residential sides, all facing the busy waterfront. Luiz Edmundo described the scene this way: "To the right in the row of buildings reaching to the water's edge stood the homes of the Telles, high vertical houses with greenish balconies and steep grey roofs, the Frenchman Philippe's canteen being on the ground floor of one of these." Initially a high-status area with access to the waterfront and the Palace Square, the Arch of Teles retained its social status after the royal family's arrival, as employees of the royal family took over the nearby housing. A fire consumed much of the complex in 1790, but the two properties around the arch survived (see photo 2.2).[45]

Long barren of vegetation, the central square was paved to serve as a site of military reviews, public festivities, and proclamations of state during the late eighteenth century, as depicted by Leandro Joaquim's painting of a "Military Review on the Palace Square," circa 1789. This panoramic view emphasizes the spatial concentration of institutional power around Palace Square, which served also as a military parade ground, port landing, and marketplace.

Photo 2.2. The Arch of Teles, showing the late-colonial buildings and commercial arcade, whose landmark status prevailed in court, despite the construction of a high-rise structure directly behind the historic façade during the 1940s. Photo by the author.

Framed by the quay and the monumental Master Valentim Fountain on the waterfront, this square featured the Governor's Palace sitting on the left, the preeminent religious institutions looming in back, and the commercial and residential complex of the Arch of Teles conveniently situated near the port on the right. This public space, surrounding the colonial symbols of power, also long centered the city's active slave trade: enslaved Africans arrived from ships docked on the square, where traders led the famished human merchandise to "fattening" storehouses nearby, where they would be prepared for sale. In fact, the city's slave markets were located within a stone's throw of the palace and cathedral until the turn of the nineteenth century, when authorities forced them to leave the city center and move out of sight to the remote Valongo Wharf on the periphery, as detailed in the next chapter. Through all of this commercial, institutional, and religious activity, Palace Square served as the city's main public space through late-colonial and early-imperial Brazil.

By the mid-nineteenth century, a water fountain (*chafariz*) and a pillary (*pelourinho*) for punishment sat in the center of Palace Square (see figure 2.2). It was here, in 1792, that Joaquim José da Silva Xavier, known as Tiradentes (the tooth puller), the leader of a revolutionary movement known as

Figure 2.2. "Military Review at the Palace Square," by Leandro Joaquim, circa 1790, shows the concentration of political power in late-colonial Brazil.

the Inconfidência Mineira, was publicly hanged and quartered for advocating independence from Portugal and the creation of a Brazilian republic. By that point, the Master Valentim Fountain had become a gathering place for those getting water and socializing after its inauguration in 1789. Visiting ships would resupply their water from the fountain, lending a cosmopolitan air, while venders sold their water, sweets, and other goods to local residents and visitors. In 1821, English lieutenant Henry Chamberlain noted: "The square is much frequented by the citizens in the cool of the evening after business is ended, to learn the news, and talk politics; and is at such hours, if any breeze be stirring, a very agreeable place of promenade."[46]

In 1835, French painter Jean-Baptiste Debret published his painting *After Dinner Refreshments on the Palace Square*. In the accompanying commentary, based on his work with the French artistic mission from 1816 to 1831, the artist described the lively scene on the waterfront near Master Valentim Fountain in the late afternoon. Well-to-do men would sit with friends, under a protective police gaze, and purchase sweets and refreshments from Black female street venders. Keen on the subtleties of street life, Debret noted that malicious customers might cheat venders by consuming the goods, then complain about their bad quality and refuse to pay. On the other hand, generous customers patronized their favorite venders on a regular basis. Such regular buyers become popular and indeed indispensable for the business of street merchants. According to Debret, the affluent men would converse until 7 p.m., when the chapel bells would alert them to rise and recite the prayer of Ave Maria. After this religious devotion, they bid each other goodbye and returned to their homes. Officials and courtiers, however, continued to pass through the square. As night fell and residents filtered away, foreign naval officers and sailors from merchant vessels came ashore to enjoy time at a café, eatery, or other sites in town. Two French establishments on Palace Square were common meeting places for strangers.[47]

IPHAN inscribed most of the historic district's twenty listings in the National Registers in 1938, during the initial frenetic phase of preservation. Seventeen of the structures date from before Brazilian independence in 1822, mostly during the eighteenth century, thereby illustrating the importance of colonial structures. Half of the landmarks are religious: the ten churches in the district are costly to maintain in good condition and, in fact, several are rarely open to the public. The other half of the protected sites are public or institutional. Notable examples include the Imperial Palace; the Church of Our Lady of Carmel; the former national cathedral; the Arch of Teles; the historic customs house (Casa França-Brasil); the cultural centers of the Bank of Brazil, the Post Office, and the Imperial Palace; and many others. Historian Gilberto Velho, as a member of the IPHAN advisory board, argued for the national importance of this central area: "The historic, architectural, and cultural importance of the area justifies its protection at the federal level, even though already preserved by municipal legislation. We are dealing with an area of major significance while old capital of the Colony, the Empire, and the Republic."[48]

Several of the landmarked sites in the vicinity of November 15th Square have prompted national debates over historic preservation, cultural politics, and urban redevelopment. Federal patrimonial legislation passed in 1937 (Decree-Law n° 25) promised to preserve notable historic monuments listed in the National Historic Register, but development pressures sometimes threatened the landmark status. The Arch of Teles, the colonial-era building and arcade, became a key legal test of the national preservation law. In April of 1938, SPHAN notified property owners of its intention to list the Arch of Teles, which in turn prompted a federal judge to question the constitutional legality of this process. Property owners wanted to demolish the deteriorated structure and replace it with a modern office tower or hotel. After the courts subsequently upheld the legality of preservation law, SPHAN director Rodrigo Andrade confirmed the listing in December 1938, retroactive to June 1938. On appeal, the case went to the Supreme Court, pitting the site's owners against the federal government and testing the constitutionality of preservation legislation. In a major legal decision, the court in 1940 upheld the federal government's right to preserve such structures in the public interest, even if this protection infringed on the traditional rights of private property.[49]

Given development pressures, the case of the Arch of Teles resurfaced in 1954–1955, resulting in a compromise between the rights of private property and preservation regulations. The real-estate development firm Companhia Carioca Imobiliária, which had acquired the two historical properties making up the arch in 1944, began to build a new eight-story office building directly behind the historic structures. In protest, the heritage department director, Rodrigo Andrade, notified the owners of the earlier Supreme Court case that confirmed the site's preservation. Andrade also cited the evaluation of architect Lúcio Costa, from a memorandum of 1954, that insisted on restoration of the original façade, according to historical depictions, but not the building interiors. In December 1955, a federal judge ruled in favor of the government's proposal to restore the façade, even as part of the high-rise directly behind and joined to it. Given continuing disputes, Governor Carlos Lacerda decreed on February 18, 1961, in the state's official newspaper, that redevelopment of the Arco de Teles could proceed under the terms specified by Lúcio Costa in 1954.[50]

Due to these legal and administrative maneuvers, today the observant visitor notes that over the restored colonial façade of the Arco de Teles looms a modern office structure, while the late-colonial and imperial buildings in the vicinity have become restaurants, bars, boutiques, and other businesses. This has long been a lively commercial area—singer and actress Carmen Miranda, although born in Portugal, grew up in her family's boarding house at Travessa do Comércio, 13, behind the Arch of Teles. Then home to working-class Portuguese immigrants and others of modest backgrounds, the area has been gentrified with implementation of the Cultural Corridor. The surrounding streets now feature such popular tourist sites as the Imperial Palace and other cultural centers, along with bars and restaurants popular after work downtown. Despite concerns of some preservation purists, the authorities arrived at a working compromise between the rights of property owners whereby the building interiors could be modernized as long as the traditional façades were maintained.

Despite this preservationist victory, urban renewal still threatened the historic district. Long fronting the city's first harbor, this area remained a vital port and warehouse district until the early twentieth century, when the modern port moved to the north on Guanabara Bay. The subsequent addition of expressways tore paths across downtown streets: an elevated central arterial constructed in phases between 1956 and 1962 separated some seven kilometers (4.3 miles) of the historic center from the shoreline of Guanabara Bay. Although it linked Santos Dumont Airport to Brazil Avenue in the northern zone of the city, the elevated arterial quickly became congested and often operated at overcapacity. In addition to creating visual blight, the elevated highway isolated the waterfront. November 15th Square, the Imperial Palace, and other historic landmarks lost visual connection and urban legibility. Nearby, the Municipal Market, built of imported iron between 1903 and 1907, was demolished to make way for the arterial, except for a single tower to be used as a restaurant. The grand market itself "could have been preserved," lamented a preservationist, "giving it another use."[51] After years of planning, civic authorities had the elevated eyesore demolished between 2011 and 2014, replacing it with tunnels for traffic and an extended plaza in front of the palace and the square, as well as by a broad boulevard elsewhere, thereby creating an open esplanade with direct access to the bay. The demolition of the expressway represented the dramatic demise of elevated freeway construction in downtown Rio, as in many other contemporary cities.[52]

Federal listing of this historic district on the National Historic Register in 1990 provided additional protection against incompatible high-rise buildings and other forms of discordant development. For example, the IPHAN advisory board had been concerned about the twenty-five-floor height of the modernist Stock Exchange (Bolsa de Valores do Rio [BVRJ]) building on the square since its construction in the early 1980s. As historic buildings in the district generally did not exceed three or four floors in height, the addition of other buildings of twenty-five stories would disfigure the local cityscape. As a result, an IPHAN report of December 19, 1984, suggested that new constructions in the proposed historic district should be limited to 10.5 meters (about 35 feet)—a recommendation incorporated into the historic district's protective guidelines. As a result, the November 15th Square district would preserve the area's physical form while reinventing the economic functions. For example, the BVRJ, Rio's venerable stock exchange, suffered by competition and subsequently merged with São Paulo's BOVESPA exchange in 2002; the modernist high-rise building is now a convention center and office building.

This part of the Cultural Corridor has also attracted stylish new enterprises, such as the upscale Vertical Shopping, located two blocks from November 15th Square at 48 September 7th Street (Sete de Setembro, 48). Opened in 2003, Vertical Shopping occupies a twelve-story repurposed office building with sixty specialized shops, beauty salons, and a food court. According to its website, "The mall is considered a reference of good taste, having followed the trend of major European retail centers, undergoing a retrofit and being fully modernized to be a smart mall, offering convenience and comfort to its customers." Besides the upscale stores, the mall also enthuses, "We are in the middle of Rio's most important historical and tourist sites, such as the Carmo and Candelaria churches, Municipal Theater, Paço Imperial, and Art Museums."[53] Reviews stress the quality, privacy, and convenience for affluent customers. What seems most significant is the high-end marketing downtown, clearly intended to compete with larger shopping malls in Rio's southern zone, after the establishment of the Cultural Corridor and November 15th Square Historic District. In this sense, the Vertical Shopping mall represents a commercial upgrading and gentrification increasingly common in this part of the Cultural Corridor.

While this historic district has seen a remarkable architectural restoration in recent decades through public and private investments, at points it has come to look like a historical theme park. As M. Christine Boyer has noted with regard to New York, "The landscape of the contemporary city seems to be composed of conflicting fragments, slices or framed views first cut out and extracted from the city fabric, then set up and juxtaposed against one another." Moreover, she adds, the "contrasting views" are "made more potent by their proximity to each other."[54] So too is it with the Imperial Capital imaginary in downtown Rio. The area north of November 15th Square and the Arch of Teles now serves as a frequent stage for historically inclined television and film dramas. By emphasizing the glories of the Imperial Capital, the district gains a public interested in cultural heritage and tourism, while local office employees and their friends enjoy "happy hour" festivities as in bygone days after work. The historic setting offers a celebration of Rio's glorious past, which seems somehow reassuring: that the district assumes a rarefied, indeed reified, air seems precisely to be its appeal. Along with the steady gentrification of local commerce, this part of the Cultural Corridor seems remote from the heady social diversity, the tawdry experience, common to much of urban life. One way to counter these trends would be to embrace alternative perspectives on the past and incorporate greater diversity of historical experience. Who would know that the African slave trade operated openly on the waterfront of Palace Square and in the surrounding markets until the late eighteenth century, when the viceroy ordered it moved to Valongo Cove? Public signage, for example, could more frequently call attention to non-elite populations in public spaces and monuments. Local cultural centers could also promote such educational diversity, as does the Imperial Palace.

ADAPTIVE REUSE OF THE IMPERIAL PALACE

In his interpretation of the Basilica of the Sacred Heart (Sacré-Cœur) in Paris, David Harvey suggests that the landmark projects an image of "perpetual remembrance. But remembrance of what?"[55] Although the basilica outwardly evokes a conservative moral order, a close reading of its history reveals intense political and ideological struggles, which the present-day cityscape serves to conceal. Overlooking Paris from the Montmartre hill, Sacré-Cœur crowns the summit of what was once a rebellious working-class neighborhood. In fact, the basilica's construction began in 1875, after a humiliating national defeat in the Franco-Prussian War and the short-lived Paris Commune of 1871. After these tumultuous events, there arose in nationalist quarters a desire for *revanche*—revenge against the country's supposed enemies, both external and internal, and a return of Alsace-Lorraine after its annexation by Germany. Given this historical context, Harvey argues that the basilica arose as kind of penance for military defeat and socialist insurrection, replaced by an uplifting symbol of French spiritual and political redemption. This case suggests that historical landscape interpretation requires a consideration of class conflict, political upheaval, and urban change.

Similarly, to appreciate Rio's Imperial Palace, we must consider the structure's long and often tumultuous history. This national monument long served as a pillar of aristocratic privilege and conservatism, but the palace's story culminated in the establishment of a public museum and cultural center in 1985. If Sacré-Cœur in Paris conceals its origins in conflict, the Imperial Palace proclaims its history through public education and heritage tourism.

The site of notable episodes in Brazilian history, the building witnessed the arrival of the Portuguese royal family in 1808, proclamation of Brazilian independence in 1822, coronation of Pedro II in 1841, abolition of slavery in 1888, and fall of the monarchy itself in 1889. Then, after a century and a half at the center of royal rule, the historic palace survived a century of republican neglect, deterioration, and threats of demolition.[56] Restoration of this monument ultimately stimulated a historic sense of place, a cultural reinvention, and the economic revitalization of downtown Rio. Thus, the saga of the Paço Imperial reflects the vicissitudes of Brazilian history as well as the appeal of historic placemaking in the Cultural Corridor (see photo 2.3).

This venerable palace dates from 1697, when regional gold and diamond discoveries prompted construction of the Royal Mint to smelt and guard the crown's revenues. By the early eighteenth century, colonial authorities added the Royal Armory and Storehouse. At this point, the crown provided governors with an allowance to rent residences. In 1733, given the growing prosperity of Brazil, the governor of Rio de Janeiro and later Minas Gerais, António Gomes Freire de Andrade, received permission to build an official residence and administrative center in Rio. In 1738, military engineer José Fernandes Alpoim arrived to build the Governor's Palace. Besides combining

Photo 2.3. The restored Imperial Palace (Paço Imperial), now converted into a cultural center in downtown Rio de Janeiro. Besides the artistic exhibitions, the Paço features a research library, bookstore, and café. Photo by the author.

and expanding the preexisting structures, Alpoim added a second floor to create a sizable palace, first occupied by the regional governor in 1743. With the transfer of the colonial capital from Salvador to Rio de Janeiro in 1763, Alpoim later made further additions to what then became the Viceroy's Palace.[57] Yet opinions of the newly enlarged building were decidedly mixed. According to Luiz Edmundo, the Viceroy's residence was "a huge rambling affair" and "ugly rectangular and low, painted white, with narrow doors and windows, the interior gloomy and dark, almost bare of furniture and smelling of mold." He cited a commentary from 1772, which described the palace "as a place of vast and deserted rooms, containing but few chairs and tables, the latter completely covered with large cloths, assuredly to hide from view their decrepitude and ugliness."[58]

Royal residence began with the arrival of the prince regent in 1808, along with his family and the royal court. Among the thousands of Portuguese arrivals, aristocrats acquired the use of the best local residences after displacing the owners. The royal family occupied the former Viceroy's Palace, subsequently remodeled into the Imperial Palace. Although relatively large, the palace lacked amenities fit for a monarch and as a result underwent renovations. A throne room, hastily arranged on the second floor, allowed for the traditional hand-kissing ceremony in which subjects awaited to pay homage to the monarch. In 1817, the addition of a third floor at the front of the building, facing the waterfront, provided a palatial façade with a prominent balcony for public events. Even so, the palace proved cramped and noisy, and so the king's family took up primary residence at the Quinta da Boa Vista, a large mansion then on the city's outskirts, which became known as the Palace of São Cristóvão. (After the fall of the monarchy in 1889, the grand suburban palace became the National Museum in 1892; it was listed on the National Historic Register in 1938 but was severely damaged by a fire in 2018.)

Despite its steady fall from grace after Pedro I declared Brazilian independence in 1822, the city palace remained the monarchy's administrative center and site of coronations, marriages, and major celebrations. It continued to serve as the monarch's official residence through the waning years of the Brazilian Empire under Pedro II, although the Palace at São Cristóvão was the actual royal residence. In the 1820s, the painter Rugendas wrote: "The Imperial Palace is a vast and irregular building of the worst architecture; and that of the Archbishop is of the best taste."[59] By the mid-eighteenth century, the Imperial Palace suffered further deterioration, according to press reports. In 1862–1863, one prominent journalist, Joaquim Manuel de Macedo, noted in his weekly newspaper column that "a few years ago the palace received from its termites the formal notice to find a substitute. . . . The palace is ruined and the nation should at least offer its first citizen a suitable building." While recognizing the historic events witnessed by the palace in the past, Macedo argued that the building "should not be conserved. . . . It is not worthy of the emperor or the nation. What we are seeing in the middle of the Palace Square (Largo do Paço) is not a palace, it is an old house in complete ruin."[60] Still, the palace remained standing during the waning years of the Brazilian Empire. Princess Isabel signed the Golden Law (Lei Aurea) here on May 13, 1888, before announcing from the balcony the total abolition of slavery to the cheering multitudes assembled in the square.

After the monarchy's fall on November 15, 1889, the new regime instituted a policy of deliberate disrespect for the symbols and structures of empire. After changing the name of Palace Square to commemorate the date of the republic's proclamation, the authorities redesigned and embellished the square, installing formal landscaping with trees to surround an equestrian statue of General Manuel Luís Osório, a military hero of the Paraguayan War. The republic almost demolished the Imperial Palace itself, but after some debate, the national Mail and Telegraph Service occupied the building in 1893 and remained there until 1982. As headquarters of the postal services, the building experienced numerous external and internal changes at odds with earlier forms. During the 1920s, the structure gained a central tower with three floors, which occupied a large internal patio. In 1929, the front façade of the old Paço acquired a neocolonial style; the third floor was extended to encompass the entire structure, while a fourth floor was added to an interior tower; the building was painted pink; and the roof style modernized. Despite suffering what critics considered misguided architectural changes, the building's role as a federal postal agency saved the structure from demolition.[61]

Even after IPHAN landmarked the palace in 1938, conflicts over building conservation continued. In 1942, for example, the postal authorities repainted the historic building in a different hue, without prior consultation with IPHAN, in violation of legal requirements, but the building's decline continued. In 1959, given mounting problems of deterioration, a special commission even recommended the demolition and reconstruction of the structure, although it ultimately was not carried out. While the postal authorities gradually abandoned use of the building, historic preservationists fumed about the lost opportunities for renovation. By the 1970s, the completion of a new headquarters for the Mails and Telegraph Department in Brasília left most of the old structure vacant: use was restricted to customer service on the ground floor, while the rest of the building deteriorated further. Finally, in 1981, the postal authorities abandoned the old palace. IPHAN noted a "complete abandonment except for two or three rooms on the ground floor. The rest of the building is in a precarious state. Higher floors, ceilings, and walls have suffered great water damage."[62]

On February 15, 1982, postal authorities agreed to transfer ownership of the Paço Imperial to the Heritage Foundation (Fundação Pro-Memória), a public-private institution that from 1979 to 1990 worked alongside IPHAN to facilitate the acquisition and preservation of important heritage sites; the foundation, importantly, drew from both public funds and private donations.[63] In this sense, the emerging neoliberal role of the state was of vital importance in recovering one of the country's most important but endangered historic monuments. According to Lauro Calvalcante, a recent director of the Imperial Palace Cultural Center, "The restoration of the old palace was very meaningful. It meant giving it a public role that could be used as a pilot project for other Brazilian monuments and that would help to revitalize Rio's downtown area." It was also a sign of confidence "that the Federal Government would do something about the debilitated city of Rio de Janeiro which, since the early 1980s, was going through the worst crisis of its 20th century history."[64]

Plans initially called for only a modest renovation of the deteriorated structure, but after deliberation, the IPHAN advisory committee recommended a full restoration to its heyday during the Portuguese monarchy's residence. Architect Glauco Campbell coordinated the plans for restoration. After much debate and some discord, the leadership team decided to return the palace for the most part to its appearance in 1818, when festive celebrations accompanied the coronation of King João VI. By this point, the structure had acquired a third floor and balcony in front—the palatial façade for which the building has become known. Authorities resolved to eliminate the architectural changes made after the monarchy's fall in 1889. Traces would also remain of the colonial origins, of the Imperial Palace of Pedro I and Pedro II, and of the room in which Princess Isabel signed into law the "Golden Law" that abolished slavery in Brazil. For public education, the extensive renovations effectively highlighted the building's colonial origins and evolution, even in one place revealing the original walls of the Royal Mint.[65]

Rio's Imperial Palace illustrates how the Cultural Corridor has remade places even as it has preserved vestiges of the past. The palace's restoration provided a model for other historic institutions, given the transparency about its historic evolution, renovation, and adaptive reuse as a contemporary cultural center. This saga also underscores the ways in which heritage is a product of institutional power and public taste, rather than a simple return to "authenticity." Compared to Sacré-Cœur in Paris, which "hides its secrets in sepulchral silence,"[66] Rio's Imperial Palace proudly proclaims its story, first as a (post)colonial palace, then as a national institution, and now as a public-private partnership. The mission statement explains: "In the Imperial Palace, the expressions of the contemporary world enter into dialogue with references to the past, inviting the visitor to pass through the times.

The diversified programming includes exhibitions of visual arts, architecture and design, performance of scenic arts, musical concerts, seminars, and lectures."[67] Engaging the visitor in a conversation about the past and present, the historic site exemplifies a "reflective" (as opposed to "restorative") nostalgia, as Svetlana Boym suggested.[68] While the Paço Imperial makes no attempt to glorify the monarchy, the building restoration provides a revealing window on national history and identity. In the end, after two centuries of royal rule, the palace survived a century of republican neglect, deterioration, and threats of demolition. With the renovation of this longtime bastion of monarchy and its inauguration as a cultural center in 1985, the Imperial Palace stimulated a historic sense of place and cultural reinvention in an entrepreneurial city.

REINVENTION AND CONTINUITY

The Cultural Corridor program has reflected a benevolent style of entrepreneurial preservation, which has renovated much of central Rio for business, tourism, and the arts. Most notably, the rebranded city center provides the historical frame of reference for a carefully crafted sense of place and environmental quality, while legitimizing a flexible regime of neoliberal accumulation. Historic periodization prompted the design guidelines. The program proved more accommodating to local communities than earlier autocratic urban planning, but arguments that the Cultural Corridor succeeded because of its "democratic" and "pluralistic" qualities ring hollow. Community participation has been driven top down in hierarchical fashion, while socioeconomic inequality remains a problem. But by moderating the demands on property owners for building renovation and obscuring the coercive forces of the market economy, contemporary preservation has promoted historic placemaking. Official histories that emphasize political elites—the monarchs, presidents, and other leaders—have limited relevance for the broad public, although cultural centers like the Imperial Palace have expanded exhibitions to include a wide variety of topics, ranging from national folklore and public history to modern art. As a result, Cariocas and tourists alike have rediscovered Rio's largely renovated historic center.

The Cultural Corridor's effusive reviews, however, often overlooked the program's uneven results, overemphasized the "public" benefits, and underestimated the state's role. While reflecting a search for roots, the rebranding program mounted a shrewd marketing campaign, appealing to memory in the context of urban political-economic restructuring. By encouraging renewed investment, the historic districts have, to varying degrees, rehabilitated much of Rio's city center. Entrepreneurial city managers and their commercial allies led a notable, if uneven, urban renaissance downtown. The upgrading process has been most successful and profitable in districts with notable cultural capital—the imperial aura of November 15th Square; the busy crowds on Rio Branco Boulevard, among the high-rises of Cinelândia; and the charm of Lapa's streets under the old city aqueduct as Santa Teresa's streetcars pass above. While the São Francisco and SAARA districts have witnessed less visible renovation and retain more popular and informal commerce, they also retain notable ethnic communities. Given this social diversity, incumbent upgrading with community stabilization would be a far better goal than an economic revitalization that displaces residents and merchants. Hyper-gentrification, as in a number of global cities, would remove the heart and soul of Rio's historic center.

Beyond rescuing much of the historic core from deterioration and irrelevance, the Cultural Corridor's restoration largely recaptured downtown's historical allure through the effective branding of urban heritage. The program proved to be a public-private collaboration in terms of infrastructural, commercial, and cultural investments: the city and state wielded the power of remembrance to benefit official heritage sites and high-end businesses. The informal sector of street venders, small businesses, and low- and medium-income residents has not benefited like capitalized enterprises and property owners, despite public markets with stalls at several transit hubs and squares downtown. The city center's vision of restoration descended from the highest levels of government and business, while appealing to the affluent population. One cannot help but applaud the adaptive reuse of the Imperial Palace and other notable historic monuments downtown. But where is mention of the African slave trade, which long operated on the Palace Square? Where are the sites of working-class struggles, women's lives, and the heritages of immigrants and people of color? Such social and racial diversity would benefit from more inclusive historical signage on the streets and squares downtown, which would then better narrate the Brazilian people's experience of the city and the nation. Despite such a need for a more diverse representation of public history, Rio's once-declining city center has reemerged as a major cultural and historic attraction: selective images of the past have created a fascinating, impressive, and grandiose image of the past.

NOTES

1. IPHAN, "Area Central da Praça Quinze de Novembro" (Processo 1213-T-86), Arquivo Noronha Santos, Rio de Janeiro, March 2, 1990.

2. IPHAN, *Bens móveis e imóveis inscritos nos Livros do Tombo do Instituto do Patrimônio Histórico e Artístico Nacional, 1938–2009* (Brasília: IPHAN/COPEDOC,

2009); and Brian J. Godfrey, "Remembering Rio: From the Imperial Palace to the African Heritage Circuit," in *The City as Power: Urban Space, Place, and National Identity*, ed. A. Diener and J. Hagan (Rowman & Littlefield, 2018): 105–20.

3. Riordan Roett, *Brazil: Politics in a Patrimonial Society* (Praeger, 1999); Anthony W. Pereira, "Is the Brazilian State 'Patrimonial'?" *Latin American Perspectives* 43, 2 (March 2016): 135–52.

4. Getúlio Vargas, president of the Republic of Brazil, "Decree Law n° 25 of November 1937," Rio de Janeiro, November 30, 1937, 1. Published by the Union's *Dally Journal* of December 6, 1937, and republished on December 11, 1937.

5. Process 99-T-38 (RJ, Arquivo Noronha Santos, IPHAN central archives), March 2, 1990.

6. David Harvey, "From Managerialism to Entrepreneurialism: The Transformation in Urban Governance in Late Capitalism," *Geografiska Annaler* 71B, 1 (1989): 3–17.

7. Veronica Crossa, "Resisting the Entrepreneurial City: Street Vendors' Struggle in Mexico City's Historic Center," *International Journal of Urban and Regional Research* 33, 1 (March 2009): 43–63.

8. Claudio de Paula Honorato, "Valongo: O Mercado de Escravos do Rio de Janeiro, 1758–1831" (master's thesis in history, Universidade Federal Fluminense, Niterói, 2008), 59–60.

9. Jaime L. Benchimol, *Pereira Passos: Um Haussmann tropical: A renovação urbana da cidade do Rio de Janeiro no início do século XX* (Biblioteca Carioca, 1990), 112–15, 134–46; and Sérgio Pechman and Lilian Fritsch, "A reforma urbana e seu avesso," *Revista brasileira de História* 8, 9 (1985), 148–49.

10. James N. Green, *Beyond Carnival: Male Homosexuality in Twentieth-Century Brazil* (University of Chicago Press, 1999), 112–15, 134–46.

11. Fania Fridman and Eduardo Cézar Siqueira, "O Bairro Judeu no Rio de Janeiro," International Seminar on Urban Form, *Conference Proceedings*, Ouro Preto, Brazil, August 2007; and Erik Steiner and Zephyr Frank, "Tenement Housing in Rio de Janeiro, 1870s–1880s," Stanford University, Spatial History Project, 2019, http://web.stanford.edu/group/spatialhistory/cgi-bin/site/viz.php?id=45&project_id=0.

12. Maurício de Almeida Abreu, *Evolução Urbana do Rio de Janeiro*, 4th ed. (IPLAN/RIO, 2006), 48–51.

13. IBGE (Instituto Brasileiro de Geografia e Estatística), *Anuário Estatístico do Brasil*, Brasília, 1996.

14. Murillo Marx, *Cidade Braslieira* (São Paulo, Editora da Universidade de São Paulo, 1980), 23–24; Jeffrey D. Needell, *A Tropical Belle Epoque: Elite Culture and Society in Turn-of-the-Century Rio de Janeiro* (Cambridge University Press, 1987); "Rio de Janeiro at the Turn of the Century: Modernization and the Parisian Ideal," *Journal of Interamerican Studies and World Affairs* 25, 1 (2003): 83–103.

15. Francisco Pereira Passos, *Melhoramentos da Cidade Projetadas pelo Prefeito do Distrito Federal* (Governo do Distrito Federal, 1903); and Giovanna Rosso del Brenna, *O Rio de Janeiro de Pereira Passos: Uma Cidade em Questão* (PUC, 1985).

16. T. Meade, *"Civilizing" Rio: Reform and Resistance in a Brazilian City, 1889–1930* (Pennsylvania State University, 1997).

17. Museu Nacional, "Arquitetura e História—Exposição de 1922," Rio de Janeiro, June 13, 2016.
18. Abreu, *Evolução urbana do Rio de Janiero*, 76.
19. José Bento Monteiro Lobato, "Não arrasen o morro do Castelo" in *Rio de Janeiro em Prosa e Poesia*, ed. Manuel Bandeira and Carlos Drummond de Andrade (Rio de Janeiro, José Olympio, 1965), 413–14.
20. Afonso Henriques de Lima Barreto, *Revista Careta*, Aug. 28, 1920. Quoted in exhibition "O Paço, a Praça e o Morro" (Rio de Janeiro: Paço Imperial, June 23–Aug. 28, 2016).
21. Leonardo Castriota, "Living in a World Heritage Site: Preservation Policies and Local History in Ouro Preto, Brazil," *Traditional Dwellings and Settlements Review* 10, 2 (1999): 10.
22. IPHAN, *Bens móveis e imóveis inscritos nos Livros do Tombo do Instituto do Patrimônio Histórico e Artístico Nacional* (RJ: IPHAN/COPEDOC, 2009); and http://www.iphan.gov.br/. For clarity and convenience of usage in English, I translate *Livros do Tombo* as National Historic Registers, comprising four registry books.
23. IPHAN, *Bens móveis e imóveis inscritos*; and http://www.iphan.gov.br.
24. IPHAN, *Bens móveis e imóveis inscritos*; and http://www.iphan.gov.br.
25. Vargas, "Decree-Law nº 25 of November 1937."
26. Anne S. Martin, "Cultural Conservation in Brazil: Saving Pelourinho" (PhD diss., University of Florida, 1993), 54–56.
27. UNESCO, "World Heritage List," http://whc.unesco.org/en/list, accessed March 2019.
28. Augusto Ivan de Freitas Pinheiro, "A cidade e o tempo," in *Rio de Janeiro: Cinco Séculos de História e Transformações Urbanas*, ed. A. Pinheiro (Rio de Janeiro: Casa da Palavra, 2010), 21–41; and Carlos Lessa, *O Rio de Todos os Brasis (Uma Reflexão em Busca de Auto-Estima)* (Editora Record, 2000), 413.
29. A. Pinheiro, "Novas Experiências em urbanismo: Barra da Tijuca e Corredor Cultural," in Capítulos da memória do urbanismo carioca, ed. A. Freire, L. L. Oliveira (Rio de Janeiro: Folha Seca, 2002), 202–21.
30. IPHAN, Arquivo Noronha Santos, Central Archives, Rio de Janeiro, http://portal.iphan.gov.br/ans/inicial.htm (accessed Sept. 13, 2020).
31. Pinheiro, "Novas Experiências em urbanismo," 202–21.
32. A. Pinheiro, "Aprendendo com o Patrimônio," in *Cidade: História e desafios*, ed. L. L. Oliveira (Rio de Janeiro: Ed. Fundação Getulio Vargas, 2002), 141–55.
33. RIOARTE, *Corredor Cultural: Como Recuperar, Reformar, ou Construir seu Imóvel* (Rio de Janeiro: Instituto Municipal de Arte e Cultura, 2002).
34. Roberta Sampaio Guimarães, "O patrimônio cultural na gestão dos espaços do Rio de Janeiro," *Estudos Históricos* 29, 57 (Jan.–April 2016).
35. Ricardo Maranhão, *Cinelândia: Retorno ao fascínio do passado* (Rio de Janeiro: Letra Capital Editora, 2003).
36. Notes from a walking tour by Professor João Baptista Ferreira de Mello, "LAPA: Roteiro Noturno no Centro do Rio a Pé," July 14, 2011.
37. Susane Worcman, *SAARA* (Rio de Janeiro: Relume Dumará, 2000).

38. Lúcio Costa, quoted in *Lúcio Costa: Documentos de Trabalho*, 2nd ed., ed. José Pessôa (Brasília: IPHAN, 1998), 286–87; and IPHAN central archives, Rio de Janeiro, Process 0986-T-78.

39. RIOARTE (Instituto Municipal de Arte e Cultura, Rio de Janeiro), *Corredor Cultural: Como Recuperar, Reformar ou Construir seu Imóvel* (Rio de Janeiro: Prefeitura da Cidade/Instituto Pereira Passos, 2002), preface.

40. RIOARTE, *Corredor Cultural: Como Recuperar, Reformar, ou Construir seu Imóvel*, RIOARTE (Instituto Municipal de Arte e Cultura, Rio de Janeiro). *Corredor Cultural: Como Recuperar, Reformar ou Construir seu Imóvel*, 4th ed. (Rio de Janeiro: Prefeitura da Cidade/Instituto Pereira Passos, 2002).

41. Vicente del Rio, "Restructuring Inner-City Areas in Rio de Janeiro: Urban Design for a Pluralistic Downtown," *Journal of Architectural and Planning Research* 14, 1 (1997): 20–34. See also Augusto Ivan Pinheiro and Vicente Del Rio, "Cultural Corridor: A Preservation District in Downtown Rio de Janeiro, Brazil," *Traditional Dwellings and Settlement Review* IV, 11 (1993): 51–84.

42. Guimarães, "O patrimônio cultural," 149–68.

43. Area Central da Praça Quinze de Novembro (Processo 1213-T-86), IPHAN.

44. Luiz C. Edmundo, *Rio in the Time of the Viceroys* (Rio de Janeiro: J.R. de Oliveira, 1936), 16–17.

45. In colonial times, Teles was spelled "Telles," but I follow IPHAN's modern spelling, except when translating historical commentaries. Process 99-T-38, Arquivo Noronha Santos, IPHAN central archives, Rio de Janeiro.

46. Lieutenant Henry Chamberlain, *Vistas e Costumes da Cidade e Arredores do Rio de Janeiro em 1819–1820* (Rio de Janeiro & São Paulo: Livraria Kosmos Editora, 1943), 195. Originally published by Columbian Press, London, 1822.

47. Jean-Baptiste Debret, *Voyage Pittoresque et Historique au Brésil* (Paris: Actes Sud, Aries, 1834). Planche 58, "Les rafraîchissements de l'après-dîner sur la place du palais," 173.

48. IPHAN, "Area Central da Praça Quinze de Novembro," Processo 1213-T-86 (Rio de Janeiro, Arquivo Noronha Santos, IPHAN central archives) Oct. 28, 1986.

49. Daryle Williams, *Culture Wars in Brazil*, 114–20; and processes 55-T-38, 99-T-38, and 1213-T-86, Arquivo Noronha Santos, IPHAN central archives, Rio de Janeiro.

50. IPHAN Process 23-9-1955 (Rio de Janeiro, Arquivo Noronha Santos, IPHAN central archives); Processes 55T and 56T, DPHAN Conselho Consultivo (Rio de Janeiro, Arquivo Noronha Santos, IPHAN central archives); and *Diário Oficial do Estado da Guanabara,* Atos do Poder Executivo, Feb. 18, 1961.

51. Alberto A. Cohen and Sergio A. Fridman, *Rio de Janeiro: Ontem e Hoje 2* (Rio de Janeiro: Rioarte 2004), 18–19.

52. Olivia Bandeira, "Derrubada da Perimetral Reformulará Sistema Viário do Centro do Rio," *Infraestrutura Urbana*, June 2012.

53. Vertical Shopping, Rio de Janeiro, http://verticalshopping.com.br/conheca-o-shopping/.

54. M. Christine Boyer, *The City of Collective Memory: The Historical Imagery and Architetural Entertainments* (Cambridge, MA: MIT Press, 1996), 421–22.

55. David Harvey, "Monument and Myth: The Building of the Basilica of the Sacred Heart," in *Consciousness and the Urban Experience* (Oxford University Press, 1985), 223.

56. Paço Imperial (Rio de Janeiro, RJ), *Livros do Tombo*, Aquivo Noronha Santos, IPHAN; and Lauro Cavalcante, "Twenty Years as an IPHAN Cultural Center," in *Paço Imperial,* ed. Lauro Cavalcanti (RJ: Editora Index, 2005), 11–16.

57. Paço Imperial, IPHAN Processo 159-T-38 (Rio de Janeiro, Arquivo Noronha Santos, IPHAN central archives), 1938; Gilberto Ferrez, *O Paço da Cidade do Rio de Janeiro*, Fundação Nacional Pró-Memória, 1984, 82; and Antonio Torres, "The Palace, Step by Step," in *Paço Imperial*, ed. Lauro Cavalcanti (RJ: Editora Index, 2005), 77–104.

58. Edmundo, *Rio in the Time of the Viceroys*, 16.

59. João Maurício Rugendas, *Viagem Pitoresca através do Brasil* (São Paulo: Livraria Martins, 1940), 19.

60. Joaquim Manuel de Macedo, *Um passeio pela cidade do Rio de Janeiro*, ed. Diogo de Hollanda (São Paulo: Editora Planeta do Brasil, 2004), I: 27–87.

61. Paço Imperial, IPHAN Processo 159-T-38 (Rio de Janeiro, Arquivo Noronha Santos, IPHAN central archives), 1938; Ferrez, *O Paço da Cidade do Rio de Janeiro*, 82; Torres, "The Palace, Step by Step," 77–104.

62. Process 0199-T-39 (Rio de Janeiro, Arquivo Noronha Santos, IPHAN central archives).

63. Maria Beatriz Rezende, Bettina Grieco, Luciano Teixeira, and Analucia Thompson, "Fundação Nacional Pró-Memória, 1979–1990," in *Dicionário IPHAN do Patrimônio Cultural* (Rio de Janeiro, Brasília: IPHAN/DAF/Copedoc, 2015) (verbete).

64. Lauro Cavalcante, "1982–1992: Dez anos na história recente do Paço Imperial," in *Paço Imperial*, ed. Sergio Pagano, Heloisa Buarque de Hollanda, and Lauro Cavalcante (Rio de Janeiro: Sextante Artes, 1999), 18–20.

65. Process 0199-T-39 (Rio de Janeiro, Arquivo Noronha Santos, IPHAN central archives); Cavalcante, "1982–1992," 21–22.

66. Harvey, "Monument and Myth," 249.

67. Paço Imperial, "Histórico e Missão," http://www.amigosdopacoimperial.org.br/.

68. Svetlana Boym, "Nostalgia and Its Discontents," quoted in *The Collective Memory Reader*, eds. J. K. Olick, V. Vinitzky-Seroussi, and D. Levy (Oxford and New York: Oxford University Press, 2011), 452–57.

Chapter 3

Little Africa

Afro-Brazilian Heritage and Historic Placemaking

> Valongo Wharf is a site that awakens memories of traumatic historic events and is bound up with aspects of pain and survival in the history of the forefathers of people of African descent, who sum over half of the contemporary Brazilian population.
>
> —International Committee on Monuments and Sites, 2017[1]

In January of 2011, workers of the "Wonderful Port" (Porto Maravilha) renewal program inadvertently uncovered remnants of Rio's Valongo Wharf, where at least a million enslaved Africans landed during the first half of the nineteenth century. If not quarantined for disease, the emaciated newcomers proceeded to "fattening houses" nearby for inspection by potential buyers. Amid growing opposition to the slave trade, the original wharf disappeared in 1843 under the stately new Empress Wharf, built to receive Tereza Cristina of Bourbon, Princess of the Two Sicilies, who would wed Emperor Pedro II. In the surrounding port district of Gamboa arose the large Afro-Brazilian community Little Africa. Subsequent waterfront expansion and renewal buried the Empress Wharf between 1903 and 1911, after which new piers, railroads, and elevated expressways devalued the residential area and dispersed the population (see figure 3.1). Then, a century later, remains of the two successive wharves reappeared under layers of pavement, landfill, and debris. While some historians and local residents knew the approximate location of the hidden wharves, most Cariocas were unaware of them and their links to slavery. As the news media reported on the archeological excavations, evidence of the transatlantic human traffic alternately shocked, fascinated, and angered the public.

In a city that largely ignored or erased the historical presence of African slaves, it was not entirely surprising that authorities initially planned to pave

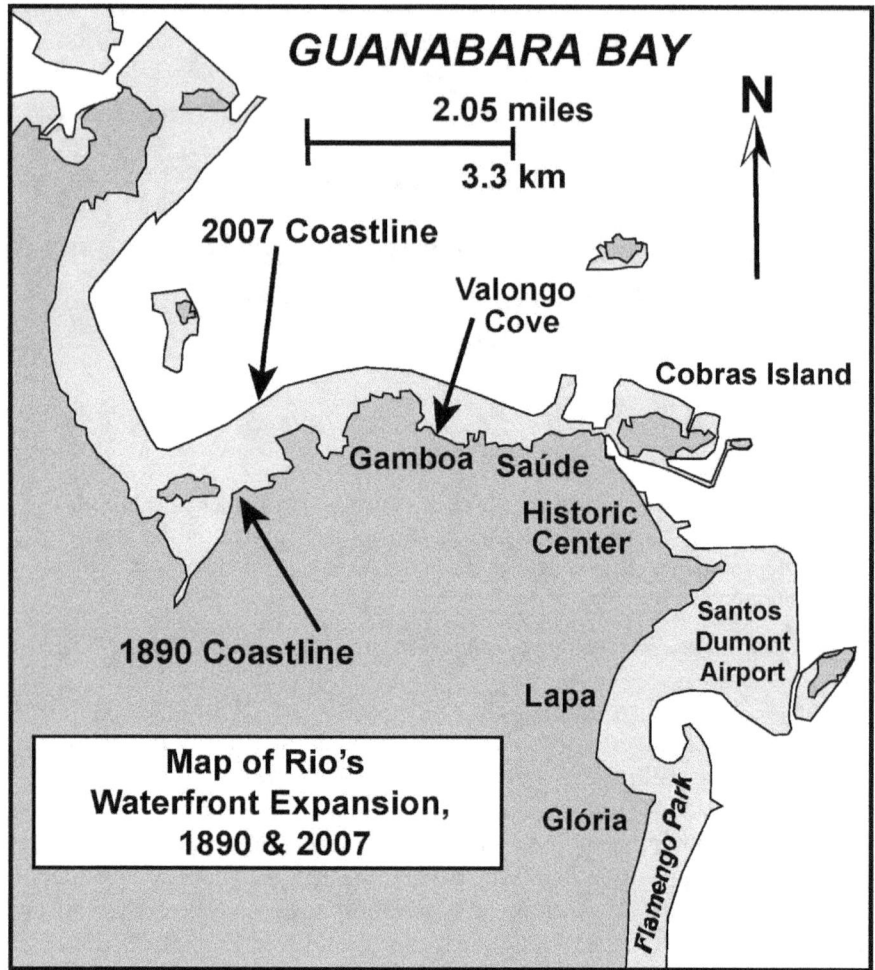

Figure 3.1. Map of waterfront expansion in Rio de Janeiro. By the author.

over the rediscovered wharf remains, so as to proceed quickly with waterfront redevelopment. Rio had long suffered from amnesia regarding its Afro-descendant past, given the government's repeated removal of slave sites and predominantly Black communities. Furthermore, urban renewal programs had repeatedly demolished poor communities in the way of "progress," including the fin de siècle downtown demolitions, destruction of Castle Hill in the 1920s, clearing of historic buildings for the construction of Avenida Vargas in the 1940s, and massive displacement of favelas in the 1960s and 1970s under the military-authoritarian regime. Despite increasingly vocal protests, the city and state of Rio de Janeiro repeatedly removed low-income residents to redevelop sites with more desirable land uses, as documented by the influential exhibition "Memory of Destruction: Rio—A History of What Was Lost (1889–1965)," held at the City Archives in 2001–2002.[2]

Given this destructive legacy, it came as no surprise that the waterfront renewal program initially resisted preservation of the wharves' ruins. For the authorities, saving the sites would require changing plans for new pipelines and roadwork, which would prove costly and further delay preparations for the 2014 FIFA World Cup and the 2016 Olympic Games. Indeed, those planning the athletic mega-events removed neighborhoods that blocked construction, even though the displacement proved unpopular and received critical press coverage. Community defense, not demolition, had come to prevail politically—rhetorically, if not always in practice. Indeed, public opinion strongly supported heritage conservation of the Valongo site. Black religious and political groups, public intellectuals, and general public opinion demanded preservation rather than redevelopment, particularly after the nearby construction of the Museum of Tomorrow and the Museum of Art of Rio de Janeiro (MAR). This controversy regarding the uncertain status of old Valongo Wharf, compared to the two trendy new museums, led to an unexpected public debate about whether the city was neglecting its past in the rush to rebuild for a revitalized future in the port district.[3]

News of the slave wharf's reappearance prompted a reactivation of place memory. Previously, in late 2010, a public-relations bulletin of the Wonderful Port program published a history of Gamboa with no mention of slavery, which would be unthinkable after Valongo Wharf's rediscovery soon thereafter.[4] As opposed to the previous perception of the port district as a deteriorated slum in need of redevelopment, alternative narratives arose of Afro-Brazilian heritage. In November of 2011, the City Council authorized an African Heritage Circuit comprising the slave wharf, a cemetery, a public square and a park, as well as other historic sites. This rapid change in community identity reflected the urban politics, the potential tourism, and the development pressures of upcoming athletic mega-events. A pivotal moment came in 2012, at the Rio Post-2016 program on the city's post-Olympic future, when Mayor Eduardo Paes endorsed the Valongo archeological project as "Rio's Roman ruins," thereby signaling official support of a potentially major tourist attraction. In other words, the city's recognition would have immediate political-economic benefits as well as long-term financial paybacks.

Valongo Wharf became the quintessential site of Rio's African heritage in short order, an occurrence that began to fill a notable racial gap in the city's array of public memorials and monuments. This unexpected but long overdue recognition illustrates the contemporary political power of repressed remembrance in our post-holocaust age. In the port district, historic placemaking revived a defunct place identity, based on the oppressions and ruins of the slave past, for such present-day purposes as ethnic pride, racial reparation, public history, and cultural tourism. According to the UNESCO World Heritage listing in 2017, the Valongo Wharf Archeological Site commemorates "the most important physical evidence of the arrival of enslaved Africans on the American continent." Beyond this historical role, the memorial site has become "a site of conscience, which illustrates strong and tangible associations to one of the most terrible crimes of humanity, the enslavement of hundreds of thousands of people, which created the largest forced migration movement in history."[5]

Given the recent revival of Little Africa's sense of place, this chapter traces the local history of Afro-Brazilian slavery and cultural heritage in terms of contested memory, placemaking, and urban change. Complicated by unexpected twists and turns, the saga also reflects Rio's evolving politics and power dynamics. While the ruins of Valongo Wharf quickly attracted a dedicated following of African-descendant spiritual and cultural groups, the site also became a new and growing tourist destination. The entrepreneurial city began to market ethnic heritage as a way to promote urban redevelopment and cultural tourism, thereby further promoting the revival of Little Africa's place memory—or more precisely, counter-memory, since the rediscovery of the Valongo site represented the exposure of a long-hidden history of oppression and violence. While beneficial for political activism and community solidarity, memorialization of Rio's Little Africa also suggests the limitations of cultural heritage in promoting social change. Despite openness to multicultural celebration, policies have encouraged heritage tourism and urban revitalization without significantly challenging the deeply embedded structural and systemic realities of racial inequality. Yet the Valongo Heritage site certainly reignited passionate debates about race relations in Brazil.

COUNTER-MEMORY AND CULTURAL REINVENTION

Michel Foucault regarded "counter-memory" as an alternative to dominant histories promoted by governments, mass media, and culture industries. He saw it as an oppositional stance, which rejected mainstream views of historical progress while rescuing the ignored, forgotten, and excluded versions of the past.[6] This critical view of remembrance provides an antidote to the numbing of historical consciousness in contemporary society, ever more dominated by televised spectacle and commercial entertainment. Given an impoverishment of memory with the spread of modern technologies, consumerism, and political disenfranchisement, Andreas Huyssen suggests that "historical memory is not what it used to be."[7] Similarly, T. J. Demos sees a "loss of historical experience and the diminishment of political agency, as collective identity is defined more and more by reactionary and intolerant forms such as nationalism, fandom, and consumerism."[8]

In a context of heritage-based cultural reinvention, counter-memory proposes a reawakening and reassertion of citizenship. Two examples serve to illustrate this oppositional concept. First, in a former colony like Brazil, counter-memory would emphasize struggles against colonialism in favor of self-determination and independence. Second, in an actual example from Rio de Janeiro, city and state governments have long sought to placate favela districts through promises of infrastructure improvements, urban services, community policing, and general socioeconomic progress, while informal communities stressed their struggles against displacement and for human rights and basic needs not met by governments. Counter-memories may not always constitute full-fledged narratives but can still challenge dominant readings of history; the suffering and unhappy fate of transported slave labor would fit this description. Such antiestablishment viewpoints may suffer in relative silence, leading to the apparent erasure of group heritage from public histories and cultural landscapes—unless there is a reactivation of counter-memory, as with the rediscovery of historic Little Africa.

Counter-memory often finds vivid expression in memorials to those who have suffered from social injustice or violence. Recognizing the ruptures, omissions, and ambiguities of remembrance, artists and cultural critics may respond with projects that confront observers with troubling issues that resist easy resolution. Such monuments aim to stimulate discussion and debate, rather than to preserve a calcified past. Given the horrors of contemporary wars and terrorism, for instance, traditional heroic tributes can seem insufficient. As a result, creative responses to violence now incorporate elements of human instability, loss, and grief. Artistic installations often question unexamined assumptions, ponder diverse perspectives on the past, and reflect on future social and political directions. Rather than build grandiose monuments to war heroes or powerful leaders, the new thinking stresses "open-endedness, complexity, ambiguity, discussion, involvement—and impermanence."[9] Provocative contemporary memorials now respond to the Holocaust, struggles of war, ethnic genocide, human rights, terrorist attacks, and the African diaspora. In Rio de Janeiro, the horrors of the slave trade have yet to be adequately memorialized, but the reappearance of Valongo Wharf and the Cemetery of New Blacks (Pretos Novos, born in Africa) has sparked related debates still not fully resolved.

Official memory and counter-memory often intersect at sites of institutional power in Rio. Large political demonstrations often occur at historic monuments and governmental buildings downtown, which provide highly symbolic targets for public outrage. Over the years, strikes by public employees and political protests by citizens have led to major disputes, both peaceful and violent. Some protests have been massive and virtually shut down the city. At the turn of the twentieth century, violent protests targeted the urban "reforms" that displaced the working classes downtown, while mandating an unprecedented smallpox vaccination in poor districts: mobs battled police, looted buildings, and burned streetcars during the "Revolt of the Vaccine" during November 10–18, 1904. More recently, large protests occurred during a national movement against bus-fare hikes, governmental corruption, and the costs of hosting international mega-events. On June 17–18, 2013, some one hundred thousand people attended a largely peaceful protest next to the old Imperial Palace, which later turned violent when splinter groups invaded the state's Legislative Chamber and vandalized banks and public buildings downtown. Beyond such intermittent protests in the historic center, the most enduring counter-memories have emerged on the city's peripheries, marginalized from the centers of state power.

Such was the case in early 2011 of the rediscovered Valongo Wharf, which reactivated the dormant place identity of Little Africa. This rescued heritage site challenged Rio's historical self-image as a racially mixed but largely European imperial city. While the northeastern city of Salvador da Bahia proudly proclaimed itself the cultural capital of Black Brazil, Rio largely ignored the heritage of its large African-descendant population. As a result, popular opinion long favored Salvador as the appropriate place to study Afro-Brazilian history and culture. But Rio also has grounds for making this claim. While both cities were major slave ports, Rio received far more enslaved Africans than did Bahia. But prevailing opinion in Rio long favored forgetting the city's slave past. Although foreign travelers often referred to Rio's slave markets, early Brazilian histories usually chronicled the city's natural beauty and elite culture with little mention of Afro-descendant Brazilians. This omission may have stemmed partly from a lack of archival materials on Black life, but it probably also reflected Rio's long role as the national and commercial capital, widespread but thinly disguised racism, and the general low status of the people of color. In any case, this oversight goes back centuries. As historian Mary Karasch observed, "Most urban histories of Rio create the impression that Rio was a Luso-Brazilian city of White faces and European culture; but it was not, as any careful reading of the travel literature reveals."[10]

The contours and magnitude of the transatlantic slave trade have long been hard to grasp, due to scattered source materials and uncertainty about accurate figures on the "middle passage" between Africa and the Americas. Fortunately, recent advances in quantitative research have greatly enhanced our understanding of the African diaspora. The Transatlantic Slave Trade Database estimates that 4.86 million African slaves disembarked in Brazil between 1561 and 1856, comprising 45 percent of all those who landed in the Western Hemisphere. Mainland North America, in contrast, received some 389,000, or 3.6 percent of the hemisphere's slave traffic. Today Brazil has the largest population of African descent outside of Africa. Within Brazil, Rio de Janeiro served as the largest slave port by far. While an estimated 1.55 million captive Africans landed in the state of Bahia, some 2.36 million slaves arrived in southeastern Brazil (see table 3.1).

These data indicate that Rio de Janeiro historically served as the largest slave port in the Americas, probably in the world. In fact, UNESCO's world heritage program regards Rio "as the biggest slave harbor in human history."[11] The massive movement of enslaved labor, driven by the emerging capitalist relations of the Atlantic world, reflected Brazil's subordinate colonial position as a producer of lucrative primary commodities—particularly gold, diamonds, sugar, coffee, and rubber. Given Portuguese economic dependence on Britain, colonial Brazil fell victim to an international web of economic exploitation. As historian E. Bradford Burns recounted: "It has been observed with some sagacity and a little exaggeration that Brazilian gold mined by African slaves financed English industrialization."[12]

Table 3.1. Slave Disembarkations in North America and Brazil, 1501–1900

Years	Mainland North America	Brazil			Hemispheric Total
		Bahia, Brazil	Southeastern Brazil (Rio)	Brazil, Total	
1501–1550	0	0	0	0	44,909
1551–1600	0	5,647	4,770	29,275	154,377
1601–1650	100	115,517	80,712	320,406	527,705
1651–1700	15,047	197,956	140,371	464,050	994,969
1701–1750	145,973	416,045	281,461	891,851	2,168,888
1751–1800	149,509	399,859	475,099	1,097,166	3,440,981
1801–1850	77,704	414,350	1,275,932	2,054,726	3,181,566
1851–1900	413	981	5,568	6,899	189,257
Totals	388,746	1,550,355	2,263,913	4,864,373	10,702,652

Source: "Voyages Database," Transatlantic Slave Trade Data Base, 2010, http://www.slavevoyages.org/assessment/estimates.

SLAVE PORT AND DIVIDED CITY

Although the transatlantic slave trade started in sixteenth-century Brazil and grew through the booms and busts of Brazilian wood, sugar cane, minerals, and other commodities, the late eighteenth century witnessed a slowdown in the importation of enslaved Africans. Many slaves were freed in Brazil as domestic and international opposition arose to the "peculiar institution." The arrival of new slaves in Rio's harbor fell to fewer than ten thousand annually, as gold and diamond production declined in colonial Minas Gerais. But soon after the turn of the nineteenth century, a massive final wave of slave landings began. Rio de Janeiro became the epicenter of this renewed African diaspora, the largest yet in terms of the numbers of slaves disembarked in the city. With the landing of the Portuguese royal court in 1808, along with the expansion of coffee plantations in southeastern Brazil, increasing labor demands pushed the yearly arrival of new slaves up to 20,000 or more. In the first half of the nineteenth century, an annual average of 25,518 enslaved Africans disembarked in Rio, not including internal migrations of Brazilian-born slaves. Mary Karasch has suggested that between 900,000 and 950,000 captive Africans, possibly a million or more, landed in Rio from 1808 to 1850.[13] Scholars now incline toward the higher figures, as the transatlantic traffic reached its peak during this period. Recent estimates suggest that 1.28 million new African slaves arrived in and around the city of Rio de Janeiro between 1801 and 1850.[14]

This period also witnessed a general shift in slave origins from the early dominance of the Guinea "Slave Coast" along the Bight of Benin in West Africa to greater numbers coming from Angola and the Congo in West-Central Africa.[15] A young Englishman who visited Rio in 1819–1820, Lieutenant Henry Chamberlain, son of the British consul, commented in his book on late-colonial Rio: "The number of wretched Africans imported into Rio de Janeiro every year from Congo, Angola, Benguella, or Mozambique may be computed to average about 20,000; rarely falling short of 18,000, and as rarely exceeding 22,000." He added: "The revenue the State derives from this inhuman traffick [sic] may be estimated at about 80,000 sterling, per Annum. The sufferings of the miserable Captives during the voyage from Africa are not to be described."[16]

After disembarking at Rio's Valongo Wharf, the main port of entry, most of the enslaved newcomers labored in such rural areas as the Paraíba Valley, where coffee plantations expanded their operations during this period. But a significant portion of the New Blacks (as newly arrived African slaves were called) stayed in Rio. When the Portuguese king ended his tropical residence and returned to Lisbon in 1821, Rio's enslaved population had reached

57,549—virtually half the total city population of 116,444.[17] During the royal residence, the city had doubled in size and grown more cosmopolitan, but also became notably more dependent on slave labor. By 1831, during the first decade of national independence, a record 335,069 captive Africans landed at Valongo. In 1826 and 1831, successive imperial decrees banned the international slave trade with Brazil, but the measures lacked full enforcement in the face of opposition from plantation owners. The transatlantic slave traffic declined after the peak years of the 1820s, due to growing internal and external opposition, but it did not stop entirely for more than two decades. The illicit human traffic continued more clandestinely, often at surrounding landing sites with less scrutiny by authorities than at Valongo. Between 1831 and 1856, slave disembarkations in the city conservatively numbered 102,772 (a yearly average of 4,100), while nearby landings reached 38,208 (an annual average of 1,528) in the larger province of Rio de Janeiro. In 1851, the British Royal Navy's West Africa Squadron intensified efforts to interdict slave vessels on the high seas—forcibly stopping them and seizing, and returning to Africa the captive slaves on board. This naval campaign dramatically diminished the transatlantic slave traffic. The last new African slaves to arrive in Brazil, on the record, landed in 1856.[18]

Before Valongo Wharf became the favored site of disembarkation, colonial slave markets proliferated on Direita Street (now Rua 1 de Março), located conveniently close to the central waterfront, the customs house, and other institutions of colonial power. By the mid-eighteenth century, dozens of slave-trading businesses could be found in central Rio. With the growing numbers of New Blacks on the streets, medical professionals and the City Council proposed the removal of slave markets from the urban core, purportedly for reasons of public health. In 1718, the City Council requested the right to require a "health visit" for all ships coming to Rio from Angola, Costa Mina, and São Tomé; the king granted the authority to do so, even suggesting that the measure be extended to ships from Bahia, Pernambuco, and parts of Europe. The city authorities then announced that the commerce in enslaved Africans would be transferred to Valongo Cove at a northern landing on Guanabara Bay. This move did not actually occur until the late eighteenth century, but the pathologizing of Africans became evident earlier. Slave traders long downplayed the risk of disease and argued that the port transfer was unnecessary.[19]

As population growth accelerated in Rio, pressure intensified to relocate the slave trade to remote Valongo Cove. In 1758, the City Council met to discuss the "grave damage done to the city by the slaves that were sold in the principal streets" and to propose policy solutions. In 1759, the city councilors ordered the transfer of the human markets to the urban periphery. Given the opposition of slave traders, however, the measure did not take effect. With the viceroys' presence after 1763, this "sanitarist" perspective gained support: according to this logic, spatial isolation would prevent newly arriving slaves from spreading diseases, while those with illnesses would be quarantined until they got healthy. But such segregation would lessen the profits from the slave trade, so merchants opposed the regulations. In 1765, the City Council republished the notice that arriving African slaves should be removed from the city center, but again the policy lacked enforcement. The measure provoked debate over whether the New Blacks endangered public health: some health professionals reversed their prior positions, apparently being paid to do so, and they again testified that newly arrived slaves did not actually pose a risk of disease.[20]

The stalemate only changed with the arrival of a forceful new viceroy from Portugal. In 1769, the Marquess of Lavradio—Luís de Almeida Portugal Soares de Alarcão d'Eça e Melo Silva Mascarenhas—became the eleventh viceroy of Brazil, the second since Rio became the colonial capital. Charged with ensuring the crown's tax income from the diamond district of Minas Gerais, Viceroy Lavradio also gave attention to the colonial capital, which faced growing pains. Lavradio was horrified by the sight of arriving slaves—virtually naked, emaciated, often sick—on the waterfront of Palace Square, in full view of the vice-regal palace, the cathedral, and elite residences. His concern centered on the disconcerting appearance, rather than the humanitarian plight of the human cargo. Lavradio described the problem in these terms:

> There was in this city the terrible custom that all the Blacks who came from the Coast of Africa to this port, as soon as they disembarked, entered the city and passed through the most public and principal streets, not only full of infinite diseases, but naked. Since that quality of people, as they do not have education, are like wild savages, in the middle of the streets, where they were sitting on boards stretched out there, they did everything that nature reminded them, not only causing the greatest fetid smell in the streets and neighborhoods, but the most hideous spectacle that could be presented to the eyes.[21]

In 1774, the viceroy ordered the transatlantic African slave trade definitively transferred away from the city center. Thereafter, New Blacks would first pass through the central customs house, before proceeding by boat to Valongo Cove. After landing on the beach there, the new arrivals would continue to nearby slave storehouses or, if necessary, to quarantine for those infected with leprosy or other diseases. Lavradio also specified that owners were not to enter the city center with more than "four or five" new slaves, who would have to be properly dressed, unless they were simply in transit to inland mines or plantations. While slave merchants began to transfer their operations to Valongo, some traders in the city center remained resistant, so the viceroy reiterated his orders on returning to Portugal in 1779. Lavradio's report to his successor emphasized the continued need to remove the slave trade entirely to Valongo. Ten years later, Viceroy Vasconcelos de Souza still complained about the presence of newly arrived slaves in the city center. Gradually, the slave trade transferred its operations, and the move had been completed by the Portuguese monarch's arrival in 1808. For the authorities and elites, hygienic rationales for the segregation of New Blacks became a central strategy of socio-spatial control.[22]

The Bavarian painter Johann Rugendas later published the lithograph *Débarkment*, which suggests what slaves' arrival experiences were like. His portrayal shows the newly arrived slaves in transit on rowboats from their vessels to the customs post on a harbor pier, where the government officials, guards, and merchants assembled for the inspections and payment of taxes. As Ana Lucia Araújo notes, the artist depicts the arriving slaves "as young men and male children, and despite the horrors of the Middle passage, as in his other idealized representations of the Black individuals, the naked slaves have strong and muscled bodies."[23] Rugendas was known as a staunch abolitionist, which helps to explain his depictions of slaves as strong and active participants in colonial life. Another of his images from *Voyage Pittoresque dans le Brésil*, published in 1835, shows a public whipping of an enslaved man in the Campo de Santana. In *Punitions publiques; sur la Place Ste. Anne*, the painter emphasizes the varied emotional responses to the public spectacle, given the diversity of classes and races in attendance. Mathew Riley suggests this interpretation: "The print thrusts forward the subjectivity of the spectator and, confronting him or her with the ambiguities of the position, forces a choice to cheer on the whippings or to stop them altogether by identifying with Rugendas's abolitionist stance."[24]

At Valongo Cove, for decades New Blacks landed on the beach in small boats. Between 1811 and 1816, construction of a stone landing in the colonial *pé de moleque* style of street paving (which fit irregular rocks together to form a flattened surface upon a layer of sand) facilitated the disembarkation. Although commentators often referred to Rio's "slave market" in the singular, the city never had a centralized market for the human cargo: trading took place in a series of commercial storehouses. In 1817, at least twenty different establishments lay along Valongo Street (now Camerino Street). By 1826, some fifty markets in Valongo exhibited a total of about two thousand slaves at a time, who according to observers were badly fed, treated, and housed. Isolated by distance, surrounding hills, and mangroves on Rio's northern shores, the Valongo district became a stigmatized place, tainted by the horrors of slavery and viewed by White observers as dirty, diseased, and disreputable. After disembarking from a horrendous transatlantic voyage that many of the involuntary passengers did not survive, the arriving African slaves proceeded to the "fattening houses," where they would be inspected by potential buyers. Historian Bráz Hermenegildo do Amaral described the markets as follows: "During the day the slaves were made to go outside these storehouses to be exhibited for sale, as is done today with cattle. Interested buyers could browse at their leisure through the human herd."[25]

Unfortunately, no written accounts by African slaves arriving in Rio have come to light, but European visitors published works with detailed descriptions of the slave trade. Lieutenant Henry Chamberlain included colorful images and descriptions of the Valongo district in his book, published in 1822. Chamberlain commented that, "properly speaking, there is no Slave Market. The lower parts of the houses are allotted for these unhappy Beings, who sit huddled together in rows, one behind the other, waiting to be purchased." Constantly watched by their keepers, the newly arrived slaves "are encouraged to sing and be merry, and whether from their enjoying greater liberty, and having better food and kinder treatment than on board ship, their countenances bear few signs of sadness." It is evident in this passage that the lieutenant takes a benign view of slavery. One of his images depicts "an elderly Brazilian examining the Teeth of a Negress previous to purchase, whilst the Dealer, a Cigano [gypsy], is vehemently exercising his oratory in praise of her perfections. The woman looking on is the Purchaser's Servant Maid, who is most frequently consulted on such occasions."[26]

French artist Jean-Baptiste Debret, who traveled in Brazil from 1816 to 1831, published an illustrated book on the subject in 1834. Debret, like Chamberlain, tends to humanize the relationships between masters and slaves in an approach often known as "soft slavery." In discussing the public torture of slaves, for example, Debret suggests that Brazil is "the part of the New World in which the negro is treated with the most humanity," but he maintains that authorities require public whippings and executions to maintain order. One of the painter's most haunting images depicts a slave market at Valongo. *Boutique de la Rue du Val-Longo* shows newly arrived slaves in a storehouse, seated in small groups, famished and wasting away at this "fattening house." In his commentary, Debret describes "the selling room" as "always infected by miasmas of castor oil, flowing from the wrinkled pores of these itinerant skeletons, whose curious, nervous, and sad faces remind one of the interior of a menagerie."[27] The corpulent Cigano, seated and watchful, provides contrasts with the emaciated slaves. Occasionally the slaves "belong to diverse owners, and because of this they can be distinguished by the color of the piece of cloth that envelops them." Above this selling room, a sleeping loft serves as a dormitory for the New Blacks, who ascend by ladder at night (see figure 3.2).

Figure 3.2.   Jean-Baptiste Debret, *Boutique de la Rue du Val-Longo*, 1835, Biblioteca Brasiliana Guita e José Mindlin, 1835.

Debret also noted that "the venders and prospective buyers had to be escorted in the boutique by a surgeon when wishing to choose a Negro, who had to undergo certain tests for inspection." These physical examinations were thorough, since buyers would no longer have the right to exchange the human cargo if any physical defects were found after the sale. The painter calculated that slaves were "valued between 1800 and 2400 francs. The female Negro a bit less, and the Negro child, around 640–800 francs." Brazilians would recognize the slaves' origins by their physiognomy and distinctive character, according to Debret. In addition, the small flags above the groups indicated their ethnic regions in Africa. The artist also described the individual variations in age, appearance, and personality in one group: "The first is already a bit old, without energy, the second with a bit better health, and a bit indifferent; the third of a sad character, the fourth patient, the fifth apathetic, and the last two very sweet." The wealthy buyer in the image, wearing a large gray hat, can be seen inspecting a child "who unfortunately has a discolored stomach, symptomatic of obstructions developed back in Africa, and those like him will likely be replaced by fresh arrivals."[28]

Even in the face of growing abolitionist sentiment, Valongo Wharf long remained active in the slave trade. After the imperial decree of November 7, 1831, ordered the end of the transatlantic traffic to Brazil, Valongo was not officially supposed to receive more New Blacks. Even so, at least sixty-five thousand more African slaves arrived there between 1831 and 1842. In addition, Rio's slave port continued to receive slaves from other parts of Brazil, many of whom were actually disguised as transatlantic slaves. The slave wharf only disappeared in 1843, buried under the new Empress Wharf, constructed to receive Tereza Cristina of Bourbon, Princess of the Two Sicilies, who would wed Emperor Pedro II. The new wharf, designed by military engineer Grandjean de Montigny, covered the earlier Valongo structure by about two feet (0.6 meters). Granite flagstones formed a wall and pier, while the paving consisted of cobblestones. In 1872, a monumental granite column, still standing, arose nearby on the Municipal Square. The Empress Wharf and monument served to conceal the sordid history of slavery, thereby replacing it with a celebratory reference to the Brazilian Empire in its heyday.[29]

The Empress Wharf, in turn, disappeared under landfill between 1903 and 1911, as part of a waterfront redevelopment program that transferred the city's port from the central waterfront to the northern shoreline. After the massive landfill project, the waterfront expanded some 344 meters (376 yards) over the bay, covering the contours of Valongo Cove. On the new shoreline arose warehouses, railroad and vehicular transportation facilities, and other infrastructure. The Municipal Square, rechristened the Journal of Commerce Square, retained the monumental column to the empress with an added commemorative plaque, inscribed as follows:

IN THIS PLACE EXISTED THE EMPRESS WHARF

In 1843, the old Valongo Wharf was widened and beautified to receive the future Empress Teresa Cristina, who arrived to marry Pedro II

As a result, memory of the slave wharf gradually receded into the mists of time. A local historian later remarked: "Why does the same column not say that the slave wharf was refashioned into an elegant, imperial one in order to conceal our past?"[30] While a few such informed residents were aware of the district's slave heritage, most people had little if any knowledge of it. Although never entirely forgotten by historians, Valongo receded from public awareness. The lack of visible ruins weakened place memory—as intended, according to observers. Washington Fajardo, former head of the city's cultural heritage agency, told newspapers: "The decision to bury the wharf was deliberate. I believe it was a strategy to erase the memory of the practice of slavery."[31]

Slavery ended gradually in Brazil. Rather than ending by civil war, slavery withered away from the increasing legal restrictions and the owners' freeing of slaves. Under abolitionist pressure and subject to the threat obstruction and of seizure by the British navy, the influx of enslaved Africans ended by 1856, when there were about three million in Brazil—42 percent of the national population. Thereafter, the proportion of Brazilian-born slaves rose steadily, while that of the foreign New Blacks declined. Rio's slave commerce became decentralized in a series of individual markets, scattered over the city, rather than concentrated in the trading houses of Valongo.[32] In 1871, the Rio Branco law, or the "Law of the Free Womb," declared future children of slaves born in Brazil to be free. Then, in 1885, the Saraiva-Cotegipe law freed all slaves at the age of sixty. By this point, plantation owners relied increasingly on hired labor by southern European and Japanese immigrants, which proved cheaper than maintaining a fixed slave population. Still, Rio remained home to the largest enslaved population of any hemispheric city until the "Golden Law" officially ended slavery on May 13, 1888.[33]

The transatlantic slave trade's human movements greatly affected Rio de Janeiro, which was the largest recipient of enslaved African in the Americas and probably the world. Influential Afro-Brazilian cultural innovations arose in the city, although Black contributions have been downplayed by White elites. While the memory of Valongo Wharf waned after the abolition of slavery and subsequent waterfront redevelopment, the site remained historically important. It had hosted an enormous number of slaves who disembarked there, spatially separated from the city center for purposes of sanitarist segregation, low visibility, and social control. These veiled strategies of racial oppression made the eventual rediscovery of the Valongo Wharf all the more important, both by reminding people of the port's role in the slave trade and by leading to a remarkable reactivation of place memory with a World Heritage site in 2017.

Valongo had become an established place name by slavery's abolition in 1888, evident in historical records and maps of the era, even if the popular memory gradually waned thereafter. In the fiction of Brazilian literary master Machado de Assis (1839–1908), the appearance of "Valongo" signified the slave traffic, slavery, and emancipation. *The Posthumous Memoirs of Brás Cubas*, first published in 1881, has the narrator pass "through Valongo," where he observes "a Negro who was whipping another Negro in the square." The Black man inflicting the beating was Prudêncio, his own childhood slave. As his former master, the narrator begs Prudêncio to grant the slave mercy, which he does. Brás then reflects on the episode: "It was a way that Prudêncio had to rid himself of the blows he had received in his lifetime—by transmitting them to someone else . . . now that he could work, relax, sleep, as he willed, unrestrained, now he rose and became top man: he bought a slave and paid to him, in full and with interest, the amount he had received from me." In the Machadian geography, "Valongo" represents slavery's lingering physical, emotional, and symbolic presence. The disappearance of the old slave wharf reflects an attempted assimilation. As Rogério Pacheco Jordão has noted, "the word Valongo suggests a double reminder: that of the history of slave trafficking and the trajectory of forgetting this past in the city."[34]

VALONGO WHARF: MAKING A WORLD HERITAGE SITE

During the late nineteenth century, Brazilian intellectuals grappled with issues of national identity, race, and development. In a country comprising largely people of color, but governed by privileged White elites, the nationalist ideology of "racial democracy" arose to obscure continuing prejudice and thereby unify the country. As a school of thought, racial democracy describes Brazilian race relations as harmonious and lacking in racial discrimination, due both to Luso-Brazilian tolerance and a relatively flexible cultural framework of race classification. Sociologist Gilberto Freyre popularized this theory in such works as *The Masters and the Slaves*, first published in 1933, which rejected apologies for Brazil's race mixture and largely praised indigenous and African contributions. Instead, Freyre celebrated miscegenation and rehabilitated the mulatto in the national consciousness: tolerant racial attitudes, he argued, helped to bridge the "social distance" between masters and slaves, thereby creating a basis for national assimilation. Indeed, as opposed to the Anglo-American model of segregation, based on the "one drop" rule of racial identity, Brazilians have tended to see race as a continuum of color, rather than a dichotomy. Although the model of equitable race relations has by now been held up for critical scrutiny and debunked, it does help to explain post-abolition efforts to eliminate reminders of slavery.[35]

The fading away of Valongo as a distinctive place also coincided with the rise of positivist ideals of freedom, progress, and capitalism in fin de siècle Brazil. Through the rebuilding of Rio's downtown, port, and waterfront, the national capital would be "civilized," the colonial past would be left behind in a new "tropical Paris," and Brazil could take its place among the world's leading countries. Construction of the new docks between 1903 and 1911 included improvements to warehouses, larger ship berths, cranes for unloading, and landfill along the waterfront. As historian Teresa Meade has pointed out, "The importance of the harbor and dock renovations should not be underestimated."[36] While Meade refers here primarily to socioeconomic impacts, urban renewal also had important symbolic implications. The disappearance of the Valongo slave wharf, first by the construction of the Empress Wharf and then by waterfront redevelopment, concealed the past. After the port redevelopment at the turn of the twentieth century, the waterfront was no longer widely connected to slavery in the popular mind.

Despite a long silence regarding the city's slave past, contemporary placemaking has reinvented Valongo's memory and better connected it to the African diaspora. UNESCO's Slave Routes Project: Resistance, Liberty, Heritage, launched in 1994, has sought to "break the silence about the slave trade and slavery" and "to enhance the understanding of diverse histories and heritages stemming from this global tragedy." This project focuses on public education related to the slave trade in the Atlantic and Indian Oceans, Arab-Muslim trade, and modern slavery. In addition, it has recognized scores of international memorial sites and places of slavery, including World Heritage sites and others linked to the slave trade. Milton Guran, a Brazilian anthropologist and participant, advocated for the recognition of Valongo Wharf in the Slave Routes project. On November 18–20, 2013, at a meeting of the International Scientific Committee of the Slave Routes Project in Rio de Janeiro, the committee inducted Valongo Wharf, while a group of Brazilian historians presented a list of one hundred other sites of memory associated with slavery and the slave trade in Brazil.[37]

Contemporary memorials to the victims of slavery have arisen around the world. One highly publicized case, akin to Rio's port district, occurred earlier in Lower Manhattan. The African Burial Ground, a late-colonial cemetery for some fifteen thousand free and enslaved Africans, long buried under the landfill and buildings of New York City, became a cause célèbre after being discovered in 1991 on the planned site of a new U.S. federal office building. When archeologists examined the site, as required by law, they discovered interred bodies from about two centuries ago. Given the pressure of construction costs, however, the General Services Administration (GSA) continued the work on the excavation and foundation of the new building. After the discovery of intact burials became publicly known, African American activists protested the rush to redevelop the site. Feeling insufficiently consulted, the descendant community demanded an archeological project for the proper study of the remains.

Given political pressure from community activists, elected officials, and involved scholars, the GSA halted construction and funded further archaeological work, which uncovered 419 bodies. Examination of the bones at Howard University provided ample evidence of slavery's stresses: many of those buried were malnourished and died young. New York City designated the "African Burial Ground and Commons Historic District" in 1991, located on highly visible blocks around City Hall and federal courts. In 1993, the U.S. Congress ordered new plans for the federal building to allow a memorial site. In 2006, the U.S. Interior Department designated the African Burial Ground as a National Historic Landmark. The memorial, designed by Rodney Leon and Nicole Hollant-Denis, features a granite monument centered on a "Circle of Diaspora." Built of stone from South Africa and North America, the memorial symbolizes the joining of two worlds. The dedication ceremony on October 5, 2007, included prayers, songs, dances, and speeches, along with 419 drummers who performed in honor of the 419 individuals reinterred. A visitor center opened in 2010 to interpret the site and teach the African American history of New York.[38]

In a similar case, Rio's long hidden Cemetery of New Blacks suddenly came to light in 1996, when a family found remains of human bones under the kitchen floor during home renovation in the Gamboa port district. The property soon became part of an archeological site overseen by the federal preservation agency. Archeologists found evidence of about six thousand deceased African slaves—estimated to be 60 percent male, 30 percent female, and 10 percent children and adolescents. Totals were undoubtedly much higher. UNESCO's World Heritage program considers the site to be "the biggest slave cemetery in the Americas with approximately 20,000 to 30,000 burials." It functioned between 1769 and 1830 as a common grave for those who died before being sold in the Valongo markets. A visiting German naturalist, G. W. Freireyss (1789–1825), left this graphic description: "In the middle of this space there was a pile of dirt from which, here and there, appeared remains of cadavers uncovered by the rain and there were also many cadavers on the ground that had not been buried yet. Naked, they had been wrapped in mats, tied above their head and below their feet." Given neighbors' continual complaints about the open graveyard and the official (if largely unenforced) ban on the Brazilian slave trade, the burial ground closed by 1831. After the burial ground closed, the growing city steadily built over the abandoned land.[39]

Unlike New York City, where both the federal and city governments supported the African Burial Ground historic landmark and memorial, Rio's Cemetery of New Blacks received little official assistance. Located on private property in working-class Gamboa, the federal government has assumed no authority over the site. City administrations have also shown little inclination to support the burial ground, reportedly due to local partisan politics and an apparent reluctance to honor the slave past. Ana Maria de la Merced, the White owner of the property where the burial ground was rediscovered, embraced the cause with support from the local community and visitors, even converting her family's original house into a memorial and cultural center. Since 2005, the Institute for Research on the New Blacks (IPN, by its Portuguese acronym) has offered educational programs on "the recovery of the memory of the ancestors buried in the Cemetery of the New Blacks."

Although the IPN received an annual stipend of US$18,000 from the Wonderful Port program between 2013–2016, since then there has been no official support. Still, most Rio residents remain unaware of the historic Afro-Brazilian burial site, although Valongo Wharf became well known.[40]

Despite the 1996 experience of uncovering the African cemetery, subsequent rediscovery of the Valongo slave wharf came widely as a shock in January of 2011. Although historically informed observers knew the old pier's approximate location—it was still indicated, after all, on the Empress Wharf monument in the Journal of Commerce Square—the rediscovery of the original Valongo Wharf surprised the port redevelopment agency as well as the general public.[41] As workers installed a new drainage system as part of the waterfront renewal program, they came upon patches of the wharf's stone paving, along with numerous objects belonging to newly arrived African slaves, buried beneath some ten feet (3 meters) of debris and pavement. Federal law required an archeological excavation, begun on January 25, 2011. Tania Andrade Lima and a team of archeologists ultimately collected 466,035 artifacts at the site, notable not just for their quantity but also the quality, concentration, and variety of objects related to the African diaspora. Most notable were the many amulets, pendants, earrings, bracelets, and other adornments, used both to ward off evil and to affirm an identity in the new land.[42] The painstaking work revealed a clear profile of both the Valongo Wharf and the subsequent Empress Wharf (see photo 3.1).

The discovery of so many artifacts attracted media attention and mobilized the local community, Black activists, and academics. Afro-Brazilian religious groups began to carry out annual symbolic cleansings of the site in 2011, along with other spiritual events. City authorities initially hoped to cover over the site again and proceed promptly with port renewal, but Black political and religious groups, supportive scholars, and public opinion demanded preservation rather than redevelopment of the ruins. The rediscovery of Valongo Wharf, however, counteracted a long preference to forget or downplay the slave past. And not just by White elites, but also by Black social movements, which found reference to slavery to be disempowering in contemporary politics. As one Afro-descendant activist told me, there had long been "memory fatigue" regarding slavery in Rio's Black movement. But by offering new possibilities for political engagement in the memorialization of slavery, Afro-Brazilians could link history with contemporary racial and urban inequality. Suddenly, a variety of stakeholders—Black social movements, local politicians, community residents, scholars, and international agencies—found common cause in preserving the historic slave pier. Under increasing pressure, the port redevelopment agency agreed to support Valongo preservation, despite delays to the infrastructure projects underway.

Photo 3.1. Valongo Wharf, rediscovered. Photo by the author, 2015.

Given the upcoming municipal elections, along with enhanced prospects for cultural tourism with athletic mega-events on the horizon, Mayor Eduardo Paes endorsed site preservation.

There followed a series of preservationist measures aimed at building support for an eventual World Heritage site. On November 29, 2011, the city landmarked the Valongo ruins as part of the African Heritage Circuit, comprising the previously rediscovered slave cemetery and several other historic sites nearby. The Valongo Wharf subsequently became part of UNESCO's Slave Route Project: Resistance, Liberty, Heritage on November 18–20, 2013, when the International Scientific Committee of the Slave Route project met in Rio and unveiled a commemorative plaque. By forming part of this international movement to recognize the African diaspora on par with the Holocaust and other genocides around the world, the Valongo ruins gained historical context and relevance in terms of global human rights struggles. The designation also encouraged cultural tourism. As in the United States, Black populations claimed such rescued heritage sites as sacred spaces to commemorate their African ancestors. Aided by supportive scholars with specialized expertise in the study of cultural heritage and archeology, Afro-Brazilians compelled governmental authorities to recognize their long-buried pasts. As rediscovery of the slave past become part of the historical narrative in Rio's port district, Brazil finally began to address the traumas of the Atlantic slave trade at public sites of memory.[43]

Still in pursuit of a World Heritage designation, IPHAN sponsored a working group of anthropologists, archeologists, architects, and historians to prepare a proposal. After Brazil nominated the Valongo Wharf site, UNESCO tentatively listed the property in January 2014, subject to local planning for historic preservation and the creation of a buffer zone to control nearby development. The preliminary report noted that the site "consists in one of the most striking testimonials to the history of slavery and its legacy in the Americas."[44] Then on July 9, 2017, the World Heritage Committee officially inscribed the Valongo Wharf Archaeological Site. The final evaluation noted that "despite the modesty of the archaeological remains, Valongo Wharf presents the most significant physical evidence of an arrival point of African enslaved people to the Americas and therefore carries enormous historical as well as spiritual importance to African Americans."[45] About a week after the UNESCO listing, I witnessed a celebration of the site's enduring importance in a festive event, featuring drumming, music, and dance by the Filhos de Gandhi (Children of Gandhi) Afro-Brazilian cultural and spiritual group (see photo 3.2). For me, this event personally demonstrated the continuing spirit of dedication, reverence, and resilience among descendants of the slave trade. It also personally reaffirmed the two criteria cited by UNESCO for Valongo's selection as a World Heritage site:

- Criterion (iii): "bears a unique or at least exceptional testimony to a cultural tradition or to a civilization which is living or which has disappeared," since "around a quarter of the Africans enslaved in the Americas reached the continent via Rio de Janeiro, thus making Valongo Wharf the biggest slave port in history."
- Criterion (vi): "directly or tangibly associated with events or living traditions, with ideas, or with beliefs, with artistic and literary works of outstanding universal significance," since Valongo Wharf "awakens memories of traumatic historic events and is bound up with aspects of pain and survival in the history of the forefathers of people of African descent, who sum over half of the contemporary Brazilian population."[46]

Anthropologist Milton Guran, coordinator of the working group preparing the UNESCO proposal, told me during an interview that this recently inscribed World Heritage site represented a significant change in the way that Brazilians viewed their past, themselves, and the kind of nation they wanted to build. Guran suggested that memory and self-knowledge were helping to

Photo 3.2. Afro-Brazilian celebration of the Valongo's enduring importance as a place of memory, featuring drumming, music, and dance by the Filhos de Gandhi (Children of Gandhi) Afro-Brazilian cultural and spiritual group. Photo by the author, 2017.

build a more inclusive nation. "Valongo's greatest importance," he noted, "is that Brazil finally assumed the responsibility of showing the world that it benefitted from a slave regime, but that the country was now willing to rethink its history and to create a nation for everyone, not just a small group of elites. This is a heroic endeavor."[47]

After an unplanned delay for implementation of the heritage sites, the city proceeded with the Wonderful Port program, which included the removal of aging elevated expressways, the placement of public art along the new Olympic boulevard, the implementation of streetcar lines, and new electrical, water, and sanitation lines. Despite fears that a proposed "creative district" for artists and technology startup firms would lead to gentrification and social displacement, local changes so far have proven to be more incremental than transformative. The port district has certainly experienced noticeable property speculation, infrastructure renovation, and redevelopment of deteriorated buildings, but there has been scant evidence of widespread residential dislocation. While there have been pressures to upgrade and secure nearby favelas, along with initial disruption from transportation projects, as discussed in the next chapter, recent changes have been more commercial than residential. Like many neoliberal urban renewal programs sponsored by the state in conjunction with private capital in Latin America, as John Betancur has observed, "they do not displace lower-class users and uses directly and constitute principally commercial rather than residential gentrification."[48]

While the creation of the African Heritage Circuit resignified the area, promoted historic placemaking, and encouraged heritage tourism, the revival of Little Africa actually sharpened critiques of redevelopment. For example, despite public presentation of the design for a memorial with grand portals and columns at Valongo Wharf, community activists opposed the design as garishly oversized, likely to detract attention from the archeological site, and possibly to put pressure on affordable housing availability in the district. A simpler design would be more appropriate in historical and contemporary terms. As a result, the Valongo Wharf ruins would remain an open-air, on-site memorial.[49] This decision proved beneficial, for as James Young argues, grandiose monuments may be counterproductive in "supplanting a community's memory work with its own material form."[50]

Future plans for the Valongo World Heritage site do include a visitor's center, a collection of urban archaeology to display artifacts, and possibly a museum of slavery and freedom in a former coffee warehouse. But the country's long economic recession has strained federal, state, and local governmental budgets, thereby calling into question the feasibility of such heritage plans. The national heritage agency, along with twenty-one Brazilian cities, recently teamed up to campaign for additional federal funding to maintain heritage sites. IPHAN director Andrey Schlee argued that "the main problem is the lack of public policies guaranteeing adequate infrastructure, which affects the heritage sites." Given that Brazil's UNESCO sites have reported significant increases in tourism, IPHAN argues that extra funding is necessary to improve the electricity, sewage, and pavement of historic districts. The organization also is concerned about the future of Rio's Valongo Wharf site, where development of a full open-air museum by 2020, as originally envisioned in the UNESCO proposal, now seems in danger.[51]

Even so, historic placemaking in the port district so far has led to a more diverse and interesting district than the bland modernist project initially envisioned. *New York Times* architectural critic Michael Kimmelman, who toured the area in 2013, before the full establishment of the Valongo site and the African Heritage Circuit, complained that "the port redevelopment is mostly a commercial real estate deal, another example, critics complain, of a government in thrall to developers. . . . There is no real master plan, no guarantee that what's good and worth preserving about the urban mix of the existing port won't be sacrificed to a sea of office towers."[52] Recovery of the Valongo

Wharf and the nearby burial ground has, at the least, led to a new historical consciousness of the legacies of slavery and Afro-Brazilian cultures. Community organizations, tourist agencies, and schools now offer walking tours of the port waterfront to highlight its long history and cultural life.

The port district has become a center of Afrocentric cultural tourism and counter-memory. Gradually, the Valongo Wharf, the Cemetery of New Blacks, Salt Point Square, and other sites in the African Heritage Circuit are being incorporated into city tours. The Gamboa district itself is now being reinvented as "Little Africa" (Pequena Africa), which now serves both to reaffirm Black cultural history and to critique redevelopment plans. In that sense, the city's progressive journalism center, Casa Pública, has launched a smartphone application with an alternative public history: dubbed the "Museum of Yesterday" (Museu do Ontem) in a playful reference to the "Museum of Tomorrow" (Museu do Amanhã) not far away on the Praça Mauá. The high-tech "app" focuses on notable historical events and revealing stories about port neighborhoods, such as that of the Portuguese royal family's residence, the slave trade and its abolition, and contemporary politics.[53] As a result, the historic placemaking programs of the Valongo Wharf and other heritage sites have unleashed creative energies in the contemporary Port District, which serve to balance the high-profile modernism of the new museums with historical monuments to the slave past.

LITTLE AFRICA AND
THE AFRICAN HERITAGE CIRCUIT

After the end of the transatlantic slave traffic in the 1850s and the abolition of slavery itself in 1888, Rio's northern waterfront remained the main center of Afro-Brazilian population and culture. The waterfront district of Gamboa, which encompasses the Valongo Wharf site and former slave markets, is the city's oldest continuously inhabited Afro-descendant community. As local slaves gained their freedom, they often stayed to live and work in the vicinity, while migrant former slaves from Bahia and elsewhere also found opportunities there for work and residence, venues to eat and drink, a strong sense of community, and places of worship for both Roman Catholic and African-based religions. Although tensions sometimes arose between Brazilian- and foreign-born Africans, generally familiar cultural and racial bonds prevailed. This community gave birth to samba dance and music, which later became the preferred style for Carnival in Rio. This area became known as Little Africa—a nickname popularized by samba singer, composer, and painter Heitor dos Prazeres (1898–1966).

Despite this cultural dynamism, Little Africa long suffered from pervasive poverty and difficult living conditions—housing, health, work, indoor ventilation and sanitation were all deficient in the crowded district. Remote from the city center, the post-abolition waterfront still retained the place stigma and low social status associated with the slave trade. Lacking basic services of water and sewerage, the port district squeezed together the Afro-Brazilian working poor as urbanization mounted during the late nineteenth century. Although there was no formal or legal segregation by race and class, the forces of uneven development served that purpose. Residents worked in the blue-collar occupations that kept the city running: the port workers, industrial and construction laborers, handy jacks-of-all trades, laundrywomen, seamstresses, maids, cooks, and others. The teeming tenements (*cortiços*), cramped rooming houses (*casa de cómodos*), and self-constructed favelas were all concentrated on Rio's northern side—a pattern perpetuated in the extensive North Zone (Zona Norte) of the contemporary metropolis, where port facilities, the international airport, oil refineries, industry, warehouses, military bases, blue-collar functions, and much of the city's population can still be found. Not surprisingly, life's daily difficulties and continuing injustices bred discontent at the turn of the twentieth century. Historian Jeffrey Needell has observed the "political alienation and hostility" of the city's Afro-Brazilian population, given that "the vitality and the repression of their distinct culture, as well as the poverty and racial abuse they had suffered for generations, formed only the backdrop to the new anguish they must have endured in post-abolition Rio."[54]

At least a thousand Black residents lived in the port district, with others living elsewhere in the city. According to a book on alternative religions of Rio first published in 1904, the speaking of African languages persisted into the early twentieth century. Written by journalist Paulo Barreto (with the pseudonym John of Rio), *As Religiões no Rio* reported that some wealthy Afro-Brazilians even sent their children on trips to Africa, where they would learn ancestral languages and religions. African languages included Igesá, Oié, Ebá, Aboum, Hausa, Itaqua, and others. Despite the linguistic diversity of Little Africa, all Africans spoke a common lingua franca, Yoruba (eubá). Antonio, a local resident and one of the author's main sources of information, suggested that "Yoruba was to Africans what English was to civilized peoples. Whoever spoke Yoruba could cross Africa and live among the Blacks of Rio."[55]

Under the regime of slavery, the most sought-after African arrivals were often young men and boys, who could work as agricultural laborers. The enslaved African females tended to be domestic servants, charged with cooking, cleaning, and childcare. In cities, the women also commonly served as "slaves of profit" (*escravos de ganho*), who frequently worked as street venders for their merchant owners, while the African men in cities worked in construction, transport, street cleaning, and other menial jobs. The women had the highest rate of emancipation, since they sometimes could buy their freedom from profits as venders. When they were free, they had marketable skills and were able to make a living from sewing, cooking and selling foodstuffs, and of course sex work. With such resources, these "Aunties" became anchors of the community of color after abolition. They often had their own houses, where they offered food, drink, and social life for diverse Afro-Brazilians, who would gather to socialize, dance, celebrate Carnival and other events, and practice African-derived spiritual rites of *candomblé* and *umbanda*, in which women played leading roles. They formed a government for their underground world, modeled after the Brazilian Empire, and each year the participants would vote for their kings, queens, and imperial courts. Over the years, this parallel structure would gradually become the "samba schools" of today.

It was in this socially polarized context that, in 1902, new president Francisco Rodriguez Alves (1848–1919) announced an ambitious program of urban renewal for the national capital. After decades of rapid growth, Rio's central streets were increasingly congested, port facilities outmoded, and tropical diseases often epidemic. Authorities planned to transform the city center with broad boulevards, seaside promenades, and new port facilities and rail connections. Besides improving infrastructures of transportation and trade, these "urban reforms" aimed to increase real-estate profits, remove poor residents from the city center, and enhance the conditions for capitalist development. Given the lack of replacement housing, many of those displaced from the city center moved to Favela Hill (now Providência Hill, the city's first favela). The city administration also worked with public health authorities, under the direction of Brazilian physician and epidemiologist Oswaldo Cruz (1872–1917), to end epidemics of bubonic plague, yellow fever, and smallpox.[56]

A program of mandatory vaccination against smallpox, which particularly targeted poor districts, provoked the violent Revolt of the Vaccine in 1904. The unprecedented immunization orders terrified the population, as opposition newspapers, labor unions, and politicians fanned anti-vaccination sentiment. Following an altercation between young Black men and the police after a community meeting, protesters marched downtown to voice their opposition to the vaccination program on November 10, 1904. The demonstrations turned violent as protesters burned streetcars, smashed streetlights, and vandalized buildings downtown. On November 14, the Military Academy joined the revolt, but after intense shooting, the cadets were dispersed. Fearing a coup d'état, the government declared a state of siege. The revolt culminated in a fierce battle over the northern waterfront district of Saúde, closer than Gamboa to the city center, where defenders set up barricades, mounted battle flags, and engaged the police and army in ferocious hand-to-hand combat. Needell notes that the defenders, "retreating before the army's pressure by land and threatened by bombardment from a navy ironclad positioned just off dockside, faded away into the maze-like squalor of the slums." On November 18, the government put down the uprising and suspended the obligatory vaccination.[57]

Popular indignation over the mandatory smallpox inoculations may have prompted the destructive spree downtown, but the Revolt of the Vaccine more fundamentally stemmed from the widespread resentment over displacement from the renovated central district. In fact, this episode served as an early counter-memory. While elites reclaimed the central areas for high-status functions, businesses, and residences, the working poor largely had to relocate from Rio's urban core to the periphery, just as Baron Haussmann's work displaced the poor in Paris. Meade argues that the displaced workers realized that public transportation improvements served to marginalize them in spatial and social terms: "Since 'civilization's' victims were aware that even if they worked in the downtown, they were not going to live there, they logically attacked the transportation service that was making this relocation a reality."[58] Needell interprets the revolt more broadly as resistance to the uneven "modernization" of belle époque Rio de Janeiro. The implications for working-class Blacks were clear: "Plainly, Afro-Brazilian Rio was being exorcised in 1904—the city was 'civilizing itself' indeed."[59] Still, it is important to remember that this narrative of civilization was not universally accepted. The fin de siècle transformation of central Rio prompted mass protests, gave the elites pause, nearly overthrew the elected government, and gave Afro-Brazilians a new voice. The Revolt of the Vaccine in 1904 generated counter-narratives of oppression and social injustice, which have continued to this day.

After the violent insurrection ended in 1904, the city authorities proceeded apace with the urban renewal plans. To facilitate international trade and urban transportation, the port moved from the waterfront at November 15th Square to new facilities on the northern waterfront, where by 1911, railroads facilitated circulation of people and products. The northern part of the central district also remained a center of Afro-Brazilian life, as indicated by the presence of Our Lady of the Rosary and Saint Benedict Catholic Church, located at 77 Rua Uruguaiana since the eighteenth century. Besides being the center of African and Afro-Brazilian religious, social, and political life, this church has long housed a Black museum, although a fire in 1967 destroyed most of the original artifacts. The museum today exhibits a small collection of artwork, handicrafts, documents, portraits, and a collection dedicated to Saint Anastasia. Opportunities for work encouraged continuing in-migration to Rio, especially from Bahia, and the Afro-Brazilian population overflowed from the port district into New City (Cidade Nova) and June 11th Square (Praça 11 de Junho, widely known as Praça Onze, or Eleventh Square). In fact, the major focus of Black cultural life in the early twentieth century shifted to Eleventh Square. Afro-Brazilian migrants crowded into the precarious rooming houses (*casas de cómodos*) here, and when these were fully occupied, the newcomers built their own improvised houses on the hills of Santo Cristo, Conceição, and Providência—the city's early favelas. A lively social, cultural, and spiritual life arose here by the 1920s, Little Africa's heyday.

Besides serving as a cultural hearth for Little Africa, Eleventh Square also hosted the city's largest Jewish concentration, as evident in the number of synagogues and Jewish social clubs. Between 1870 and 1910, foreign immigrants made up nearly 30 percent of the city's population, and many of them settled in this district. Here they found work and cheap housing, including hundreds of rundown tenement buildings (*cortices*). The area was known to feature prostitution, particularly by young women from Poland, who often had been promised Brazilian husbands on arrival, only to find themselves trapped in sex work. By 1910, Eleventh Square was the heart of Rio's Jewish community—in fact, the largest Jewish concentration in the city's history—but with the displacement in the early 1940s, due to the construction of the President Vargas Boulevard, most of the Jews moved to the Copacabana, Tijuca, and Madureira districts.

A major historical figure in Little Africa was Aunt Ciata (Tia Ciata), a migrant from Bahia, whose house near Eleventh Square became a gathering place for Afro-Brazilian *candomblé* ceremonies, samba music and dance, and other occasions. Born a free Black woman as Hilária Batista de Almeida (1854–1924), Aunt Ciata became a cook, a spiritual leader, and an influential figure in the development of samba. Born in Santo Amaro, Bahia and initiated into *candomblé* in Salvador, she was a devotee of the deity Oshun and became a spiritual leader in a Rio assembly (*terreiro*). "Ciata," the nickname by which she became known, was a common feminine name in Rio's Muslim community from Portuguese Guinea. She arrived in Rio de Janeiro from Bahia in 1876 at the age of twenty-two and worked initially as a food vendor. After marrying João Batista da Silva, they had fourteen children and became respected figures in Little Africa. Ciata became one of the main forerunners of contemporary Afro-Brazilian culture in Rio. While the celebration of Carnival already was popular, it consisted primarily of European-style bands, polkas, and masquerade balls. At Aunt Ciata's home in late 1916, Donga

(Ernesto Joaquim Maria dos Santos) and Mauro de Almeida composed the first recorded samba Carnival song, "By the Telephone" ("Pelo Telefone"), released commercially in early 1917. After this, the community of Little Africa reinvented the celebration's style of music and costume, while broadening public participation. Tia Ciata was honored annually at the Rio carnival until her death in 1924.[60]

Thereafter, the increasing police persecution encouraged composers to form samba schools, a euphemism for social and recreational associations, as a way to meet for practice of song and dance without arousing the suspicion of authorities. Such enduring samba schools as Estácio de Sá, Mangueira, and Portela arose in this district. Given the growing popular appeal of samba schools, Mayor Pedro Ernesto organized in 1933 the first official Carnival parade and competition of samba schools, which took place on Eleventh Square and resulted in a victory for Mangueira. Ever since then, the carnival parades have been annual events in the city. The city's public carnival celebrations centered here for many years, before a disruptive urban renewal program of the early 1940s, which prompted such protest songs as "Praça Onze" by Herivelto Martins and Grande Otelo, and "Rancho de Praça Onze" by Dalva de Oliveira. The construction of Vargas Avenue in the early 1940s destroyed Eleventh Square and its community, however, and the famous square now only exists as the name of a Metro station in the subway system.

Another of Little Africa's important cultural sites has long been Salt Point (Pedra do Sal), now featured in the African Heritage Circuit, where slaves once traversed massive geological formations as they carried sacks of salt from the waterfront wharves to the neighborhoods above. To make the work easier, they chiseled steps into the stone that remain clearly visible today. Even before it was considerably widened by landfill in 1904–1911, the strip of land along the bay provided a place to socialize at Salt Point, protected by the huge rocks, which created a protected space for Afro-Brazilians. For generations, the local community gathered at Salt Point's historic square to celebrate the samba style of music and dance, the African orixá spiritual tradition, migration of Bahians to Rio, Carnival groups, and elements of popular Catholicism. Dockworkers once gathered here to drink and sing. Improvised Carnival parades and parties began here, and now the square is home to Slaves of Mauá (Escravos da Mauá), one of the most famous *blocos*, or street parties, during Rio's Carnival season. On many evenings, street parties still occur in the winding streets and intersections around Salt Point Square. A growing number of local walking tours also visit the site and reinforce historic placemaking.

The case of Salt Point has not been limited to heritage tourism, though. It has also involved a controversial battle for ethnic recognition and property rights, which pitted a newly declared *quilombo*—traditionally considered a historical settlement of runaway African slaves—against the powerful Roman Catholic Church. The saga goes back decades. In 1984, the state government landmarked Salt Point as a heritage site of popular culture. The official listing called attention to the site's role as cultural witness of Afro-Brazilian identity as the oldest standing monument linked to the origins of Carioca samba and carnival.[61] The city of Rio then recognized the site's value for Afro-Brazilian culture, the history of slavery, and African religions in 1987. This heritage designation encompassed elements of both spiritual and ethno-racial identity. The federal constitution of 1988 included in article 68 the basis for ethnic-racial land ownership through creation of a "remnant quilombo community," as quilombo residents historically did not own the land on which they settled. Since colonial times, quilombos have been regarded as places of rural residence for runaway slave communities, but the new constitutional definition broadened the term to include a "remnant" concept, which allowed a reparative "right to memory" for black and indigenous groups that had suffered histories of displacement. The concept also referred to the "commons," in which natural resources have been shared among local families. In sum, a "quilombo community" reflected a distinctive culture, including "a unique historical trajectory," "specific territorial relationships," and "Black ancestry."[62]

Beginning in 2001, several Afro-Brazilian families living near Salt Point organized to oppose the Catholic Venerable Third Order of St. Francis of Penance, owner of properties at the foot of the Conceição Hill. The Church had begun an eviction process against the opposing local families. Roman Catholic religious orders planned to consolidate their real-estate holdings and to expand educational and social-welfare programs in the port district. In late 2005, the African-descendant families officially incorporated as a "remnant quilombo," which allowed for ethnic recognition and land ownership of previously disenfranchised ethnic communities. While the families threatened with eviction practiced Afro-Brazilian religion, they were not native to the Salt Point area. But citing the "right to memory," they broadened the constitutional rationale for a quilombo to include an ethnic territory in an urban context, justified territorial occupation based on a mythic historical narrative, and claimed the cultural heritage of a generic "Black city." In December of 2005, the quilombo sought possession of the hill, square, and surrounding properties. To strengthen its claim, a working group asserted a religious and ethnic-racial identity for the Quilombo of Pedra do Sal, based on the historical narratives of Little Africa:

> After slavery was abolished, Blacks continued to live around Rio de Janeiro's port zone, and the area was appropriated as a social space for rituals, religious

cults, drumming, and capoeira. Popular culture flourished around Pedra do Sal and traditional samba artists drew inspiration from the community.... In the same port zone, "Brazil's Little Africa" was established, a refuge for Blacks escaping Pereira Passos *bota abaixo* ("tear it down"), an urban renewal project in the first decades of the twentieth century.[63]

In addition to documenting spiritual and social identity, the proposal for a quilombo required claims to territory. The state's landmark designation noted that historic Catholic and military sites on Conceição Hill had been listed by the National Heritage Institute since the 1930s. To demonstrate their own Afro-Brazilian historic site, the Salt Point Quilombo proposed the Pedra do Sal and the adjacent square. In this sense, the quilombo has made great strides in recent years, although the issue of land ownership has still not been resolved. In July 2014, the city recognized the quilombo as an Area of Special Cultural Interest. Subsequently, at a ceremony held on December 12, 2015, the quilombo celebrated the ten-year anniversary of its formal incorporation. The ceremony began with a breakfast and an Afro-Brazilian *candomblé* ritual at the historic site, before local drummers led a procession of residents and supporters around the ruins of Valongo Wharf and finally to Mauá Square, near the Museum of Tomorrow. The group maintains an active Facebook site, which advocates greater governmental support and recognition of quilombo land rights. One resident, Damião Braga, voiced a community sentiment of "fighting for cultural and territorial recognition in the context of real-estate speculation in Rio's port district. With the Wonderful Port program, the challenges have increased. Our region is undergoing gentrification, which occurs in disguised form."[64] Agencies of the federal government have also recognized the Pedra do Sal as a legitimate quilombo, in reviewing its historical presence and dispossession.

Besides the landmarked Valongo Wharf, Salt Point Square, and the Cemetery of New Blacks, the African Heritage Circuit includes several other historic sites (see figure 3.3). Near the wharf lies Stevedore Square (Praça dos Estivadores), previously known as Warehouse Square (Largo dos Depósitos) when it concentrated slave markets in the late eighteenth and early nineteenth centuries. It was here that houses and shops called "fattening houses" prepared the human merchandise for sale. Above the square lies the Hanging Gardens of Valongo, a classically inclined park inaugurated in 1906 during the fin de siècle urban renewal and beautification campaign in the former slave district led by Mayor Francisco Pereira Passos. In a strange historical twist, Mayor Eduardo Paes rededicated the park in 2012, while a new urban renewal program unintentionally revealed so much of the port district's brutal slave-trading past. Finally, the last site in the circuit is the José Bonifácio Cultural Center, named after a notable nineteenth-century abolitionist, which

Figure 3.3. Street map of African Heritage Circuit, Port District of Rio de Janeiro. The map includes the following historic sites: (1) Valongo Wharf and Express Wharf, (2) Salt Point, (3) Hanging Garden of Valongo, (4) Warehouse Square, (5) Cemetery of the New Blacks, (6) José Bonifácio Cultural Center.

Dom Pedro II founded in 1877 as a public school to educate low-income residents. Closed in 1977, the renovated structure reopened in 2013 as a community center with a particular focus on Afro-Brazilian culture.

The rapid succession of events suggests that more than memory and heritage has been at stake: the Valongo World Heritage site and the entire accompanying Afro-Brazilian Heritage Circuit have encouraged broad debates over racial identity, civil rights, and affirmative action. The emphasis on countermemory suggests a novel philosophy of multiculturalism and racial difference—a far cry from the assimilationist discourse of "racial democracy." As a result, the reemergence and promotion of Little Africa may signify a further break from the traditional belief in a race-blind nationalism with equal opportunity, assimilation, and social mobility. While effectively debunked, given the country's vast socioeconomic disparities of race, in practice, mixed-race assimilation remains a persistent, if deceptive ideology. The revival of Little Africa provides a step forward in terms of race consciousness and recognition. From the perspective of place branding, however, the African Heritage Circuit may be less of a cultural rupture than an accommodation to prevailing neoliberal policies of urban revitalization and cultural tourism. Racial and social equality will depend on further political-economic change. The social impacts of memorializing slave sites and Afro-Brazilian historic districts will depend largely on the implementation of supportive social policy and the rising political status of Afro-descendant identities.

COMMUNITY IDENTITY AND CULTURAL POLITICS

This reactivation of Little Africa illustrates both the potential value and limitations of counter-memory in urban planning, public history, and historic preservation. Formed in opposition to dominant official histories, narratives of Little Africa have contested mainstream assumptions of irrevocable historical progress and rescued long ignored, forgotten, buried, and otherwise excluded versions of the past. City authorities initially hoped to cover up the Valongo site soon after its rediscovery in 2011, so as to proceed promptly on the planned Wonderful Port program, but Afro-Brazilian political and religious groups, supportive scholars, and public opinion demanded preservation rather than redevelopment of the ruins. As a result, the port area is now being reinvented as Little Africa through a convergence of urban politics, civil rights, public history, and cultural tourism. For example, Line 3 of the light-rail streetcar system, which passes through the port district, has incorporated historical Afro-descendant themes in the naming of stations, including "Little Africa" (Pequena África), "New Blacks" (Pretos Novos, or newly arrived slaves), and "Black Roses" (Rosas Negras, nineteenth-century Black female entrepreneurs).

Such naming of historic sites is an integral part of historical placemaking and rebranding. While heritage institutionalization lessens the oppositional edge of counter-memory, it serves to legitimize a multicultural project on local, national, and international scales. The preservation of slave sites incorporates counter-memory as an "official national narrative that now recognizes the importance of the Atlantic slave trade and Brazil's crucial role in it."[65] Contemporary placemaking has revived the once defunct place identity of Little Africa, based on the rediscovery of remnants of the past. To preserve a site is to reinvent it: heritage status inevitably involves cultural innovation. While not immune to political cooptation and cultural commodification, even an entrepreneurial city counter-memory still emphasizes a pride in survival against the odds, wariness toward state authority, and alternative readings of history. Through oppositional public and journalistic exhibitions, activists have sought to empower marginalized communities through the remembrance of past struggles. The African Heritage Circuit has yet to receive the official support accorded to the downtown Cultural Corridor in Rio, but the 2017 listing of the Valongo Wharf Archeological Site as a World Heritage property may alter the equation in the future. As the UNESCO World Heritage Center states, the site "can therefore be seen as unique and exceptional both from a material point of view and with regard to the spiritual associations to which it is tangibly related."[66]

An important lesson from this case is that in neoliberal cities, which depend on entrepreneurial dynamism and public-private partnerships, the politics of memory turn on marketable branding campaigns with the broadest shareholder support. Despite initial opposition of the Wonderful Port program, Rio's African Heritage Circuit arose from the convergence of Afro-Brazilian counter-memory, urban politics, civil rights, and cultural tourism. But even with the power of place branding, heritage sites cannot by themselves correct socioeconomic inequities of race, gender, and class. Thus, 131 years after the abolition of slavery, official statistics indicated in 2019 that White Brazilians continued to enjoy much higher salaries than those of color. The Afro-descendant majority, including both Blacks and mixed race individuals (Pardos), earned on average only 55.8 percent to 57.3 percent, respectively, of the White population's pay. Levels of education, longevity, informal work, gender, and other indicators showed similar gaps.[67]

True equity surely depends in large part on whether city, state, and federal governments implement corrective educational, socioeconomic, and related programs. While the saga of Little Africa is inspiring in many ways, innovative policies need to promote racial and social equality. The recovery of lost place memory, however, has engaged and educated many observers in Rio and beyond. Although the city long prioritized urban renewal, the recognition of Afro-Brazilian heritage supported a more inclusive society with greater acceptance and understanding of racial difference. The rediscoveries of Valongo Wharf and other heritage sites illustrate how oppositional sensibilities have contributed to historic placemaking and cultural reinvention, thereby opening new opportunities for debate on the causes, consequences, and corrections of social inequality in Rio de Janeiro.

NOTES

1. International Committee on Monuments and Sites (ICOMOS), "Valongo Wharf (Brazil)," *World Heritage List* (UNESCO, March 10, 2017), 337, http://whc.unesco.org/en/list/1548/documents/.

2. Arquivo da Cidade, *Memória da Destruição (Rio—Uma História que se perdeu, 1889–1965)*, (Prefeitura da Cidade do Rio de Janeiro, 2002).

3. Theresa Williamson and Maurício Hora, "In the Name of the Future, Rio Is Destroying Its Past," *New York Times*, Aug. 12, 2012.

4. André Cicalo, "From Public Amnesia to Public Memory Rediscovering Slavery Heritage in Rio de Janeiro," in *African Heritage and Memories of Slavery in Brazil and the South Atlantic World*, ed. Ana Lucia Araujo (Amherst, NY: Cambria Press, 2015).

5. ICOMOS, "Valongo Wharf (Brazil)," 337.

6. Michel Foucault, *Language, Counter-Memory, Practice: Selected Essays and Interviews*, trans. Donald F. Bouchard and Sherry Simon (Cornell University Press, 1977).

7. Andreas Huyssen, *Past Presents: Urban Palimpsests and the Politics of Memory* (Stanford University Press, 2003), 1.

8. T. J. Demos, "Sites of Collective Counter-Memory," Scribd, posted 2012, https://www.scribd.com/document/103447935/Sites-of-Collective-Counter-Memory-by-T-J-Demos.

9. Jon Spayde, "Monumental Changes: New Thinking about Historical Monuments is Embracing Inclusivity—and Ambiguity," *Public Art Review* 29, 57 (2018): 40–49.

10. Mary Karasch, *Slave Life in Rio de Janeiro, 1808–1850* (Princeton University Press, 1987), xv.

11. African Origins Project, Voyages: Trans-Atlantic Slave Trade Database, Emory University, http://www.slavevoyages.org; and ICOMOS, "Valongo Wharf (Brazil)," World Heritage List, no. 1548 (UNESCO, March 10, 2017), 335.

12. E. Bradford Burns, *A History of Brazil*, 3rd ed. (New York: Columbia University Press, 1993), 68.

13. Karasch, *Slave Life in Rio de Janeiro*, xxi–30.

14. African Origins Project, *Voyages: Trans-Atlantic Slave Trade Database*. The database uses the regional category of "Southeast Brazil," for which Rio de Janeiro was by far the dominant slave port during the period under study.

15. Claudio de Paula Honorato, "Valongo: O Mercado de Escravos do Rio de Janeiro, 1758–1831" (master's thesis in history, Universidade Federal Fluminense, Niterói, 2008), 47; and *African Origins Project, Voyages: Trans-Atlantic Slave Trade Database*, 2010.

16. Lieutenant Henry Chamberlain, *Views and Costumes of the City and Neighbourhood of Rio de Janiero, Brasil* (Thomas McLean, 1822), 229.

17. Karasch, *Slave Life in Rio de Janeiro*, xxi–30.

18. African Origins Project, Voyages: Trans-Atlantic Slave Trade Database. These data refer to documented disembarkations, which are lower than the estimated landings cited elsewhere.

19. Honorato, "Valongo"; and Carlos Eugênio Líbano Soares, *Valongo, Cais dos Escravos: Memória da Diáspora e Modernizaçao Portuária na Cidade do Rio de Janeiro, 1668–1911*, Programa de Pós-Graduação em Arqueologia, Museu Nacional and Universidade Federal do Rio de Janeiro, Depto. de Antropologia, 2013.

20. Honorato, "Valongo," 59–60.

21. Soares, *Valongo, Cais do Escravos*.

22. Honorato, *Valongo*, 59–60.

23. Johann Moritz Rugendas, *Voyage pittoresque dans le Brésil* (Paris: Engelman, 1835); and Ana Lucia Araujo, *Shadows of the Slave Past: Memory, Heritage, and Slavery* (Routledge, 2014), 87.

24. Mathew Francis Riley, "Counterwitnessing the Visual Culture of Brazilian Slavery," in *African Heritage and Memories of Slavery in Brazil and the South Atlantic World*, ed. Ana Lucia Araujo (Amherst, NY: Cambria Press, 2015), Kindle edition.

25. Amaral and Debret, "Valongo, a Notorious Slave Market," 42.

26. Chamberlain, *Views and Costumes of the City*, 228–29.

27. Jean-Baptiste Debret, *Voyage Pittoresque et Historique au Brésil* (Paris: Actes Sud, Aries, 1834), *Boutique de la Rue du Val-longo*, Planche 73, 210–11.

28. Debret, *Boutique de la Rue du Val-longo*, Planche 73, 210–11.

29. Tania Andrade Lima, Glaucia Malerba Sene, Marcos André Torres de Souza, "Em busca do Cais do Valongo, Rio de Janeiro, Século XIX," *Anais do Museu Paulista* 24, 1 (Jan.–April 2016), 299–391, http://dx.doi.org/10.1590/1982-02672016v24n0111.

30. Quoted in André Cicalo, "From Public Amnesia to Public Memory: Rediscovering Slavery Heritage in Rio de Janeiro," in *African Heritage and Memories of Slavery in Brazil and the South Atlantic World*, ed. Ana Lucia Araujo (Amherst, NY: Cambria Press, 2015), Kindle edition.

31. Associated Press, "Unearthing of Rio Slave Port Sparks Debate over Black Space," *New York Times*, Dec. 28, 2015.

32. Frank and Berry, "The Slave Market in Rio de Janeiro circa 1869."

33. Thomas A. Skidmore. *Black into White: Race and Nationalism in Brazil* (Oxford University Press, 1974).

34. Rogério Pacheco Jordão, "Machado's Valongo in Rio de Janeiro's Cartography: Urban Slavery in Motion," *Machado de Assis em Linha* (Dec. 8, 16, 2015), http://dx.doi.org/10.1590/1983682120158166.

35. Gilberto Freyre, *The Masters and the Slaves: A Study in the Development of Brazilian Civilization* (University of California Press, 1987).

36. Teresa A. Meade, *"Civilizing" Rio: Reform and Resistance in a Brazilian City, 1889–1930.* (University Park: Pennsylvania State University Press, 1997), 87.

37. UNESCO, "The Slave Route: Preservation of memorial sites and places," http://www.unesco.org/new/en/social-and-human-sciences/themes/slave-route/spotlight/preservation-of-memorial-sites-and-places/; and Ana Lucia Araújo. *Shadows of the Slave Past: Memory, Heritage, Slavery* (Routledge, 2016), 89.

38. National Park Service, African Burial Ground National Monument, New York, https://www.nps.gov/afbg/index.htm.

39. ICOMOS, "Valongo Wharf (Brazil)"; Ana Maria de la Merced Anjos and Júlio Medeiros da Silva, *Saga dos Pretos Novos* (RJ: Prefeitura do Rio de Janeiro, 2015), 20; and Julia Barbassa, "Brazil's Black History, Uncovered," *Americas Quarterly* 11, 1 (2018), which provided the translated quotation from the published work of Freireyss.

40. Anjos and Medeiros da Silva, *Saga dos Pretos Novos*; Araújo, *Shadows of the Slave Past*, 88–89; Cicalo, "From Public Amnesia to Public Memory," Kindle edition; and Julia Barbassa, "Brazil's Black History, Uncovered."

41. Julia Carneiro, "Brazil's Hidden Slavery Past Uncovered at Valongo Wharf," BBC Brasil, Rio de Janeiro, December 25, 2014; and Simon Romero, "Rio's Race to Future Intersects Slave Past," *New York Times*, March 8, 2014.

42. Lima, Sene, and Torres de Souza, "Em busca do Cais do Valongo," 299–391.

43. UNESCO, "The Slave Route Project: Resistance, Liberty, Heritage," http://www.unesco.org/new/en/social-and-human-sciences/themes/slave-route/; and Araujo, *Shadows of the Slave Past*, 108–9.

44. Valongo Wharf Archaeological Site. World Heritage Center, "Tentative Lists," January 31, 2014.

45. ICOMOS, "Valongo Wharf (Brazil)," no. 1548, World Heritage Center, UNESCO, March 10, 2017.

46. UNESCO, World Heritage Center, "Valongo Wharf and Archeological Site," http://whc.unesco.org/en/list/1548/.

47. Interview with Milton Guran, Rio de Janeiro, July 31, 2017.

48. John J. Betancur, "Gentrification in Latin America: Overview and Critical Analysis," Urban Studies Research, 2014, 9.

49. Araujo, *Shadows of the Slave Past*, 99.

50. James Young, "Memory and Counter-Memory: The End of the Monument in Germany," *Harvard Design Magazine* 9 (Fall 1999): 2.

51. Sophie Foggin, "Brazil's 14 UNESCO World Heritage Sites in Need of Extra Funding, Say Local Governments," *Brazil Reports*, August 24, 2018, https://brazilreports.com/brazils-14-unesco-world-heritage-sites-in-need-of-extra-funding-say-local-governments/.

52. Michael Kimmelman, "A Divided Rio de Janeiro, Overreaching for the World," *New York Times*, Nov. 25, 2013.

53. Casa Pública, Museu do Ontem, https://apublica.org/museu-do-ontem/; and Lisa Hollenbach, "A Groundbreaking App Exposes the Nefarious History of Rio de Janeiro's Port," Rio on Watch: Community Reporting in Rio, July 19, 2017, http://www.rioonwatch.org/.

54. Jeffrey D. Needell, "The Revolta Contra Vacina of 1904: The Revolt Against 'Modernization' in Belle-Epoque Rio de Janeiro," *Hispanic American Historical Review* 67 2 (May 1987): 254.

55. João do Rio, *As Religiões no Rio* (first published in 1904; most recent edition by Editora Nova Aguilar, 1976).

56. Maurício Abreu, *Evolução Urbana do Rio de Janeiro* (Rio de Janeiro: Editora Jorge Zahar, 1988).

57. Needell, "The Revolta Contra Vacina of 1904," 233–69, 269.

58. Meade, *"Civilizing" Rio*, 110.

59. Needell, "The Revolta Contra Vacina of 1904," 233–69.

60. Roberto Moura, *Tia Ciata e a Pequena África no Rio de Janeiro* (Rio de Janeiro: Secretaria Municipal de Cultura, 1995).

61. State Institute for Cultural Heritage (INEPAC), "Pedra do Sal," Process Number E-18/300.048/84, http://www.inepac.rj.gov.br/index.php/bens_tombados/detalhar/20.

62. Roberta Sampaio Guimarães, "Urban Interventions, Memories and Conflicts: Black Heritage and the Revitalization of Rio de Janeiro's Port Zone," *Vibrant* 10, 1: 208–27.

63. Quoted in Guimarães, "Urban Interventions, Memories and Conflicts," 214–15.

64. Damião Braga, "Uma palavra da comunidade Quilombola Pedra do Sal," Facebook, January 18, 2017, https://www.facebook.com/notes/quilombo-pedra-do-sal/uma-palavra-da-comunidade-quilombola-pedra-do-sal/757175007770605/.

65. Araújo, *Shadows of the Slave Past*, 100.

66. UNESCO, World Heritage List, "Valongo Wharf Archaeological Site," http://whc.unesco.org/en/list/1548.

67. Nicola Pamplona, "Aumenta desigualdade salarial entre brancos e pretos, diz IBGE: Diferença nos rendimentos atingiu o maior patamar desde 2016," Folha de São Paulo, May 6, 2020, https://www1.folha.uol.com.br/mercado/2020/05/aumenta-desigualdade-salarial-entre-brancos-e-negros-diz-ibge.shtml.

Chapter 4

Resilient Favelas

Pride of Place, Memory of Resistance

> If you enter a *favela*, don't look at it superficially, see in depth what a *favela* really is all about.
>
> —Amaro, resident of the Favela da Maré[1]

Largely self-constructed and underserved, the informal communities known as *favelas* have often settled on difficult sites, including steep hillsides, transit corridors, and low-lying wetlands. While place stigma persists, affirmative images emerge over time as *favelados*—the residents of favelas—organize politically, improve their homes, and lobby for urban services. According to a recent survey, thirty-six favelas have established community museums (nearly all out-of-doors "ecomuseums") to preserve local heritage, while promoting pride of place and resisting displacement.[2] Despite their distinctive histories, locations, socioeconomic conditions, politics, and cultural practices, favelas still largely define themselves in terms of their past and present struggles for survival. I believe that this collective counter-memory of resistance serves as a common denominator that unites diverse favelas, whatever their current conditions.

These struggles reflect a city divided largely by where one lives. As Brazilian journalist Zuenir Ventura argues in *Cidade Partida* (Divided City), Rio encompasses two interrelated but distinct sectors: the "visible city" or "formal city," where the affluent classes dwell; and the "invisible city" or "informal city," where the working classes reside in favelas. Ever since the fin de siècle urban renewal of Pereira Passos, Ventura notes, "the option was always separation, if not outright segregation. The city became civilized and modernized while expelling the lower classes to the hills and peripheries. The result of this policy was a divided city."[3] Historically, a broad north-south division has marked Rio's social geography: favelas with concentrated poverty have clustered in the North Zone (Zona Norte), which still has the largest number of them, although in recent decades they have grown more rapidly in the West Zone, near the affluent seaside district of Barra da Tijuca. Yet favelas remain visible throughout the city, including in the upscale South Zone (Zona Sul). Officially comprising close to a quarter of the city's population, informal settlements have grown faster than the formal city for decades. The 2010 census found that 23 percent of the city's 6.3 million residents lived in 763 favelas of "substandard" and "irregular" housing. But the true proportions of informal settlement are most likely higher, given the city's frequent irregularity of property titles. Rio had the country's largest official population of favela residents with a total of about 1.4 million in the last decennial census, even more than in the larger city of São Paulo.

This continuing favela growth reflects a persistent shortage of affordable housing, which has made informal urbanization commonplace in Brazilian cities. The country experienced the world's highest rate of urban growth between 1920 and 1980, as the proportion of city dwellers rose from 20 to 80 percent of the total population in 60 years.[4] Squatting on unoccupied land has allowed for auto-construction among arriving migrants, those displaced by urban redevelopment, and others in urgent need of cheap residential solutions. If favela residents can find ways to remain on legally precarious sites, living conditions and services tend to improve in time. Even though property titles remain difficult if not impossible to obtain, certificates of occupancy provide proof of residence and enhance the prospects for permanency. Early in the resettlement process, new favelas still appear slum-like. Over time, however, many favelas transition into predominantly working-class neighborhoods comprising mainly low- and middle-income residents, often with a class of professionals and even *gringo* expatriates in gentrifying districts.[5]

Given their collective memory of struggle for survival, resistance to removal continues to energize favela residents. A heritage movement began in the mid-1990s, when the "Viva Rio" NGO began the Favelas Have Memory advocacy program with oral histories and community profiles. Based primarily on an informative website, the digital campaign's goal was to "rescue and preserve the social memory of Rio de Janeiro through narratives and life histories of *favela* residents."[6] Subsequently, favelas created community museums, walking tours, public exhibitions, and other programs to promote awareness of local history and struggles. These museums also educate visitors on other issues by forming eco-museums, digital museums, eviction museums, and cultural museums. One of the first was in the Favela da Maré (Favela of the Tide), where a local organization established a community museum focused on local history in 2006. According to Gitanjali Patel, "The museum is used as a tool to directly invert power dynamics by addressing the absence of the community in national records, reframing public perceptions, and actively shaping the process of historical production to produce the community's own narrative."[7]

One of the most contested favela narratives has been about urban ecology. Indeed, favelas have often borne the brunt of environmental problems and have gotten unduly blamed for them, given the multiple and complex causes. As Mario Fuks has argued, "The declared aim is now not to 'socially integrate' the 'contaminated' sectors, but to protect or recover environmental resources. That is, the favela dweller is not seen simply as contaminated by the surrounding filth, but as a causative agent of pollution of the urban environment."[8] As he notes, this hostile argument for displacement stresses the environmental degradation, deforestation, and flooding caused by favela growth, along with the dumping of trash and inadequate sewage. Real-estate developers have long argued that favela eradication would allow for the construction of sturdier structures, thus making the areas more resilient to rains and landslides. While such environmental issues are real problems, they are widespread and not confined to favelas. Elite gated communities on the urban periphery, for example, also contribute to pollution, untreated sewage, and flooding.

Deforestation, construction, and compaction of soils on Rio's hills and lowlands have increasingly resulted in urban flooding from heavy storms. A century ago, the city's forests would have absorbed some 70 percent of the heavy rainfall and released the rest slowly. Not so today. In the city's remaining forests, increasingly fragmented and impermeable due to growing settlements and roads, less than 30 percent of precipitation now sinks into the soil—leaving more than 70 percent of the rainfall to run off impervious surfaces into swollen streams, storm drains, and low-lying areas.[9] Contemporary climate change exacerbates urban flooding due to more extreme and irregular patterns of precipitation. As meteorological variability becomes more notable, growing cities intensify the human impacts. As a result, calls for favela removal often unfairly blame the victims—the *favelados*—for environmental problems. Without many other viable options for affordable housing, where are residents to go?

To counter widespread prejudice against favelas as destructive, those near forests, parks, and nature reserves now demonstrate their environmental stewardship. Babilônia has become an "ecological favela" known for ecotourism and conservation of the surrounding "natural park." Similarly, in Rio's West Zone, the Vale Encantado water park has offered eco-tours to demonstrate its use of solar panels and biodigestors, which convert gases from waste into fuel. The Favela of Horto (Garden), historically located on the Botanical Garden's edge and now threatened with displacement, promotes environmental education and organic agriculture. Although local in scale, these cases reflect a significant attitudinal shift. Such sustainable models are noteworthy as they show that poor communities can invest in green practice and technology. These informal settlements demonstrate that people's basic needs and responsible environmentalism can coexist side by side. According to Jennifer Chisholm, "These sustainable, ecological *favelas* have the potential to lead in the movement for a greener Rio de Janeiro, and by doing so, nullify an argument in favor of favela removal."[10]

Environmental injustice suffered by poor communities, particularly those of color, has with good reason been the subject of increasing scholarship.[11] Yet there has been little study of how ethnic and marginalized communities have contributed to livable and resilient landscapes. Despite the hardships faced by poor and working-class communities, evidence shows that immigrants, regional in-migrants, and ethnic and racial groups often bring benefits to troubled cities: repopulation, businesses and jobs, tourist promotion, building renovation, colorful street murals and public art, and so on.[12] Economic vitality and cultural diversity contribute to resilient landscapes by providing an enduring sense of place, strong social networks, and political activism. Such social participation is a prerequisite of urban sustainability, as June Thomas has argued, "not solely because of unjust treatment of certain categories of people—the active and even clustered presence of different racial and ethnic minority groups may indeed be an important characteristic of healthy, vibrant, and sustainable cities."[13]

This chapter explores how favelas have drawn upon counter-memory to justify their existence, oppose displacement, and promote pride of place. Rather than focus narrowly on the historic preservation of architectural landmarks and civic monuments, I extend the traditional concept to include the defense of people and place, cultural and environmental heritage, and memory of resistance. The overarching theme is urban resilience, which has been defined by the "100 Resilient Cities" network as "the capacity of individuals, communities, institutions, businesses, and systems within a city to survive, adapt, and grow no matter what chronic stresses and acute shocks they experience."[14] I argue here that remembrance and heritage contribute greatly to the resilience of Rio's favelas, as seen in the distinctive favela landscapes, alternative place narratives, and cultural tourism (see figure 4.1). Two main questions here interrogate favela sense of place: how has resistance to displacement and socioeconomic marginalization fostered counter-memories of struggle? And how have resilient favelas arisen through the politics of place, environmentalism, and networks of solidarity and resilience?

Figure 4.1. Rio de Janeiro: Selected Favelas and Landmarks. Google Maps, adapted by the author.

CONTESTED ORIGINS: INVENTION OF THE FAVELA

Scholars have traced the origins of favelas to Brazilian urbanization at the turn of the twentieth century. While massive rural-urban migration undoubtedly served as the prime mover, it is also important to factor in the political-economic context and ideological discourse that brought informal communities into such decidedly negative focus. In fact, makeshift housing had existed for centuries, but it was so commonplace as to escape special attention. As Brodwyn Fischer has succinctly noted: "Latin America's poor, informal cities existed long before they were named."[15] Slaves and the free poor had dwelled in shacks (*barracos*), runaway slave communities (*quilombos*), slave quarters (*senzalas*), African neighborhoods (*bairros africanos*), tenements (*cortiços*), and other improvised dwellings. Such informal settlements gained notoriety, however, as postcolonial cities became integrated into the world capitalist system. As a result, this integration was intellectual as well as structural. Brazil and its Latin American neighbors felt a new fin de siècle self-consciousness about their standards of "civilization," sanitation and public health, housing, architecture, and urban planning.

Such issues cast critical light on informal urbanization, just as Rio de Janeiro received streams of migrants from rural areas and small towns of Brazil, along with contingents of foreign immigrants from Portugal, Spain, Italy, and elsewhere. The migration to cities accelerated with the emancipation of Afro-Brazilian slaves, even before complete abolition in 1888. As the demolition of central *cortiços* (tenements) increasingly displaced the working classes, improvised settlements appeared on Rio's hillsides by the 1880s. After a naval revolt in the mid-1880s, the Municipal Council allowed the construction of shacks on Santo Antônio Hill, next to a colonial-era Catholic Church. One of the city's oldest documented informal settlements, Santo Antônio already had forty-one squatters' shacks when a favela arose on Providência (Providence) Hill. That is, although the settlement of Santo Antônio Hill began earlier, Providência has generally gotten the credit as Rio's first favela. While plans to remove the informal village of Santo Antônio date from 1901, the settlement provided cheap housing for low-paid soldiers and sailors, so authorities allowed it to remain for decades. Santo Antônio Hill was demolished in the 1950s, which obscured contemporary remembrance of the early informal settlement there.[16]

Although the squatting on Santo Antônio Hill arose a decade beforehand, the first one called "favela" appeared on Providência Hill in 1897–1898. This latter episode reflected the republic's early history. After the fall of the monarchy in 1889, soldiers decommissioned from the northeastern War of Canudos (1895–1897) began to squat on what they initially called "Favella Hill" (as originally spelled). The area had been known for its slave market, euphemistically called a "warehouse of Black merchandise" (*depósito de mercadorias Negras*), but the transfer of the city's slave trade from downtown to Valongo Cove during this period, as discussed in chapter 3, spelled the end of the remote hillside warehouse. Still, property tax records from 1838 demonstrate that the hill continued to be occupied, if sparsely. While some sources suggest that "Providence" referred to the spiritual protection given to the veteran soldiers and others who later settled on the hill, historical cartography indicates otherwise. By the mid-nineteenth century, city maps indicate that Providência already was the toponym affixed to the hill. In the mid-1890s, after public-health officials forced the demolition of a large tenement, authorities allowed the evicted tenants to build their own homes on the adjacent hillside, using debris salvaged from the *cortiço* ruins.[17]

The term *favela* also reflects specific issues related to the War of Canudos, when the Brazilian army repeatedly attacked the messianic community of Antônio Conselheiro in the backlands *sertão* of Bahia. Afterward, many soldiers moved to the capital with hopes of back pay and housing. The former combatants occupied areas near the War Ministry, often squatting on Providência Hill, near both the city's train station and the War Ministry on Campo. Said to resemble the Mount Favela military encampment near Canudos, this hill even contained vegetation similar to a northeastern flowering shrub, popularly known as "favela" (*Cnidoscolus quercifolius*), a medicinal plant with an edible oil, protectively covered by stinging bristles. Newspapers soon began to refer to any informal village built on the city's hillsides as a "favela," so the term gradually became generic by the 1920s. Rio's original Favella Hill then reverted to being called Providência Hill.[18]

Still, there is the question of why the term *favela* became popular, since other improvised settlements arose before Providência. Lícia Valladares has suggested that the term resonated because of concurrent events: the rise of Rio's first favela coincided with the influx of veteran soldiers from Canudos, which provided a major test of the new republic. Soon after the war ended, Euclides da Cunha's journalistic account of the rebellion, *Os Sertões*, provided a detailed report on the army's campaign against Conselheiro. First published in 1902 and later translated into English as *Rebellion in the Backlands*, this book became a foundational text of the early republican regime. Although Cunha did not use *favela* in the urban context for which we now know it, his famous work called attention to conditions of the northeastern campaigns. Thus, the term arose during a national crisis, publicized by the press and the subject of a major national book, just as the new republic struggled to establish itself in the global context of Eurocentric "civilization."[19] In a similar vein, historian Bradford Burns suggested that to the author Euclides da Cunha, "the rebellion symbolized the struggle of man against nature, of civilization against barbarism. The tragedy of the backlands, he [Cunha] believed, was that civilization had abandoned both the area and its inhabitants to barbarism."[20] According to this logic, the favela arose just as rural-urban migration projected "barbarism" into a "civilizing" city with aspirations of becoming a "tropical Paris." It was in this ideologically charged context that Rio's Favella Hill faced the modernizing republican regime at the turn of the twentieth century. As we have seen before, the changing favela toponyms reflect the power of placemaking in Rio.

Besides Providência Hill's role as the first favela, even if historically debatable, the community also reflects common patterns of cultural innovation, resistance to redevelopment, ecological restoration, and counter-memory. Located in the Gamboa port district, Providência Hill overlooks the harbor where at least a million African slaves arrived during the early nineteenth century. In fact, the population of the historic favela remains predominantly

Afro-Brazilian today. Two sisters of the Costa family, Almerinda, 85, and Telma, 61, who were born and raised with their family on the hill, remember the community fondly. "The beautiful landscape is our joy," said Telma, when interviewed in 2007. "It's a wonder, the best thing in our lives, watching ships come and go." From the window, Almerinda and Telma also witnessed the changing urban landscape: construction of the Rio-Niterói bridge, new expressways, waterfront redevelopment, and downtown skyscrapers. This panorama has long been an attraction for visitors. One local landmark is the Oratory of the Cross, dedicated as the "commemorative monument of the century's passage" on January 1, 1901. Centered on the high point of the community, Providência Hill reaches an elevation of 377 feet (115 meters), for a spectacular view.[21] From the beginning, this citadel-like topography represented both confinement and resistance. Daniela Fabricius suggests: "For the government, it served as a prison-like space with clearly defined borders that contained unassimilable populations; for its residents, the borders are used to defend a territory long under constant threat of eviction, invasion, and exploitation."[22]

Providência Hill soon acquired a distinctive popular culture, along with a suggestive naughtiness. The rise of Carnival blocks (*blocos*) in the 1920s distinguished the favela: the Gossipy Neighbor (Vizinha Faladeira) group, formed in 1923, may have been Rio's first samba school. The group won the championship of the first official parade with samba schools in 1937. The hill's other Carnival blocks also attracted wide followings, including Speak My Love (Fala Meu Loro), Barroso Block (Bloco do Barroso), and Stay Firm (Fique Firme). The legendary film *Favela of My Loves* (*Favela dos Meus Amores*), released in 1935, depicted the musical and romantic sagas of two young men, business partners who began a cabaret on the hill. One of them fell in love with beautiful Rosinha, a local muse for samba composers. A film review called her "a rare flower, who preserves her beauty among those perverted people of the *favela.*"[23] Although later lost or destroyed, the film provided one of the earliest depictions of a real favela: besides the leading professional actors, the movie featured Afro-Brazilian residents and a largely Black band. The film received an enthusiastic reception for its "pioneering critical realism."[24] Although Favela Chic arose later, the early cultural vibrancy of Providência attests to prior origins for the use of spectacle in placemaking. Thus arose a Janus-like imaginary: as observers fetishized the samba music and dance, sexual mystique, and popular culture, the favela itself was seen as a place of poverty and squalor, moral depravity, violence, and crime.

The hill soon acquired a disreputable reputation. On November 4, 1900, for example, a police officer complained of the district's rampant criminality: "Policing is impossible in this area, rife with deserters, thieves and squaddies.

There are no streets, the houses are all made of wood and covered in zinc, and there is not a single gas light on the whole hill."[25] By 1910, the hill was widely regarded as "the village of the bad," the most violent place in the city.[26] According to residents, however, the community was long tightknit and relatively peaceful, despite the stigma of crime. Almerinda da Costa recalled in 2007 that the hill had *malandros* (tricksters or con artists), but that they were not a big problem. "They did not come with a gun and did not mess with anyone. Now, they want to face the police, and they have here." Urban services, of course, were long lacking: most houses used kerosene lanterns, although residents had by then begun to tap illegally into the electrical lines. But along came the drug traffickers, beginning in the 1970s. Due to increasing insecurity, Almerinda believed that life on the hill had become harder than it used to be: "When I was little, life was simpler," she said. "There were not the advantages we have today. There was no water, no light. The supermarkets did not deliver the purchases up here, we had to climb up ourselves with the goods. But even with all the difficulties, it was better, because today we have no security. A lot of shooting!"[27]

Providência has grown steadily but moderately over the years, given the restricted site, pressures of urban renewal in the port district, and environmental problems discussed below. By 1904, the favela had 100 houses; by 1933, there were 1,500. By 2010, the decennial census conservatively found 4,094 residents living on Providência Hill, housed in 1,237 dwelling units—98.8 percent of the houses reportedly enjoyed piped water and access to electricity, while only 80.2 percent had sewage connections. Despite the general improvements, 20 percent of the houses were still without sewerage. The vast majority of houses remained without legal property titles. Public safety became another major concern during the late twentieth century. The Red Command (Comando Vermelho) drug cartel controlled illicit traffic in Providência until installation of a Pacifying Police Unit (UPP) on April 25, 2010. Despite promising beginnings, a combination of budget cuts, loss of personnel, and increasingly violent clashes soon aggravated community-police relations. Even these UPPs, of course, represented only a small percentage of Rio's favelas. A study found in 2013 that paramilitary "militias" controlled 45 percent of the city's favelas, drug-trafficking cartels dominated 37 percent, and nonaligned communities represented only 18 percent of them.[28]

Providência Hill has been the site of environmental tragedy as well. Settlement on the granitic hill coexisted with the economic activity of mining for decades. Quarrying of hard-rock stones transformed the local topography, giving rise to an abyss more than 100 meters deep and 50 meters wide on the hill's southern side (see figure 4.2). These excavations led to environmental problems on more than one occasion. An explosion and subsequent landslide

Figure 4.2. Providência Hill, Rio de Janeiro. Google Maps, adapted by the author.

in 1968 buried and killed more than fifty residents; in 1975, another landslide forced the removal of more residents and their homes. The authorities, in turn, have repeatedly cited landslide risk as reason to remove houses considered to be on precarious sites: these are telling examples of *favelados* getting blamed, despite being the ones victimized. More evidence of blaming the victims came with the Wonderful Port program in 2010. With regard to the local condemnations for "environmental risk," one resident argued: "Actually what they want to do is remove as many people as possible because a *favela* doesn't fit with the grand plans for the port."[29]

Despite Providência's historical importance, urban renewal guidelines stipulated that about a third of the favela's homes should be removed, due to insecure foundations and to make room for a new cable-car tram system up the steep hill. The municipal housing agency even marked houses for demolition on the pretext that they were structurally unsound and in areas of risk, as evidenced by previous landslides. Although the government promised to resettle those displaced, as stipulated by law, the options included monetary compensation, monthly rent vouchers, and distant housing projects with little economic opportunity. Residents struggled to keep their houses as the community organized and went to court. One of the major complaints of residents was that, as often happened during urban renewal, the housing agency held few if any public hearings in the community. Ultimately, fewer houses were removed than initially planned. But the tramway, completed in 2015, soon went out of service and remained so intermittently. In addition, the neighborhood-revitalization program prompted a sudden increase in property values and the eviction of longtime residents without the means to stay.[30]

In this age of the Internet, favela residents and activists now have new digital tools and social media to promote their causes. Providência Hill gained international visibility in 2008–2009 with a provocative outdoor art exhibition titled "Women Are Heroes." In a dramatic hillside spectacle conceived by French artist JR in collaboration with the community, huge black-and-white photos of the faces and eyes of local women suddenly appeared on the hill's walls, stairways, and buildings. This installation followed the murder of three young men, reportedly caught in a battle between the Brazilian Army and the Red Command narco-traffickers, which led to a public rampage in which several buses were burned. As the favela subsequently entered an uneasy truce, JR arrived unannounced to get to know the community and to mount an artistic gesture of healing. With his creative and financial support, along with the local supervision of photographer Maurício Hora and the participation of neighborhood children and adolescents, a local cultural center called The Yellow House (A Casa Amarela) served as the operational headquarters of the remarkable spectacle.[31]

From afar, the favela's haunting female eyes seemed to return the outsiders' gaze, thereby serving notice that the hill's residents were watching back. Then, as news media investigated the unexpected phenomenon, enigmatic JR disappeared to let the local residents speak for themselves. As he later explained, "More and more, people are conscious of how the media portray them. They want to control their image."[32] Subsequently, the Cannes Film Festival enthusiastically received JR's documentary film about the favela's artistic installation, set to music with local interviews. Posted online in 2012, the video version of "Women Are Heroes" shows the hill's narrow passageways, colorful buildings, and densely packed homes with a focus on the lives of women and children intent on remaining in their homes. The artist's intention was "to highlight the dignity of women who occupy crucial roles in societies, and find themselves victims of wartime, street crime, sexual assault, and religious and political extremism."[33]

More recently, Providência has also gained local attention for its environmental restoration and activism. The Intelligent Garden project, launched in 2015, has recruited volunteers to take part in agro-forest management and environmental education. One project under development since early 2019 has focused on a long-desolate area above the Gamboa port district's João

Ricardo Tunnel, constructed in 1919. As one of the main entrances to the Morro da Providência, the space became a virtual garbage dump full of tall invasive brush, which created a risk of mosquitos and other vectors of tropical disease. The collective action (*mutirão*) has involved trash removal, cutting back the grass, and caring for the species-diverse garden of flowers, vegetables, fruit trees, blackberries, cassava, sunflower seeds, and more. After nine months of volunteer work, the space above the tunnel has been transformed: beyond maintenance, the volunteers have built a reading corner for book donations and exchange; offered environmental education for some four hundred children, with recycling, planting, culinary, and art activities; and organized environmental workshops at local fairs and in neighboring Gamboa.[34]

Besides being the first favela in Brazil, by tradition, Providência was also among the first to have a museum. In 2005, through the Favela-Neighborhood (Favela-Bairro) infrastructure program, Mayor César Maia established an open-air museum there as part of port revitalization, which also included the Samba City carnival center nearby. Besides funding for piped-in water, sewerage, squares, and streets in Providência, the infrastructure program included a tourist itinerary. This initiative represented the city's first effort to play an active role in the promotion of favela tourism. Without denying the problems of poverty, informal housing, lack of services, and violence—in fact, by playing them up and commodifying their authenticity—the local authorities hoped to convert an urban problem into a solution. Conceived by architect and planner Lu Petersen, the touristic route followed markers up to the top of the hill, along the granite stairway carved by African slaves in the early eighteenth century. This pathway gave access to points of interest: Oratory of the Cross, Our Lady of the Penha Church, and the panoramic viewpoints of Rio de Janeiro. The city initially proposed a virtual theme park with enhanced lighting and the historic restoration of several houses to their original fin de siècle ramshackle state. Criticism that it would romanticize poverty, along with the violence from drug traffic, discouraged the project.[35] Cosme Felippsen, 27, a local resident and tour guide, includes the city paths as well as those he chose personally. "There are residents who still do not know what the metal markers are for!" says Cosme, suggesting how little known the Open-Air Museum is today.[36]

For another resident, Eron César dos Santos, 49, the fact that César Maia's mayoral administration created the open-air museum discouraged subsequent mayors from supporting the project. Eron has also suggested that Providência now receives more tourists than in 2005, due to the installation of the cable-car tramway in 2015. Eron and another local resident, Roberto Marinho, created the Providência Community Museum in 2014. This digital museum operates virtually through a blog: residents conduct research, promote local heritage, and lead tours of the favela. Topics of interest include the history of

Our Lady of Penha Church, residential issues on the hill, criticism of the port area's renewal program, erasure of African memory in the port, dismay at the "Olympics of exclusion," and, most of all, community memories of life on the hill. On Providência Hill's 120th anniversary in 2017, the community blog voiced a message of continued hope, resistance, and resilience:

> One life, one hope! A favela, a story!
>   Struggling and resisting to achieve a dream!
>   Morro da Providência, more than a century of existence, struggle, resistance and perseverance.[37]

FAVELA EXPANSION, REMOVAL, AND RESISTANCE

As *favela* became a generic term for informal settlements, their proliferation became increasingly visible by the 1920s. While authorities condemned the growth of improvised villages, the news media alarmed the public with lurid accounts of ramshackle housing and human misery. Maurício Abreu found that newspapers pathologized Rio's "multidirectional and uncontrollable" favela expansion in the early twentieth century.[38] According to authorities, the official number of favelas increased from 7 in 1900, to 26 in 1920, and 116 in 1940. To use Elizabeth Bishop's evocative imagery, the "fearful stain" was clearly expanding on the "fair green hills of Rio."[39] Given the concurrent rise of urban planning, the discourse of favela removal soon moved from idle disdain to serious urban renewal. From 1926 to 1930, French architect Donat-Alfred Agache proposed to transform Rio into a "monumental city," as discussed in chapter 2, through modernist high-rise redevelopment, new traffic arterials, and favela eradication. His denunciation of informal urbanism illustrates the dogmatic elitism of the age:

> Built contrary to all rules of hygiene, without piped water, without sewerage, without garbage collection, without order, with irregular materials, the *favelas* constitute a permanent risk of fire and epidemic infections for neighborhoods they infiltrate. Their leprosy fouls the beaches and neighborhoods gracefully endowed by nature, strips the hills of their adorning greenery, and corrodes even the edges of the forest on the lower slopes of the coastal hill range. . . . Their destruction is important for social order and security, as well as the general hygiene of the city, to say nothing of aesthetics.[40]

After the Revolution of 1930, President Getúlio Vargas centralized federal power and sponsored large-scale urban renewal, which included leveling historic hills, and creating modernist high-rises, monumental boulevards, new airports, state-subsidized industries, and so on. Given his populist leanings, the president generally left the favelas intact. Yet local pressures to remove the proliferating informal communities did not abate. The Federal District began to plan for their removal in 1937, when favelas were first defined as "groups of two or more irregular shacks, constructed of improvised materials." In 1947, the Commission for the Eradication of Favelas even proposed "returning *favela* residents to their states of origin, committing *favela* residents over the age of 60 to State Institutions, and expelling from the *favela* all families whose income exceeded a minimum."[41] Although a shortage of political willpower and financial resources initially prevented such draconian measures, Rio's authorities clearly regarded the informal settlements as a blight on the capital's landscape.

The early postwar decades, noted by massive regional and urban-rural migrations, witnessed the number and size of favelas rise dramatically. It was also a time of new statistical metrics of data collection. In 1948, the Federal District of Rio carried out the first systematic survey, which initially found 119 informal settlements with a population of 280,000; later, using stricter criteria, these figures were revised to 105 favelas with 138,837 residents. In 1950, the census began to gather standardized national data on "subnormal agglomerations." While recognizing regional variations—such as *mocambos* in Recife, *baixadas* in Belém and Manaus—this technocratic term suggested an implicit stigma toward all of the "subnormal" settlements. Officials defined favelas, and their regional equivalents, as groups of 51 or more dwellings of a "rustic appearance" without land titles, and with a shortage of public services and an absence of street paving, numbers, and signage. The census of 1950 found 58 favelas with 169,305 residents in Rio, or 7 percent of the city's population. The decrease from 105 favelas, as found by local authorities in 1948, reflected the new criteria of larger settlements with at least 51 dwellings. By 1970, the number of favelas officially leaped to 300, representing more than half a million residents or 13.2 percent of the city's total population (see table 4.1).[42]

The coup d'état of 1964 provided an authoritarian state with the ideology, motivation, and power required for massive favela removal. The military regime created the Coordination of Social Interest Housing of the Greater Rio Metropolitan Area (CHISAM) to assure that there would be "no more people living in the slums of Rio de Janeiro by 1976." Between 1962 and 1974, Rio's authorities forcibly displaced some 80 informal communities, 26,000 homes, and 139,000 residents, often relocated to public housing long distances from the city center. Not coincidentally, favela growth slowed during the 1970s, before again exceeding city growth thereafter. No doubt the city's economic downturn with the loss of the national capital, financial restructuring, and

Table 4.1. Census Data on Favela Populations in the City of Rio de Janeiro, 1950–2010

Year	Total Rio Population	Total Favela Population	Favelas as % of Rio Population	Number of Favelas	Annual % Change in Favela Population	Annual % Change in City Population
1950	2,375,280	169,305	7.1	58	—	—
1960	3,307,163	337,412	10.2	147	4.9	2.8
1970	4,251,918	563,970	13.2	300	4.0	2.2
1980	5,093,232	628,170	12.3	372	1.0	1.6
1990	5,480,778	882,483	16.1	525	2.8	0.7
2000	5,857,879	1,092,958	18.6	704	1.9	0.6
2010	6,323,037	1,443,773	22.8	763	2.4	0.7

Sources: Instituto Brasileiro de Geografia e Estatística (IBGE), http://www.ibge.gov.br/, various years; Instituto Pereira Passos, "Favelas na cidade do Rio de Janeiro: O quadro populacional com base no Censo 2010," Prefeitura da Cidade do Rio de Janeiro, 2012.

industrial shifts played an important role, but the massive displacement was unprecedented. CHISAM concentrated primarily on the demolition of favela communities in the South Zone, where real-estate interests benefited the most from urban redevelopment.[43]

One of the largest and most visible favelas removed was Catacumba (Catacombs), which once overlooked the scenic Lagoa Rodrigo de Freitas, a freshwater lagoon in the South Zone. Amid the lagoon, beaches, and mountains, luxury high-rises have now replaced the informal community once there. The area was a farm during the late nineteenth century, owned by the Baroness of Lagoa Rodrigo de Freitas, who, according to some reports, transferred the land to her former slaves after abolition. If that was the case, the land titles unfortunately did not endure, for in 1925 the state divided the area there into 32 large residential lots. The origins of the favela go back to an influx of rural migrants in the 1930s, largely from Minas Gerais. In-migration mounted during World War II, and a major land invasion by migrants occurred in 1942. After construction of a direct highway from Rio to Bahia in 1952, another wave of migrants moved into the growing favela. In 1954, the city's public works department installed standpipes with water spigots in the lower-lying streets, along with facilities to wash clothes along the lakeshore.[44] A newspaper report from 1967 describes the community as enterprising:

> At five o'clock in the morning, Catacumba begins to evict its residents. Maids, cooks and nannies go down the community stairs, leaving for the "madam's houses." Workers (many in construction) line up at the two bus stops or walk in the direction of Copacabana, Ipanema and Leblon. A little later, the people who go down the hill already have another appearance: it is time for civil servants,

the children who go to school, and the great movement of the washerwomen, who leave the house early to enjoy the weak morning sun for washing and then the sun to dry clothes.[45]

Given Catacumba's convenient location in the well-to-do South Zone, there were abundant service jobs available. Based on ethnographic fieldwork carried out in the late 1960s, Perlman characterized the Catacumba community as hardworking, close-knit, and despite the poverty and lack of basic services, highly optimistic about the future: "A family can easily multiply its sources of income by the wife taking in washing, ironing, or sewing, daughters selling sweets, and sons shining shoes, watching parked cars, or selling scraps. And construction work or repair work is often available for able-bodied men."[46]

By the time it was demolished in 1970, Catacumba had grown to more than ten thousand residents. While the government considered the favela to be an ugly blight on the stunning landscape, the community reportedly had a strong class-consciousness and industrious work ethic, which in turn fostered solidarity, reciprocity, and mutual support. But the military-backed governor, Negrão de Lima, and CHISAM were determined to remove the informal settlement. Besides their general disdain for the rudimentary houses, irregular ground plan, and general poverty, they undoubtedly had designs on the spectacular location and its real-estate potential. On October 10, 1970, the military police descended on Catacumba, demolished 1,420 dwellings, and evicted 2,207 families. Most of the displaced families relocated to the distant Guaporé and Quitango public-housing complexes, while several hundred moved to the City of God and Vila Kennedy projects. When the residents of Catacumba were separated and moved into the public-housing *conjuntos*, many of them felt a loss of community, even if their new locations ultimately allowed some upward mobility. Authorities also displaced several smaller favelas around the lagoon during the 1960s, including the Praia do Pinto.[47]

After the community's removal, the city reforested the hillside and in 1979 inaugurated a park, dedicated to the arts, sculpture, and music. The free musical concerts proved so popular that huge crowds overwhelmed the park and contributed to its deterioration. Renamed the Natural City Park of Catacumba in 2003, the focus shifted to "the basic objective of preservation of the ecosystems of ecological and scenic importance." Having reforested the hillside and built trails overlooking the lagoon and ocean, the park thereafter would be managed by the Municipal Secretary of the Environment. This case illustrates the long-held perception that the favelas detracted from the Rio's spectacular natural environments, although the historical images of Catacumba made it seem vibrant, picturesque, and well adapted to the hillside. But at the time of the favela's demolition, justification for removal rested primarily on the need to "integrate" the *favelados* into society through "the economic, social, moral, and hygienic reclaiming of the slum families. . . . These families then become completely integrated in the community, especially in the way that they live and think."[48] Such ideologically charged stereotypes were questionable, since evidence showed that favelas already were integrated into the work force and social institutions, if excluded from participation on equal terms.

Still, such ideologies have largely survived in new guises, as they continue to serve vested interests. Despite the rhetoric of marginality, favela eradication concentrated largely on valuable real estate in the South Zone. In fact, historically Rio's South Zone once had an extensive array of favelas: 33 of the city's total 147 informal settlements in 1960 were in southern Rio, but the military regime removed many of them during the 1960s and 1970s. Urban renewal further marginalized the poor: a 1966 study found that relocated residents had to commute two hours each way on public transportation, costing one-third of their wages. The spatial distribution of informal settlements shifted away from the South Zone, while the number of favelas in the North Zone reached 58 percent of the total by 1980. Overall, the favela populations continued to grow, albeit somewhat more slowly during the 1970s. Thereafter, the favelas have consistently grown much faster than the city's general rate of demographic increase.[49]

Studies also suggest changes in how favela residents view the city. Instead of the "slums of hope" once described by scholars, there is evidence of a shift to a perspective of "despair," even with improved material conditions. In selective follow-up interviews based on the original 1968–1969 study, more than three decades later (1999–2003), Perlman found a transformation from "the myth of marginality" among previously aspiring migrants to "the reality of marginality" among residents now faced with limited social mobility. Although living standards, urban services, and education improved among those interviewed in three favelas, previously upbeat attitudes had soured: the inability to move into affluent neighborhoods and to achieve better jobs frustrated *favelados*, while pervasive fear and insecurity heightened their pessimism. In one telling measure of place stigma, the follow-up study indicated that among those with equal educational attainment, residents of favelas earned significantly lower incomes than those from conventional neighborhoods and even public housing.[50] While her intergenerational survey was relatively small and cannot be considered definitive, it raised important questions about blocked upward mobility and resulting pessimism among once-enthusiastic *favelados*.

Favela displacement waned as the military regime, facing renewed labor activism and political opposition, allowed a gradual democratization in the early 1980s. Return to electoral democracy also meant that political parties again courted the favela vote with promises of services and other improvements. Yet community displacement resumed under entrepreneurial regimes after the turn of the millennium, particularly with regard to athletic mega-events. New campaigns to demolish Rio's favelas began with the approach of the Pan American Games of 2007, then intensified with preparations for the FIFA World Cup of 2014 and the Olympic Games of 2016. The latter two international spectacles, intended to promote Rio's prospects as a global city for investment and tourism, occurred paradoxically as the city created the Valongo Wharf slave site and the African Heritage Circuit in the port district. While the brutal large-scale displacement of informal communities under the military regime was a thing of the past, contemporary eviction by neoliberal public-private partnerships remained a threat, if a somewhat more selective one. Between 2009 and 2015, these mega-events displaced an estimated 22,059 families and 77,206 residents from redevelopment sites in Rio de Janeiro—about half the number evicted by the military regime over a longer period, from 1962 to 1974.[51]

In contrast to the earlier authoritarian style of favela removal by state decree and police enforcement, contemporary neoliberal displacement reflects a greater reliance on the dynamics of housing markets (e.g., rising rents and property values), cash buyouts, and of course legal loopholes to force evictions. These strategies now rely less on the state's brute force and more on financial lure and legal coercion. Such tactics reflect the entrepreneurial city's reliance on private capital, city branding, governance as business management, and a general attempt to limit citizen rights to the city. International mega-events have become dependent on public-private infrastructural provision and private profit from the television rights, advertising, and sponsorships. In response, favela activists encourage social mobilization through related counter-narratives: the undue profits of elites, rising socioeconomic inequality, impoverishment of the masses, critiques of urban redevelopment, and efforts to divide broad pro-growth coalitions.[52]

Vila Autódromo became a symbol of favela community resistance to Olympic removal. This informal settlement began in the mid-1960s near Barra da Tijuca on the city's West Side. Given the lack of affordable housing for workers, low-income families squatted on unused land, often near the area's many lagoons. Fishermen and their families settled in what they initially called Lagoinha (Little Lagoon), but later they took the name Vila Autódromo after an adjacent Formula 1 racetrack built there in 1970. In 1987, with the addition of construction workers' families, the village established the Association of Residents and Fishermen of Vila Autódromo, which divided the land into lots, opened roadways, and began to install basic services—the energetic and self-reliant Association of Residents even designed and began to install its own sewerage system. A long-running dispute with the city of Rio began in 1993, when Mayor César Maia filed a lawsuit to redevelop the area, including the racetrack, given the potential real-estate development. Fortunately for residents, the city and state governments were not aligned on this issue. In fact, after the city lost the court case, the state of Rio issued eighty-four families titles of possession (*títulos de posse*), which allowed them to occupy the land for 40 years, renewable for 99 years. But the city did not give up easily. In 2009, after Rio won the bid to host the 2016 Summer Olympics, new mayor Eduardo Paes announced plans to remove 123 favelas, including Vila Autódromo, without prior consultation with the targeted communities.[53]

With Vila slated to become part of the 291-acre Olympic Park and Athlete's Village, the community launched a vigorous campaign of resistance, which counted on the support of allied favelas, political activists, city universities, segments of the government, the Catholic Church, and the local and international news media. The *New York Times* reported in a front-page article on Rio's Olympic preparations that "one of the fiercest battles is over Vila Autódromo," where the residents "took their fight online, posting videos of sharp exchanges with officials. They began working with state prosecutors to file injunctions aimed at blocking their removal, though they lost a critical ruling in recent days."[54] Indeed, the social drama of Vila Autódromo, magnified by the reports of news media, subsequently heated up to the fever pitch of a Brazilian *telenovela*. Although the winning design of the Olympic Park did not require removal of Vila Autódromo, the city of Rio was still determined to do so. The city initially cited environmental degradation as the main reason for eviction, but then it argued for a security perimeter around the Olympic Park, which the informal settlement allegedly would jeopardize, despite its peaceful history and the absence of the drug traffickers and paramilitary militias.

Given these circumstances, the city's insistence on removing Vila Autódromo may have resulted from real-estate speculation and exchange of favors among politicians and business interests. Most notably, the Olympic Village would include 3,604 apartments to house the 17,000 competitors: built by public-private partnership, the units would go on the market after the games. The favela proposed a Popular Plan to include about 500 households, while resettling only 82 households located on low-lying areas prone to flooding. But under intense pressures, including both evictions and cash settlements, only about 50 households remained by January 2016. In the glare of global media, as the Olympics approached, the mayor relented and allowed 20 households—4 percent of the original community—to remain. Despite the vastly reduced population, many observers regarded the deal as a symbolic victory. In the end, the city had to negotiate with *favelados* and allow some to remain legally. The political solidarity forged a large group of activist supporters. As Sukari Ivester concluded, the residents "exercised their right to the city and to their community. Their victory demonstrates that when people are organized in purpose, even in the face of powerful urban growth machines, resistance is not futile."[55]

In the aftermath of the Olympic Games, remembrance of Vila's resistance to removal became an important objective of community and housing activists. Founded on May 19, 2016, the Evictions Museum (Museu das Remoções) became a new favela institution with the slogan "memory cannot be removed." According to the founders, the Evictions Museum aspires to remember the local struggle against displacement and to inspire other communities to organize as well. Conceived as an open-air museum with both an online and a physical presence, archival material of the community's struggle for survival appears on the museum's Facebook site,[56] while seven outdoor memory sites incorporate the debris from demolitions to recall the multifaceted efforts to remain at the original settlement:

1. *The Light That Doesn't Go Out*, beside St. Joseph Workers Church (São José Operário), honored where residents held activities and left remnants from demolished homes.
2. *Pillar of Strength* recalls former resident Jane Nascimento, who worked tirelessly to save her home from demolition before it ultimately fell on August 1, 2020.
3. *Sweet Childhood* refers to the restored children's playground where residents held community-building events during the resistance to removal.
4. *Occupation Space/Conceição's Home* commemorates the efforts that took place as activists used a supporter's house to create an Occupation Space next door.
5. *The Vila of All Saints* depicts Heloisa Helena's former home, which served as an Afro-Brazilian *candomblé* center before its demolition on February 24, 2016. This installation includes a poem on community resilience, which in part reads: "One day everyone will remember, That when the people fight back, Destruction cannot be justified."
6. *The Many Faces of Penha* honors the political activism of Maria da Penha, a community leader and recipient of the city's Woman Citizen's award on March 8, 2016, International Women's Day, just as bulldozers demolished her house in the Vila.
7. *I Am the Association of Residents* symbolizes the fight to preserve the Vila Autódromo Neighborhood Association Building from destruction.[57]

The last site particularly evokes a sense of collective memory. In fact, before the authorities finally succeeded in demolishing the Neighborhood Association Building on February 24, 2016, activists spray-painted "Association of Residents" on the walls of all the Vila's remaining houses to strengthen group solidarity. As resident Sandra Regina argued with regard: "The Association of Residents is not a house to be demolished; the Association represents every resident. We are the Association."[58] Thus, resistance to displacement forged a resilient community in Vila Autódromo, as in other favelas under threat of removal in Rio de Janeiro.

FAVELA AS SPECTACLE: "THEY DON'T CARE ABOUT US"

> Rio de Janeiro, Botafogo, South Zone,
> Community of Santa Marta
> 73 years of resistance, my partners.
>
> —"788" by Repper Fiell from the album
> *Pedagogia de Dominação*, 2013[59]

One of Rio's most famous favelas, Santa Marta is located on the steep slope of Dona Marta Hill, visible above the Botofogo district in Rio's South Zone (see figure 4.3). While not on the beachfront, the favela enjoys scenic views of Guanabara Bay, Sugar Loaf Mountain, and Corcovado Mountain. The name Dona Marta Hill goes back to 1680, when Catholic father Clemente bought the lands of present-day Bogofogo and named one of the nearby hills after his mother, Marta. Favela Santa Marta dates from the 1920s, when an elderly female follower of biblical Saint Martha carried her image to the hilltop. During the 1930s, Catholic father Veloso had a chapel built to house the saint's statue and to serve as a place to rest after the strenuous climb. The Saint Ignacio School nearby owned the property and allowed its employees to live on the hillside, which gave rise to the favela. Many early residents were migrant agriculturalists, who came to work in construction of the church and school. The confusion about the place names goes back to the 1980s, as the news media began to refer to the favela as Dona Marta, due to its namesake hilltop viewpoint. Christian evangelical churches also preferred this name, since they did not refer to Catholic saints, whereas "dona" was a term of respect for a mature woman. Although the general preference now seems to have returned to favor "Favela Santa Marta," the way people refer to the community still reflects a local power struggle.[60] While such toponyms reflect historical placemaking,

Figure 4.3. Favela Santa Marta. Google Maps, adapted by the author.

the contemporary power of place also reflects the depictions of the news media, film, and music. The case of Santa Marta, like other favelas, shows how the use of spectacle may pit community resistance against institutional power.

Favela Santa Marta became well known over the years, largely through such media representations. Filmmaker Eduardo Coutinho directed a 54-minute film documentary, *Santa Marta: Two Weeks on the Hill*, which, on release in 1987, got enthusiastic reviews for its realistic yet respectful portrait of the urban poor. Regarded by many to be the country's greatest documentary filmmaker, the late Coutinho (1933–2014) favored filming multiple life stories (rather than a single narrative) and the expression of diverse voices (with no voiceovers), which is why his style has been called "conversational cinema." As Verônica Ferreira Dias has noted, Coutinho featured "the *favela* inhabitants as they would like to be seen."[61] In fact, the film begins on a morning as residents descend from the hill and say where they are going to work, followed by others who disclose their jobs on returning home. Community life appears in the context of meetings, religious services, songs and music, and home visits with residents. While those interviewed complained of frequent police searches for illegal drugs, the viewer never sees any drug dealing, although the narco-traffic was already firmly established by the 1980s.[62]

Compared with the focus of so many contemporary films on drug-related violence, the 1987 documentary was notable for its concern with the residents' lives and aspirations. In fact, commentators have praised Coutinho's work on favelas as ethically responsible filmmaking, given the director's refusal to engage in what Beatriz Jaguaribe calls "the spectacularization of the real undertaken by reality shows and sensationalist media coverage."[63] Mainstream media—newspapers, magazines, television newscasts, documentary and feature films—have for decades routinely depicted horrific violence in Rio's favelas and in the process stigmatized *favelados*. The bloodshed depicted in the film *City of God* (2002), based on the novel by Paulo Lins, follows the negative storyline of young male *favelados* of color who become involved in the drug trade and related conflicts. Melanie Gilligan notes that the film "renders most of the substantive history in quick strokes," while mesmerizing the spectator with "a style of fast cutting, abbreviated exposition, tinted color palettes and perpetually moving handheld photography; techniques which have undeniably become a reified visual 'pre-set' for representing Latin American experience below subsistence level."[64]

Residents of Rio's real City of God (Cidade de Deus) have resented the overly negative portrayals of the community in the news media and popular films. When Kelly Graham carried out field research on several favelas in 2006, she interviewed public high school students in Cidade de Deus and two other favelas. "Outraged at the depiction of their community in City of God," she noted, "the students filmed their own video in an effort to show the positive elements of their community." In fact, many of the teenage students hoped to be doctors, lawyers, teachers, or military personnel. They resented the news media's emphasis on violence rather than their affirmative aspirations. Similarly to Perlman's contending that the "myth of marginality" has now become more of a "reality of marginality," Graham found that the students felt pessimistic about their prospects in the favelas: "When asked what their hopes were for the future, almost all the students responded that they hoped to leave City of God and escape the economic and social marginalization and depression they were currently trapped in."[65]

Given such criticism, Fernando Meirelles and Katia Lund, directors of *City of God*, subsequently released a televised mini-series *City of Men* (2005), which centers on the fictionalized stories of two young Black men growing up on an unnamed hillside similar to Morro Dona Marta. The likable best friends try to avoid the pitfalls around them, often through mischief—similar to Mark Twain's classic adventures of Tom Sawyer and Huckleberry Finn. The young *favelados* struggle to fulfill their aspirations amid poverty, gangsters, romantic affairs, and parental pressures. Similarly, the documentary *Favela Rising* (2006) tells of the Grupo Cultural AfroReggae, which used musical genres and dance—including hip-hop, soul, funk, percussion, and *capoeira*—to offer young *favelados* educational alternatives to drug traffic and gang violence. Vibrant Afro-Brazilian cultures emanate from favelas and strive to affirm the everyday struggles of residents. Even with such occasional realistic content, some critics have bemoaned the depoliticized consumerism common to most corporate film and media on favelas. Ivana Bentes famously quipped that Brazil's politically engaged New Cinema (Cinema Novo) of the mid-twentieth century, once known for its "aesthetic of hunger," has now degenerated into a commodified "cosmetic of hunger" with the contemporary rise of Favela Chic.[66]

While already well known in Rio, Favela Santa Marta became internationally famous for hosting the filming of a music video by Michael Jackson on February 10–11, 1996. The song he performed, "They Don't Care About Us," was one of his most controversial. It protests the marginalization of poor communities, ethnic and racial prejudice, and insensitive governmental institutions. Largely inspired by the case of Rodney King, a Black man who suffered a brutal beating by Los Angeles police in 1991, Jackson probably also based the song on his own experience with the police and legal systems during an adolescent-sex case in 1993 (settled out of court). While Jackson stressed an antiracist line in the song, charges of anti-Semitism (which he denied) caused him to alter some of the lyrics. In fact, in composing the song in 1995, some critics even claimed that Jackson appropriated the cultural capital of the civil rights movement and Black nationalism to promote his career.[67] Still, the song proved widely popular, besides being a powerful denunciation of racism with an infectious pulsating chorus.

Film director Spike Lee wanted to film the music video in a Rio favela, which would illustrate the theme of marginalization. He was correct, of course, since police-community relations in favelas have been fraught with violence. Although the event organizers considered the huge favela of Rocinha, they decided that smaller Santa Marta was more self-contained and less of a security risk. The announcement of the superstar's plans to perform on Dona Marta Hill—along with an initial segment in Pelourinho Square, the Black heritage site in Salvador, Bahia—made headlines in Brazil. (While the Brazilian music video took place in predominantly Black communities of Rio and Salvador, the U.S. version focused on the conditions of U.S. prison inmates, mainly Black and Latino.) Rio's authorities particularly feared and resented Jackson's equation of U.S. and Brazilian racism, given the historic claims of "racial democracy," however long debunked, in the South American country. Cristina Becker of Rio's Convention Bureau reflected the official opinion when she complained, "We've always oriented producers to show the good that Rio has. If Michael Jackson only wants to show the bad side, it is better that he not come." A Brazilian judge initially barred the film crew from filming in Favela Santa Marta. After resolving the judicial problem, the music-video project circumvented the formal authorities and made arrangements for the filming, at a fee, directly with the local drug lord. Revelations that Jackson's company paid the Red Command (Comando Vermelho) cartel confirmed the existence of Rio's parallel and informal political-economic structures.[68]

In arranging Jackson's visit to Santa Marta, the film crew initially asked for assistance from the president of the Association of Residents, but he in turn had to get authorization from the local drug boss, Márcio Amaro de Oliveira, who belonged to Rio's dominant Red Command cartel. Born into a poor migrant family from the Brazilian Northeast, Oliveira grew up working on his strict father's food-and-drink vending cart. As he grew up in the favela, drug traffic's lucrative profits lured Oliveira into the illicit business. Journalist Caco Barcellos recounted the human saga of "Juliano VP," the pseudonym for "Marcinho VP," also nicknamed the "Poet" due to his literary interests. As he climbed in the organization's hierarchy, he maintained a reputation as a Robin Hood figure who supported community groups, local schools, and celebrations. Oliveira even led Michael Jackson's security squad in the *favela*, which exposed his identity and whereabouts to authorities: he gave boastful but indiscreet press interviews, after which the journalists broke their promises of anonymity and revealed his name, personal details, and insider drug-dealing information in Rio's daily newspapers. This strategic reversal led to a cat-and-mouse game in which the drug lord would spend the night with different girlfriends, rather than sleeping at his own house, so as to hide from the police. Yet, as Barcellos notes, the previously unknown drug trafficker suddenly "became the target of a relentless police hunt, as if he were the biggest public enemy of Rio de Janeiro."[69]

Oliveira subsequently gained even more notoriety in the documentary film *News from a Personal War* (1999), directed by João Moreira Salles and Kátia Lund. Using Favela Santa Marta as a case study, the film examines urban violence from the battles among drug dealers, police and favela residents. Based on two years of interviews with those directly involved in the drug traffic, the film drew even more attention to Marcinho VP. In interviews with the print press, he reportedly boasted that he did not drink or smoke tobacco cigarettes (he was well-known to favor marijuana) but that he was most addicted to killing. Although the drug lord claimed he had been misquoted, his fierce image made him an even more important target for police. In an odd twist, the authorities charged the film director with aiding a criminal, since Salles admitted to paying the drug dealer a "research grant" for help with the documentary. The director was not convicted, as he claimed that the payment aimed to help the drug dealer leave crime and write a book about his life. Meanwhile, the increasingly isolated and introspective drug boss recalled twenty-three traffickers killed in action. After the police captured Marcinho VP, authorities sentenced him to twenty-five years in Rio's infamous Bangu Prison complex. Ironically, two months after the publication of *Abusado*, the book about his life, rivals strangled Oliveira to death in prison on July 29, 2003. According to the police, he revealed too many details about the functioning of Rio's criminal factions, which caused problems within his own cartel, the Red Command. Dumped into a trashcan, his dead body covered with his beloved books, Oliveira joined fifty-four of his cartel partners who lost their lives in summary executions during the three years he was in prison.[70]

After Jackson's performance publicized Favela Santa Marta, a stream of celebrities, singers, and action-movie teams descended on the community. On November 13, 2009, the American singer Madonna visited the favela, escorted by both Governor Sérgio Cabral and Mayor Eduardo Paes. In February of 2010, the community hosted the filming of a music video by singers Alicia Keys and Beyoncé. Then, on June 26, 2010, a year after the death of American singer Michael Jackson, the State Department of Tourism, Sports and Leisure unveiled commemorative works of art on the public space where Jackson performed, located above a new cultural center with musical instruction for young people in the community. The site now features a colorful mural of Jackson by Romero Brito and a statue of him by Ique.

Given the community's high visibility, coupled with Michael Jackson's music video and Marcinho VP's notoriety, the initial choice for a UPP location seemed highly symbolic. In fact, the police station moved into the former house of the drug lord, located at the top of the hill, providing strategic and symbolic domination over the community. Timed to coincide with subsequent athletic mega-events, including the 2014 World Cup and the 2016 Summer Olympics, the UPP initially provided security and helped to consolidate physical improvements: the Favela-Neighborhood program installed sewage lines, water pipes, electrical cables, a free wireless internet network, and a cable-car tramway up the steep hill. After initial success in reducing the violence, the UPP program faltered after 2016, due to budgetary shortfalls and protests against police violations of human rights.

The hillside community now has some 8,000 residents, who dwell in some 500 wooden and 2,000 brick houses. Someone approaching the favela from the Botofogo neighborhood below is likely to enter through a colorful square, Praça Cantão, center of a small commercial district with brightly painted buildings. As a result of the Favela Painting project, an art program under the collaborative direction of Dutch artists Jeroen Koolhaas and Dre Urhahn (known as Haas&Hahn), the community painted 75,000 square feet (7,000 m2) around Santa Marta's main square in 2010. The colorful tableau of this main square served as the cover of the exhibition and, later, the book *Design with the Other 90%: Cities*, an exhibition by the Cooper-Hewitt Museum at the United Nations Headquarters in 2011. In addition, the *Herald Sun* newspaper of Australia called the Praça Cantão one of the world's "most colorful places" that year: having transformed "the hillside slum of Santa Marta, the project aims to inspire the community."[71] As one proceeds up the narrow and winding land, up the steep hill, the houses become progressively newer and more rustic, while the climbing becomes more strenuous. The cable-car tramway system up the hill has been a godsend for residents and visitors, but it does not always work.

With the arrival of UPP community policing, the city and state asserted new power over environmental issues in favelas. Thus, landscape optics became another kind of spectacle for the authorities, intended to demonstrate that deforestation and pollution made informal communities detrimental to the city's quality of life, urban ecology, and property values. Indeed, real-estate interests have long argued that the prime locations made available through favela eradication would allow construction of luxury homes, thus making the areas safer and more "sustainable." Interestingly, such arguments are not directed so much at favelas in the working-class North Zone as in the posh South Zone. For example, after torrential rains led to widespread landslides and the collapse of scores of hillside shacks in February 1998, Rio's leading newspaper, *O Jornal do Brasil*, called favelas the city's "biggest urban problem":

> The city has 223 areas of risk, which every summer create floods and landslides. There are *favelas* like Rocinha in which urbanization is the only solution, such is the area occupied. But a *favela* like Santa Marta should be eradicated, as it poses an eternal threat to its residents. Before being swallowed by *favelas*, Rio needs to revive old plans to urbanize *favelas* that are urbanizable, and to remove *favelas* that are removable.[72]

The state of Rio began to construct ten-foot-high (3 meters) walls around thirteen favelas in March of 2009, purportedly to prevent further expansion into Tijuca Forest (see photo 4.1). First proposed in 2004, the stated rationale was to protect pedestrians, passing vehicles, and nearby neighborhoods from stray bullets. Although not implemented initially, given community opposition, the plan subsequently reappeared under a cloak of environmental responsibility: to protect the tropical forest, the project would build seven miles (11 km) of ten-foot-high walls and displace 550 families in thirteen communities. It provoked widely divergent opinions. Some observers concurred with Sergio Cabral, the state governor, who argued: "It is a wall of inclusion,

Photo 4.1. A view of Favela Santa Marta, showing the "eco-barrier" installed in 2009. Photo by the author, 2011.

not segregation. It means the end of the state's omission." *Veja*, a leading Brazilian news magazine, commended the project: "The government of Rio has shown courage to fight without demagogy the problem of favelas." On the other hand, affected residents and many other observers suspected that the "eco-barriers" were less about environmental protection than enclosing and removing from sight the most visible favelas. José Saramago, the Portuguese winner of the 1998 Nobel Prize for Literature, wrote: "The idea, now, is to surround the *favelas* with a concrete wall of three meters' height. We had the walls of Berlin, the walls of Palestine, and now Rio's."[73]

The conservation of the Atlantic Forest (Mata Atlântica) has long been an important environmental cause, since more than 90 percent of the original forest has disappeared, initially as a result of clearing for vast sugar and coffee plantations, and more recently due to rapid urbanization as well. Biodiversity has declined steadily with deforestation. Authorities also point to the danger of landslides as informal settlements climb up the steep mountain slopes above the city. But *favelados* and other observers suspected that the ecological concerns also served the less-benevolent purpose of curtailing favela growth. The fact that all but one of the thirteen favelas to be walled were in Rio's affluent South Zone added to suspicions about the ulterior motives of the "eco-walls." In this sense, the program aimed to install eco-barriers around the most strategically located favelas of the city's southern seaside , including Chacará do Céu, Pavão-Pavãozinho, Chapéu Mangueira, Rocinha, Babilônia, Cantagalo, Vidigal, and Santa Marta. Only one of the designated favelas, Parque da Pedra Branca, was located in the West Zone, where informal communities generally were growing the fastest in the city. As a result, it is difficult to see the eco-barrier strictly in environmentalist terms; instead, it appeared to be an apartheid-like desire to secure and contain the poor communities in the affluent Rio.

Former governor Sérgio Cabral—now in prison for corruption—who authorized the eco-barriers, explicitly noted that the favela walls would assist the city in monitoring "drug trafficking and vigilantes, by putting limits on uncontrolled growth." The concurrent appearance of community policing with the UPPs (given the approach of athletic mega-events in 2014–2016) added credibility to the security concerns. There have also been reports that drug cartels used adjacent forests for training and escape routes when confronting rival gangs, militias, and police forces. In fact, given the furor about the eco-barriers in Santa Marta, the state government agreed to a different approach in Rocinha. Given a population of more than one hundred thousand, significant social diversity, banks and schools, and a booming commercial strip, Rocinha is increasingly seen as a neighborhood rather than a favela. Instead of the 8.7 miles of high walls initially planned by the government, the community proposed a partially open, user-friendly barrier with the forest, including parks, playgrounds, picnic tables and barbeques, nature trails, and space for community events. While walls would still protect the forest on much of the community's circumference, the barriers would be lower—no more than three feet high—with the taller ten-foot walls reserved for areas with high risk of landslides. One wonders why this happy solution for moderated, locally adapted eco-barriers was not more widely adopted. It would have provided, instead of an image of environmental confinement, a more inspiring spectacle of environmental respect and stewardship for the favela.

THE RISE OF "FAVELA CHIC"

Despite the socioeconomic marginalization of favelas in Rio, their styles of dress, music, dance, food, and imagery have become fashionable in many affluent, even elite quarters. Favela Chic is now an international phenomenon that celebrates the "undercity's" popular culture, innovative recycling of materials and ideas, and opposition to elite pretentions. It also glamorizes poverty in stylistic terms, while largely ignoring its causes and consequences.

The focus of attention is on favela couture, restaurants and bars, *funk carioca* music, and favela tourism—all depoliticized products for global consumption. Of course, there has long been a voyeuristic fascination among affluent outsiders for the quaint "authenticity" of the struggling poor. "To slum" entered the English language as a verb in the Victorian period, as it became fashionable for the well-to-do to engage the lower classes out of curiosity, entertainment, or philanthropy. While "slumming" once involved visiting poor but distinctive districts, often in modest or tattered clothing, now it may refer to high-fashion runways where favela couture mixes luxury and poverty. The favela motif becomes a variation of Poor Chic, as Karen Halnon describes: "Rio's 'shantytown chic' funk balls and on the catwalks of São Paulo where leggy models parade *favela* fashions, including skintight 'Gang Jeans' selling for $200 a pop. Local companies even offer popular *favela* tours." Halnon adds that "what is distinctive about Poor Chic today is that the 'lower class' masquerade is now center stage in the historical theatre of downward impersonation," and "takes place in the contexts of the increasing and extreme polarization of classes."[74]

The most obvious but, to many observers, surprising indicator of Favela Chic's rise has been its global visibility. Tom Phillips has suggested that *favela* has become a "tropical prefix used to spice up western places and products."[75] International venues include, for example, favela-themed nightclubs in Paris, London, and Munich. Besides a slew of Brazilian restaurants, New York City features the popular Miss Favela restaurant, with Brazilian music in Williamsburg, Brooklyn, and the Favela Cubana restaurant with dishes and drinks from both Brazil and Cuba in Lower Manhattan. La Favela bar and restaurant may be found in Amsterdam and Bali. Favela-style restaurants also diversify the culinary choices in Tokyo and Sydney. Miami even features the Brazilian-style Favela Beach Party! This international trendiness seems to stem from the name association with authentic roots, popular cultures, and opposition to elitist pretentions. "The force of the *favela* brand has become," Bianca Freire-Medeiros notes, "capable of transcending geographical and territorial referentials, promoting Brazil as well as anything wishing to present itself as 'alternative' and 'recycled.'"[76]

This branding becomes evident in the commercial enterprises modeled on favelas. Miss Favela, in Brooklyn, prides itself as a true replica of the favela aesthetic, as the *New York Times* reported on the ratty look of the restaurant: "With a corrugated metal ceiling and walls painted bright Brazilian colors, battered tables and chairs and the hard-to-find Devassa beer, this is the closest you'll come to a traditional working class *botequim*."[77] By painting the walls with bright colors and using worn-down furniture, the restaurant assumes the quintessential favela style. With a Brazilian variation of Poor Chic, an affluent clientele consumes a stylistic representation of favela life. The menu includes many Brazilian standards, and as is traditional on Saturday afternoon, Miss Favela serves *feijoada*, the country's national dish of black bean, pork, and vegetable stew. Similarly, the owner of the Favela Chic club in Paris regarded the favela as primarily a matter of style, rather than a community constructed historically from uneven development and inequitable social relations: "All of our work aims to show that the *favela* is valuable, that the dignity we preach does indeed exist. It's not shameful anymore to speak of the favela, favela is luxury, favela is chic!"[78]

While Favela Chic gained popularity globally, upper-class Brazilians avoided favela imagery in their home country, due to the social stigma, perceived violence, and awkward proximity in cities. Elites considered such informal settlements as embarrassments to be hidden away. Since Michael Jackson performed at Favela Santa Marta in 1996, when authorities tried to block both his performance and the attendant publicity for the city's "bad side," perceptions began to change as entrepreneurs began to recognize the potential publicity and profits to be made from variations of Favela Chic. One of them is from the realm of world music. Dance parties known as *bailes funk* go back to the 1980s, as Brazilian DJs influenced by American hip-hop and funk innovated with local sounds in such hillside favelas as Santa Marta, Rocinha, and Vidigal. The result was *funk carioca*, a popular dance craze that went global in the new century. The international spread of this new popular music, according to James McNally, "glamorized global perceptions of impoverished Latin American communities and perpetuated a troublesome history of Western producers using source material from the Other for novelty and financial gain."[79] In other words, Favela Chic meets the Global Remix.

In recent years, even long-resistant Brazil has been susceptible to Favela Chic. In 2001, the trendy Favela Bar opened in São Paulo, subsequently followed by others. The original bar and restaurant quickly became popular with affluent Paulistanos, who could enjoy a favela without any risk to their social status or security. The owners boasted of the accuracy of the décor, menu, slang, and general ambience as the key to success. Teresa Caldeira, on the other hand, explains this attitudinal shift in terms of spatial separation. She writes that the upper classes "depend on distantiation: *favelados* are out of the way physically and socially and therefore may be incorporated aesthetically." Caldeira describes the bar's interior as "a décor that imitates the details of a favela's shacks: a 'kitsch style,' saints and religious objects, clothes hanging on lines, and imitations of improvised and often illegal electricity connections."[80] Turning this folksy style and lack of amenities into a caricature of poverty serves to obfuscate and romanticize the lived experience of those in favelas.

Contemporary Rio has also experienced an increasing trendiness and commodification of favela styles. A decade ago, Perlman argued that there were few signs that Brazilians shared the international sentiment of Favela Chic: the *morro* (hill, or informal city) and the *asfalto* (asphalt, or formal city), she suggested, seldom interacted socially outside of work.[81] This socio-spatial segregation still prevails, but a heightened visibility of favelas in city life and imagery has been unmistakable in recent years. Despite the continuing place stigma among the affluent sectors of Rio society, favela depictions have proliferated in commerce and the arts. Even the televised opening ceremony of the 2016 Rio Olympics, held in Maracanã Stadium, featured a vivid tribute to favelas with the sounds of samba and *funk carioca*, diverse contemporary singers and rappers, and an illuminated hillside settlement. As in São Paulo, the phenomenon of distantiation insulates the upper classes, since social space remains fragmented by physical barriers, surveillance technologies, and security personnel in Rio. From their fortified residential and commercial enclaves, elites may selectively appropriate a favela aesthetic without a fear of real-life intrusions. There is now a growing wave of bars, restaurants, and cafés with favela references in Rio. On the edge of the Santa Teresa district, in the South Zone, there is Favela Hype, a popular restaurant. In gentrifying favelas, such as Vidigal, Babilônia, and Chapeu da Mangueira, there are now numerous upscale commercial establishments that attract Brazilians and foreigners alike. This oppositional sensibility proves attractive to many outsiders, even as it fetishizes favela ways of life.

Favela Tourism first emerged during the early 1990s in Rio, where most accounts trace the global origins of Slum, Poverty, or Reality Tourism. The first and still a prominent company, Favela Tours, began in Rocinha in 1992. It quickly grew to a profitable enterprise and inspired half a dozen competitors in Rio. An average of about three thousand tourists still visit Rocinha monthly, according to estimates among the several tourist agencies. The original Favela Tours takes groups of up to twelve passengers in mini-vans or jeeps to Rocinha; most of the foreign tourists come from Europe. The company's publicity states that the tour is, "beneficial to the community, informative and surprising, not voyeuristic at all." Stressing the need to correct misconceptions of the favela and to bridge the gap with the formal city, Favela Tours' online reviews on TripAdvisor are overwhelmingly positive. According to the company's founder, Marcelo Armstrong: "Not all favelas are over-run by drug lords. For an insightful look at life in Rio's favelas, it is highly recommended you book a tour with a reputable favela guide. A good tour will include a visit to a school and an opportunity to positively impact the community."[82]

Given all the hype, I went on the Favela Tour to Rocinha in June of 2003, along with a group of curious European and American colleagues from an academic conference in Rio. I too was interested, since in previous trips my middle-class Brazilian friends had always told me that as a foreigner, Rocinha was off limits, given the drug traffic and associated violence in battles with the police. While there was not much interaction with local residents, other than random parting glances and stops to visit craft venders, we all enjoyed sightseeing on the trip. Besides the stunning views of Rocinha and the coast, I could not help but notice the adolescents working as sentinels for the drug lords, as we entered and left the district. We also climbed up narrow, winding pathways in the hills, observing the many small businesses, the tightly connected houses, and the huge bundles of assorted cables for electricity and television. The commercial center was vibrant and crowded. At the final stop, we visited a computer center for young people, a fair-trade craft store, and space for local artists to display their work for sale. The guide indicated that Favela Tours supported these activities.

The Rio Top Tour Project, inaugurated in August of 2010, promoted a more community-based tourism in selected favelas. This federally funded program began in Santa Marta, where the famous favela, it was hoped, would help invigorate the local tourist industry. The program provided English signage to indicate the location of 42 different attractions, including the Dona Marta observatory, churches and chapels, samba schools, and Michael Jackson Terrace. I went on the tour there with a small group during July of 2011. Since the cable-car tramway was not operating that morning, we had a vigorous walk up the hillside of Rio's steepest favela. It was an informative and friendly visit to the community, led by a local guide, which culminated in a visit to the viewpoint from which Michael Jackson sang to the multitudes in 1996. The many viewing stations allowed visitors to enjoy the spectacular views of Christ the Redeemer Statue above, along with many other local landmarks. Toward the top of the hill, we passed by the small, one-room Nega Vilma Ecomuseum, launched in 2010, with its photographs and stories about the area, but it was closed at the time. Overall, we left with the sense of the positive features of favela life—the sense of community, steady improvements, affordable housing, vibrant music and dance—while appreciating that living in a favela remains challenging. The president of the local Association of Residents, José Mário, estimated in 2015 that Santa Marta received "around 10,000 tourists, 3,000 of them foreign, per month." As for the pros and cons, he observed that "it improves business, people are interested in speaking other languages: English, Spanish, French. There is that positive side of it, but the negative is that the community feels like an attraction park where people come here and see the community like animals at a zoo."[83]

Proponents of Favela Tourism stress community participation as tour guides and merchants, which makes the experience less voyeuristic, while channeling paid fees back into the community. Some of those who would otherwise work in the informal sector are employed through tourism. A community leader in Rio's Rocinha asserted: "If our children can support themselves through being guides then that is great. Without English you are totally lost these days and some of the children get the chance to learn because of this."[84] Indeed, the tourist industry may be seen as a source of financial and educational opportunity to the degree that it is controlled locally. After-school programs for at-risk favela youth, for example, have proven to be particularly worthwhile. I have visited, with educational groups, the inspiring Mangueira Social Project in that favela and the We of the Hill program in Vidigal. Both educational programs, run by NGOs, benefited directly from visitors' contributions, while the students seemed to enjoy and benefit from the visits. Yet when managed by external companies, Favela tourism entails a more unequal division of profits: the residents whose lives are featured receive relatively little benefit, while most profits end up with high-level managers at the tour companies. While entrepreneurial residents, artists, and their representatives may benefit to some degree, the bulk of the profits usually go to corporate interests.

Ideally, an equitable Favela tourism involves collaboration between visitors and residents to gain a realistic sense of the lived experience, while profits are invested locally. It involves significant input from the community, along the participatory lines of the Tip Top Tours or organized school visits. These approaches encourage residents to tell their own favela stories—uncensored versions of their experiences, hopes, and dreams. A social justice approach might include discussion of local political issues, the diverse layers of community, crime and security issues, service improvements underway, environmental concerns, and the range of housing to put "informal" residence in perspective. Only with such heightened community input can there be more equitable tourism. Until then, the socioeconomically hierarchical nature of reality tourism will continue to reinforce misguided notions of favelas as fitting a singular definition of poverty.

In consuming favela style, privileged groups tend to reproduce stereotypical representations. While outside forces largely define favela life and culture, they can by no means totally control the imagery. Branding campaigns require a realistic connection with local realities. Resistance movements have emerged to act against some of the absurd depictions of favela life. An album by a local artist aptly titled *Favela Chic* has a song with these lyrics: "you must be crazy—you think favelas are chic, come on, stay a while, see for yourself, here *favelas* are not chic, not in the least."[85] Such songs, poems, and other expressive forms have emerged to assert personal accounts and lived experiences of community members. Contemporary *favelados* have witnessed how national and foreign elites have constructed a fashionably "authentic" style for marginalized communities, but residents now understand their objectification through Favela Tourism and Favela Chic. Along with their firm resistance to displacement, residents push for pride of place through more balanced representations of favelas as neighborhoods and homes. Empowered by their right to the city—and its corollary, the right of remembrance—*favelados* increasingly articulate their own sense of place.

FAVELAS AS INFORMAL URBANISM

The historical and contemporary evidence shows favelas to be highly resistant to removal by authorities, despite the widespread stigma arrayed against them. While informal communities have unique stories and distinctive identities, they share a strong sense of comradery with other *favelados*. Anti-displacement networks had been active during the military regime of 1964–1985, for example, and have been more recently during redevelopment for athletic spectacles. In addition, community organizing makes favelas resilient opponents of displacement and strong advocates incumbent to upgrading. Only forcible eviction by police or military forces has succeeded in displacing informal communities from their homes. This oppositional spirit reflects landscapes of struggle for survival and a long-term cultural and environmental resilience. While constructed over time, the built heritage of favelas comes to symbolize counter-memory in the present, diffused through local experience, neighborhood block associations, local museums, NGO activities, social media, documentary videos, public art, popular music and dance, and increasingly environmental activism. In a sense, community organizing becomes a form of placemaking with multiple benefits: building community identity, public recognition, political clout, environmental conservation, and localized commercial profits.

As opposed to gentrification in European and North American cities, where residential renovation of working-class districts has long featured the influx of more affluent populations and a change in social status, Latin America has experienced more commercial than residential upgrading in historic centers. The state has consistently overlooked the interests of longtime residents in the rush to renovate historic districts as quaint settings for idealized native or colonial pasts. Street vendors and others of the informal sector commonly face eviction as authorities renovate heritage sites. Such contemporary programs of historic preservation tend to promote social inequality, rather than inclusion. Similarly, Favela Chic often appropriates stylistic "roots" and recycled "images" over the lived experience of informal communities, while

Favela Tourism affects only a relatively few *favelados*, especially when one considers that only about a half dozen informal communities, in a city with some eight hundred favelas, receive the bulk of the attention. This selectivity also applies to the relatively small number of favelas experiencing contemporary gentrification—locally often called "white eviction" (remoção branca). Affected communities are generally in the South Zone and accessible to the beach, although, potentially, gentrification could spread more widely if there is a continuing lack of affordable housing.

In July of 2017, the passage of federal law 13465/2-17 encouraged the titling of property in informal settlements on federal lands. This law stimulated real-estate markets in favelas, particularly those with relatively good public security. Desirable locations with access to public transit, good views, and proximity to beachfronts experienced rising property values. The settlements undergoing gentrification lay primarily in the South Zone, such as Babilônia, Cantagalo, and Vidigal. Given the tendency over time for favelas to "verticalize," with the addition of new floors to buildings, the law also promised a "right to the slab" (direito à laje). Referring to the reinforced concrete slabs that support additional floors, this legal provision has multiplied properties and stimulated favela real estate. Subsequent land speculation, however, has endangered land tenure for low-income residents. For this reason, some analysts recommend providing essential urban services—piped water, sewerage, transportation, education, and health care—before titling properties. Premature titling, before long-term residents benefit from improved services, may destabilize favelas through rapid population turnover. Community planner and advocate Theresa Williamson, for instance, has proposed adopting the model of community land trusts to combat displacement in Rio's favelas.[86]

We certainly have much to learn from favelas about resilient urbanism. Favelas are part of a long tradition of vernacular architecture, self-built housing reliant on local materials, and still evident in contemporary sites around the world. Many historic districts in Europe and on Mediterranean islands, for example, evolved in similar "informal" fashion. I have been to ancient hill towns in Portugal that remind me of Rio's hillside favelas. In the contemporary world, favelas embody many of the morphological characteristics of the "new urbanism," a design movement promoting sustainable communities, walkable neighborhoods, transit-oriented development, and diverse housing types and occupational types. The Congress of New Urbanism, founded in 1993, began its charter with the following list of principles:

> We advocate the restructuring of public policy and development practices to support the following principles: neighborhoods should be diverse in use and population; communities should be designed for the pedestrian and transit as well as the car; cities and towns should be shaped by physically defined and

universally accessible public spaces and community institutions; urban places should be framed by architecture and landscape design that celebrate local history, climate, ecology, and building practice.[87]

Despite the different socioeconomic and political contexts, favelas correspond to many of these basic design principles: affordable housing, often in central areas; adaptive architecture in creatively designed buildings; relatively high density of homes and businesses; pedestrian orientation; reliance on bicycles and public transportation; mixed land use; and concern with local environmental quality. Rio's favelas also reflect collective action, cultural incubation, adaptive improvisation, and entrepreneurship. Theresa Williamson has called such notable characteristics "the power of informal urbanism."[88] What favelas need to achieve their potential is high-quality public services, but given the dangers of housing speculation, I agree with Theresa that provision of needed urban services and infrastructures—piped water, sanitation, health care, transportation, education, and job training—generally should precede titling favela properties. Although many problems of poverty, discrimination, and environmental degradation remain, community-based social movements have succeeded in promoting awareness of favela heritage, alternative narratives of the past, and a built heritage based on auto-construction and adaptive growth. Even the current challenges of COVID-19 within informal settlements are largely contingent on the provision of adequate public health, rather than an inevitable result of population density and housing morphology. As Amaro, a resident of Favela Maré, once said, "If you enter a *favela*, don't look at it superficially, see in depth what a *favela* really is all about."[89]

NOTES

1. Favela Tem Memória, "Depoimentos," http://www.favelatemmemoria.com.br/, accessed Oct. 15, 2015.
2. Rede Favela Sustaintável, *Guia de Museus e Memórias* (Rio de Janeiro, Novembro de 2020).
3. Zuenir Ventura, *Cidade Partida* (São Paulo: Companhia das Letras, 1994), 13.
4. Zhongjie Lin, Fernando Diniez Moreira, and Aline de Melo Nascimento, "Changing Informality: Gentrification in the Favelas of Rio de Janeiro," in *Rio de Janeiro: Urban Expansion and the Environment*, ed. José L. S. Gámez, Qhongjie Lin, and Jeffrey S. Nesbit (New York: Routledge, 2020), chapter 4, Kindle edition.
5. Robert Gay, *Popular Organization and Democracy in Rio de Janeiro: A Tale of Two Favelas* (Temple University Press, 1994); and Jake Cummings, "Confronting Favela Chic: The Gentrification of Informal Settlements in Rio de Janeiro, Brazil," in *Global Gentrifications: Uneven Development and Displacement*, ed. Loretta Lees,

Hyun Bang Shin, and Ernesto López-Morales (Bristol University Press/Policy Press, 2015), 81–99.

6. Viva Rio, Favela Tem Memória, http://www.favelatemmemoria.com.br/, accessed March 2012.

7. Gitanjali Patel, "Museums of Counternarratives and Resistance," RioOnWatch, May 16–20, 2018, https://www.rioonwatch.org/?p=43384.

8. Mario Fuks, "Environmental Litigation in Rio de Janeiro: Shaping Frames for a New Social Problem," *International Journal of Urban and Regional Research* 22, 3 (1998): 394–408.

9. "Uma cidade despreparada," *O Globo*, Feb. 21, 1998, 12.

10. Camila Moraes, "A Invenção da Favela Ecológica: Um Olhar Sobre Turismo e Meio Ambiente no Morro Babilônia," *Estudos sociológicos*, 18, 35 (July–Dec., 2013), 459–74; and Jennifer Chisholm, "A Sustainable Favela? How Favela Residents in Rio Are Fighting Back against Threats of Eviction by Forging New Identities Based on Ecological Preservation," *NACLA*, November 10, 2017, 1–7.

11. Robert D. Bullard, *Dumping in Dixie: Race, Class, and Environmental Quality* (Westview Press, 2008); Laura Pulido, "Rethinking Environmental Racism: White Privilege and Urban Development in Southern California," *Annals of the Association of American Geographers* 90, 1 (2000): 12–40.

12. Mike Davis, *Magical Urbanism: Latinos Reinvent the US City*, updated ed. (Verso, 2012).

13. June M. Thomas, "The Role of Ethnicity and Race in Supporting Sustainable Urban Environments," in *Urban Sustainability: A Global Perspective*, ed. Igor Vojnovic (Michigan State University Press, 2012), 475–508.

14. 100 Resilient Cities, "Resilient Cities, Resilient Lives Learning from the 100RC Network," July 2019, 6, http://100resilientcities.org/wp-content/uploads/2019/07/100RC-Report-Capstone-PDF.pdf.

15. Brodwyn Fischer, *A Century in the Present Tense* (Duke University Press, 2014), Kindle edition, 11.

16. Maurício de Almeida Abreu, "Reconstruindo uma história esquecida: Origem e expansão das favelas do Rio de Janeiro," *Revista Espaço & Debates* 37 (1994): 38; Kátia da Costa Bezerra, *Postcards from Rio Favelas and the Contested Geographies of Citizenship* (New York: Fordham University Press, 2017), Kindle edition; and Fischer, *A Century in the Present Tense*, 14.

17. Plantas da Cidade do Rio de Janeiro, 1850 and 1858, National Library, Rio de Janeirio, http://objdigital.bn.br/objdigital2/acervo_digital/div_cartografia/cart 161233/cart161233.jpg and http://objdigital.bn.br/objdigital2/acervo_digital/div_cart ografia/cart230730/cart230730.jpg; and Fischer, *A Century in the Present Tense*, 14.

18. Janice Perlman, *Favela: Four Decades of Living on the Edge in Rio de Janeiro* (Oxford University Press, 2010), 24–28; and Secretaria Municipal de Habitação (SMH), *Cadernos Favela-Bairro Comunidades: A Brief History* (Rio de Janeiro: Prefeitura da Cidade), 2007.

19. Licia do Prado Valladares, *A Invenção Da Favela: Do Mito de Origem A Favela.Com* (Rio De Janeiro: Fundação Getúlio Vargas, 2005), 28–36.

20. Bradford Burns, *A History of Brazil*, 2nd ed. (New York: Columbia University Press, 1980), 317.

21. Centro Cruzeiro: Um Comunitário de Providência, "Um pouco de história," http:// http://www.casacruzeiro.org/; and Favela Tem Memória, "Depoimentos," accessed Oct. 2015, http://www.favelatemmemoria.com.br/.

22. Daniela Fabricius, "Resisting Representation: The Informal Geographies of Rio de Janeiro," *Harvard Design* 28 (2008): 4–17.

23. Bruce Douglas, "The Story of Cities #15: The Rise and Ruin of Rio de Janeiro's First Favela," *Guardian*, April 5, 2016.

24. Rafael de Luna Freire and Leticia de Luna Freire, "The Rio *Favela* in Musical Comedy Films: From Cradle of Sample to Public Problem," *Comun. Mídia Consumo*, Sao Paulo, 15, 43 (2018); and Robert Stam, "Slow Fade to Afro: The Black Presence in Brazilian Cinema," *Film Quarterly* 36, 2 (Winter 1982–1983): 16–32.

25. Quoted in Douglas, "The Story of Cities #15."

26. Romulo Costa Mattos, "Aldeias do mal," *Revista de Historia da Biblioteca Nacional*, March 30, 2007.

27. Favela Tem Memória, "Depoimentos," accessed Oct. 2015, http://www.favela temmemoria.com.br/.

28. Gustavo Goulart, "Milícia domina 45% das favelas cariocas, revela pesquisa," *O Globo*, Dec. 3, 2013.

29. Secretaria Municipal de Habitação (SMH), *Cadernos Favela-Bairro Comunidades: A Brief History* (Rio de Janeiro: Prefeitura da Cidade), 2007; and Haimy Assefa, Director, "Providência: 115 Anos de Luta," produced by RioOnWatch, Aug. 10, 2012, https://www.youtube.com/watch?v=it=bdOXxq14.

30. Bezerra, *Postcards from Rio*, section on Providencia, 112–22.

31. Raffi Khatchadourian, "In the Picture: An Artist's Global Experiment to Help People Be Seen," *New Yorker*, Nov. 28, 2011.

32. Khatchadourian, "In the Picture," 2–9.

33. JR, "Women Are Heroes," Vimeo, https://vimeo.com/42286795, posted May 16, 2012.

34. Carla Souza, "The Urban Agroforestry Unfolding in Providência, Brazil's First Favela," RioOnWatch, February 28, 2020, https://www.rioonwatch.org/?p=57952.

35. Bianca Freire-Medeiros, "Favela como patrimônio da cidade? Reflexões e polêmicas em torno de dois museus," *Estudos Históricos* 38 (2006): 49–66.

36. "Museu aberta do Morro da Providência completa 11 anos," *O Cidadão*, Feb. 4, 2020.

37. Museu Comunitário da Providência, "Olimpíada da exclusão—A luta e resistência das favelas," July 18, 2016, https://www.facebook.com/museuprovidencia/, May 25, 2020.

38. Abreu, Maurício de Almeida. "Reconstruindo uma história esquecida: origem e expansão das favelas do Rio de Janeiro," *Revista Espaço & Debates* 37, (1994): 38.

39. Elizabeth Bishop, *The Complete Poems, 1927–1979* (New York: Farrar, Straus, Giroux, 1983), 112.

40. Quoted in Abreu, *Evolução Urbana do Rio de Janeiro*, 89 (my translation).

41. Greg O'Hare and Michael Barke, "The Favelas of Rio de Janeiro: A Temporal and Spatial Analysis," *GeoJournal* 56 (2002): 232.

42. Lícia Valladares, "A gênese da favela carioca," *Revista Brasileira de Ciências Sociais* 15, 44 (2000): 5–34; and Silva, "Favelas do Rio de Janeiro," 176–201.

43. Janice Perlman, *The Myth of Marginality, Urban Poverty and Politics in Rio de Janeiro* (University of California, 1976), 200–202; and Gay, *Popular Organization and Democracy in Rio de Janeiro*, 19.

44. Favela Tem Memória, "Favelário: Catacumba (Leblon)—extinta," accessed Oct. 2015, http://www.favelatemmemoria.com.br/.

45. *Jornal do Brasil*, Aug. 7 1967, quoted in Favela Tem Memória, "Favelário: Catacumba (Leblon)—extinta," retrieved October 2015, http://www.favelatemmemoria.com.br/.

46. Favela Tem Memória, "Favelário"; Perlman, *The Myth of Marginality*, 24.

47. Favela Tem Memória, "Favelário"; Perlman, *The Myth of Marginality*, 24.

48. Secretaria Municipal de Meio Ambiente (SMAC), "Parque Natural Municipal de Catacumba," www.rio.rj.gov.br, accessed April 20, 2020. Quoted in Fabio Soares and Yuri Soares, "The Socio-Economic Impact of Favela-Bairro: What Do the Data Say?" Working Paper OVE/WP-08 (Washington, DC: Inter-American Development Bank, August 4, 2005), 5.

49. Instituto Brasileiro de Geografia e Estatística (IBGE), http://www.ibge.gov.br/, various years.

50. Janice E. Perlman, "The Metamorphosis of Marginality: Four Generations in the Favelas of Rio de Janeiro," *Annals of the American Academy of Political and Social Science* 606 (2006): 154–77, https://doi.org/10.1177/0002716206288826.

51. World Cup and Olympics Popular Committee of Rio de Janeiro, *Mega-Events and Human Rights Violations in Rio de Janeiro Dossier*, Dec. 2015.

52. Sukari Ivester, "Removal, Resistance and the Right to the Olympian City: The Case of Vila Autódromo in Rio de Janeiro," *Journal of Urban Affairs* 39, 7 (2017): 970–85; https://doi.org/10.1080/07352166.2017.1355665.

53. Daniel Bin, "Rio de Janeiro's Olympic Dispossessions," *Journal of Urban Affairs* 39, 7 (2017): 924–38, https://doi.org/10.1080/07352166.2017.1319237; and Christopher Gaffney, "Gentrifications in Pre-Olympic Rio de Janeiro," *Urban Geography* (2015), https://doi.org/10.1080/02723638.2015.1096115.

54. Simon Romero, "Slum Dwellers Are Defying Brazil's Grand Design for Olympics," *New York Times*, March 4, 2012.

55. Bin, "Rio de Janeiro's Olympic Dispossessions," 924–38; and Ivester, "Removal, Resistance," 970–85.

56. Facebook, "Museu das Remoções," https://www.facebook.com/museudasremocoes/?ref=br_rs.

57. Miriane Peregrino, "Museu das Remoções é inaugurado na Vila Autódromo," *O Cidadão*, May 26, 2016, http://jornalocidadao.net/museu-das-remocoes-e-inaugurado-na-vila-autodromo/.

58. Gitanjali Patel, "Museums of Counternarratives and Resistance, Part 5: The Evictions Museum," RioOnWatch, March 2018, https://www.rioonwatch.org/?p=43516.

59. See music video "788" by Fiell on YouTube, https://www.youtube.com/watch?v=EqKWxkLmJCE.

60. Favela Tem Memória, "Favelário: Santa Marta—também chamado de Dona Marta (Botafogo)," accessed Oct. 2015, http://www.favelatemmemoria.com.br/.

61. Verônica Ferreira Dias, "A Cinema of Conversation: Eduardo Coutinho's Santo Forte and Babilônia 2000," in *The New Brazilian Cinema*, ed. Lúcia Nagib (I.B. Tauris, 2006), 106.

62. Caco Barcellos, *Abusado—the Owner of Morro Dona Marta* (Rio de Janeiro: Record, 2003).

63. Beatriz Jaguaribe, "Cities without Maps: Favelas and the Aesthetics of Realism," in *Urban Imaginaries: Locating the Modern City*, ed. Alev Cinar and Thomas Bender (University of Minnesota Press, 2007), 114.

64. Melanie Gilligan, "Slumsploitation: The Favela on Film and TV," *Mute* 2, 3 (Sept. 5, 2006): 2.

65. Kelly Graham, *The Asphalt and the Favela: A Critical Examination of Contemporary Urban Segregation*, senior thesis in geography-anthropology (Vassar College, 2007), 50, 53; and Perlman, "The Metamorphosis of Marginality," 154–77.

66. Ivana Bentes, "The Sertão and the Favela in Contemporay Brazilian Film," in *The New Brazilian Cinema*, Lúcia Nagib (New York: I.B. Tauris/The Center for Brazilian Studies, University of Oxford, 2003), 121–37.

67. Brian Rossiter, "'They Don't Care about Us': Michael Jackson's Black Nationalism," *Popular Music and Society* 35, 2 (2012): 203–22.

68. Diana Jean Schemo, "Rio Frets as Michael Jackson Plans to Film Slum," *New York Times*, Feb. 11, 1996.

69. Barcellos, *Abusado*, 557.

70. Lívia Marra, "Traficante Marcinho VP é assassinado no complexo do Bangu," *Folha de São Paulo*, July 28, 2003.

71. Favela Painting, https://favelapainting.com; Cynthia E. Smith, *Design with the Other 90%* (Cooper Hewitt Museum, Smithsonian Design Museum, 2011).

72. "Cabeça de Avestruz," *Jornal do Brasil*, Feb. 13, 1998, 8.

73. Duanne Ribeiro, "A Shattered City: Eco-Limits and Rio de Janeiro," *Latismo*, Sept. 21, 2009, http://www.latismo.com/a-shattered-city-eco-limits-and-rio-de-janeiro.

74. Karen Halnon, "Poor Chic: The Rational Consumption of Poverty," *Current Sociology* 50 (2002), 501.

75. Tom Phillips, "Brazil: How *Favelas* Went Chic," *Brazzil*, December 2003, http://brazzil.com/2003/html/news/articles/dec03/p105dec03.htm.

76. Bianca Freire-Medeiros, "The Favela and Its Touristic Transits," *Geoforum* 40 (2009): 583, https://doi.org/10.1016/j.geoforum.2008.10.007.

77. Seth Kugel, "So, You Were Maybe Expecting Carmen Miranda?" *New York Times*, Aug. 27, 2008, http://www.nytimes.com/2008/08/31/travel/31weekend.html?_r=0.

78. Quoted in Bianca Freire-Medeiros, "The Favela and Its Touristic Transits," 583.

79. James McNally, "Favela Chic: Diplo, Funk Carioca, and the Ethics and Easthetics of the Global Remix," *Popular Music and Society* 40, 4 (2017): 434.

80. Teresa P. R. Caldeira, "From Modernism to Neoliberalism in São Paulo," in *Other Cities, Other Worlds: Urban Imaginaries in a Globalizating Age*, ed. Andreas Huyssen (Durham, NC: Duke University Press, 2008), 68.

81. Perlman, *Favela: Four Decades of Living on the Edge in Rio de Janeiro* (Oxford University Press, 2010), 332.

82. Trip Adviser, "Rio de Janeiro," https://www.tripadvisor.com/Attraction_Review-g303506-d1637149-Reviews-Favela_Tour_Marcelo_Armstrong-Rio_de_Janeiro_State_of_Rio_de_Janeiro.html (accessed Sept. 14, 2020).

83. Mariane Peregrino, "Tram, Tourism, History and Resistance in Santa Marta: 'Each Brick Has Its Story,'" RioOnWatch, March 6, 2015.

84. Phillips, "Brazil: How Favelas Went Chic."

85. Quoted in Perlman, *Favela*, 332.

86. Theresa Williamson, "Community Land Trusts in Rio's Favelas," *Land Lines,* Lincoln Institute of Land Policy 30, 3 (July 2018): 8–23; and Lin et al., "Changing Informality," ch. 4.

87. Congress of New Urbanism (CNU), "Who Are We?," the official website, https://www.cnu.org/who-we-are, 2019.

88. Theresa Williamson, "Rio's Favelas: The Power of Informal Urbanism," in *Perspectiva 50: Urban Divides*, ed. Meghan McAllister and Mahdi Sabbagh (Cambridge, MA: MIT Press, 2017), 213–28.

89. Favela Tem Memória, "Depoimentos," accessed Oct. 2015, http://www.favelatemmemoria.com.br/.

Chapter 5

Environmental Heritage

Protecting Carioca Landscapes

> Lofty mountains, rocks of clustered columns, luxuriant wood, bright flowery islands, green banks, all mixed with white buildings; each little eminence crowned with its church or fort; ships at anchor or in motion; and innumerable boats flitting about in such a delicious climate, combine to render Rio de Janeiro the most enchanting scene that imagination can conceive.
>
> —Maria Graham, 1824[1]

Rio de Janeiro's dramatic setting has long captivated observers. From a patchwork of low-lying alluvial lands, the densely packed metropolis arises amid towering mountains, successive hills, tropical forests, scenic bays and lagoons, and white beaches. These elements coalesce into a scenic panorama, as Maria Graham commented in 1824, so that the natural landscape coexists with the cityscape to create "the most enchanting scene." Indeed, observers have repeatedly remarked on the city's breathtaking site. In 1835, artist Johann Moritz Rugendas exclaimed: "Perhaps in all the world there does not exist a place like Rio de Janeiro, with its varied landscapes and beauties, along with the contours of its beaches." In 1973, a newspaper editorial on the landmarking of Rio's most famous hills and mountains enthused that the city had finally "begun to find its defenders."[2] More recently, in 2003, journalist Ruy Castro noted how Rio's physical geography retained its long-standing appeal: "Of all the great modern cities, it's one of the few that can be easily recognized on seventeenth-century maps and engravings—there one can see the mountains that to this day form the Carioca skyline."[3]

These historical perspectives attest to how Rio's landscapes have often inspired reflection on city-nature relations. The city has also been widely associated with sustainable development since hosting the United Nations

Conference on Environment and Development in 1992. Popularly known as the "Earth Summit," this assembly of 170 countries ratified the "Rio Declaration," which maintained that "development must be fulfilled so as to equitably meet developmental and environmental needs of present and future generations."[4] The "Agenda 21" action plan stressed the reconciliation of economic growth, social equity, and environmental conservation—the "three E's" of Economy, Equity, and Environment.[5] Yet this framework ignores how urbanism affects sustainability: What are the impacts, for example, of population density, architecture, social diversity, transportation, and intensive land uses?

Agenda 21 reflected the long-standing intellectual dichotomy between "natural" and "cultural" landscapes, which dominated twentieth-century intellectual discourses. Accordingly, environmental studies traditionally focused on the conservation of rural settings, wilderness areas, and natural resources, while urban studies prioritized architectural, historical, political, socioeconomic, and cultural concerns. Presumed to exist independently of their bio-physical environments, modern cities long seemed to dominate nature—at least until contemporary climate change dramatized urban vulnerability to heat islands, sea-level rise, extreme weather events, and other ecological problems. To be sure, there were early exceptions to the polarized nature-versus-culture perspective, but for the most part, environmental and urban fields long followed divergent paths. Contemporary sustainability discourse has begun to bridge the environmental, urban, and other fields, but it still retains misconceptions about the role and impacts of cities.[6]

In addition to the forty issues of sustainability identified in Agenda 21, the Earth Summit approved the Convention on Biological Diversity and the Climate Change Convention in 1992. Yet only one measure addressed "sustainable management of all urban settlements, particularly in developing countries, in order to enhance their ability to improve the living conditions of residents, especially the marginalized and disenfranchised."[7] This provision ignored possible human-environmental advantages of urbanism. While cities do concentrate a variety of environmental and other challenges, they also provide economies of scale, social mobility, cultural innovation, infrastructural investment, and collective action. Given energy efficiencies that stem from human density, locational proximity, rapid transit, and high-rise buildings, big cities may even be considered relatively sustainable. But Agenda 21 viewed cities as problems rather than as places with certain advantages for human-environmental coexistence.

A major conceptual gap in Agenda 21 lay in the absence of any sense of "culture" in the broad sense of collective ways of life, ethnic and social traditions, and creative freedom. An alternative approach, promoted by United

Cities and Local Governments (UCLG), sought to incorporate cultural issues into governance. Between 2002 and 2004, UCLG proposed the Agenda 21 for Culture, also known simply as "Culture 21," "to work towards a healthy, safe, tolerant and creative society" and to enhance "the rights of citizens to freedom of expression and access to information and resources." The organization pushed for culture to serve as a fourth pillar of sustainable development, thereby including issues of identity and creativity, memory and belief, spirituality, gender and family issues, and health and well-being. In 2014–2016, the UCLG began the Culture in Sustainable Cities: Learning with Culture 21 Actions program, which encouraged a series of pilot cities to develop sustainability programs at local levels.[8]

This contemporary cultural turn in urban studies complemented concerns about the narrow purview of economic globalization, including the rise of "global cities" with clusters of multinational corporations, stock exchanges, financial services, and technological hubs. Given growing preoccupation about climate change, global cities have also taken leading roles in sustainability programs. There has also been growing concern with resilience in facing acute shocks—earthquakes, fires, floods, and so on—along with the chronic stresses that weaken the urban fabric. Indeed, cities have contended for the most innovative plans to face such challenges. After the Earth Summit of 1992, Johannesburg hosted a follow-up meeting in 2002 and Rio hosted another in 2012, known as "Rio+20," aimed to review progress, renew political commitment, and build a green economy. In 2016, the United Nations "Habitat III" conference in Quito renewed commitments to sustainable urbanization.

Along with such international efforts, a growing academic literature has emerged on sustainable cities, eco-cities, and green urbanism. The field of landscape analysis provides particular insights into urban environments, given its focus on the built form of cities and urbanized regions, grounded on the earth's surface with material, spatial, and symbolic components. Classical works stressed how visible landscape features could be "read" to reveal historical change, cultural values, and environmental adaptation. Contemporary approaches to landscape have focused on symbolic dimensions, multiple meanings, and questions of agency and causation. Accordingly, I regard "culture" as a complex concept with competing meanings, rather than as a unified, self-apparent, homogenous entity. Landscape studies, in my view, should interrogate the dominant "authors" or "symbolic bankers" of human environments, be they powerful individuals, political institutions, economic interests, or social groups.[9]

This chapter extends the conception of historic preservation to include the making of environmental heritages, particularly with regard to the creation and conservation of distinctive cultural landscapes. The politics of memory become evident as forces that shape the city's scenic terrains, just as they do with the historic districts. In fact, many of the city's strongest visual images are scenic views of environmental landmarks: after all, who could conceive of Rio without its giant statue *Christ the Redeemer* atop Corcovado Mountain, Sugar Loaf's massive granitic peak at the entrance to Guanabara Bay, and the great crescent-moon arc of Copacabana Beach? These and other touristic sites reflect the urbanization of nature. As a result, instead of emphasizing Rio's exceptional panoramas—although they are indeed stunning—it is more useful to focus on what can be learned from the city's environmental history and policy. In my view, the success of early conservationist activism has led to more ambitious social agendas, including community-based activism for environmental justice. In addition, given the entrepreneurial demands of neoliberalism, environmental policy also has become important for quality of life, real-estate investment, tourism, international mega-events, and global-city aspirations. Such trends inevitably raise questions about the historic origins, evolving political contexts, and contemporary concerns of urban environmentalism.

CARIOCA LANDSCAPES: MAKING A WORLD HERITAGE SITE

To begin with contemporary issues before delving into the past, Rio de Janeiro's spectacular interplay of environments and cityscapes has resulted in a new kind of world heritage. In 2012, UNESCO's World Heritage Center inscribed the first urban cultural landscape, "Rio de Janeiro: Carioca Landscapes between the Mountain and the Sea." According to the official online description, the heritage site presents "an exceptional urban setting encompassing the key natural elements that have shaped and inspired the development of the city: from the highest points of the Tijuca National Park's (TNP) mountains down to the sea." Set upon narrow strips of land, wedged between coastal mountains, Guanabara Bay, and the Atlantic Ocean, the city became home to a series of striking landscapes with interconnected physical, biotic, and human elements. This urban-heritage property, owned in its entirely by the federal government, includes four basic components (see figure 5.1).

Tijuca National Park comprises three of the four major parts of the "Carioca Landscapes" World Heritage project: first, there are the central Tijuca highlands, which rise to a peak of 3,350 feet (1,021 meters) above sea level; second, the Pedra Bonita and Pedra da Gávea peaks tower over the Atlantic Ocean; and third, the Carioca mountain range includes Corcovado Mountain with the iconic statue, along with the historic Botanical Gardens. The

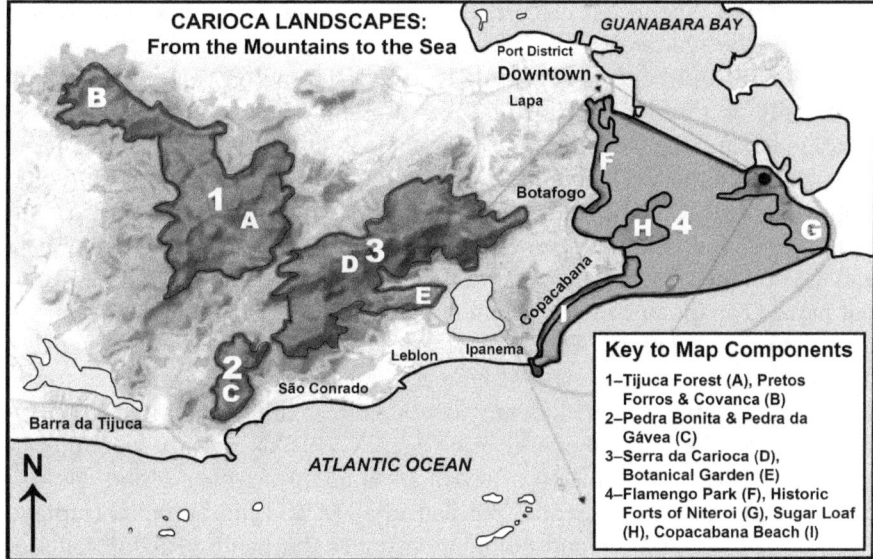

Figure 5.1. Map of the major components of "Carioca Landscapes between the Mountain and the Sea."
Source: Site Management Plan, *Rio de Janeiro: Carioca Landscapes Between the Mountain and the Sea*, IPHAN, February 2014. Adapted by the author.

fourth component, which hugs the seaside near the entrance to Guanabara Bay, includes Sugar Loaf Mountain; nearby hills; the historic fortresses of São João (where the city was first founded) and Santa Cruz (in Niterói); and the designed beachfronts of Flamengo Park, Botafogo Bay, and Copacabana Beach—all of which have contributed so much to the "outdoor living culture of the city." The International Council on Monuments and Sites (ICOMOS), after reviewing other scenic cities, doubted strongly that any other metropolis "could be similar to Rio in terms of the articulation of nature and culture and the strong sense of identity that this fusion has created."[10] I beg to differ on this point, however. While the Carioca Landscapes are undeniably breathtaking, many other cities also manifest notable nature-culture identities, which is precisely why Rio's environmental heritages serve as such promising aspirational models for others.

This novel framework of nature-culture synthesis arose after an earlier unsuccessful nomination, which had attempted a more limited and conventional approach. On February 29, 2002, the National Heritage Institute (IPHAN) had nominated "Rio de Janeiro: Sugar Loaf, Tijuca Forest and the Botanical Garden" as a hybrid natural-cultural site, based on established heritage categories. After an ICOMOS technical visit to Rio in September 2002, however, the World Heritage Committee deferred on this initial nomination.

The committee suggested that Brazil fundamentally rethink the proposal by appraising the "cultural values" inherent in the city's setting, which would in turn redefine and better safeguard Rio's diverse environments. Rather than focus only on three distinct natural or cultural landmarks—Sugar Loaf, Tijuca Forest, and the Botanical Garden—the committee encouraged a broader perspective on the city's integrated natural-cultural identity. Specifically, the World Heritage Committee suggested that in addition to the mountains and forests, the new nomination should also include Guanabara Bay's entrance and the designed beachfronts nearby. The committee also urged authorities to put in place an integrated management plan for the seashore, including stronger land-use regulations. These changes to the nominating package signaled a new and more original view of how cultural landscapes contributed to the city's human-environmental identity. Besides an enlargement of the protected heritage area, the national coordinating agency, IPHAN, revised the project's name "to reflect the inclusion of urban areas bordering the sea and the idea of an overall cultural landscape." On January 27, 2011, the National Heritage Institute submitted a second nomination under the name "Rio de Janeiro, Carioca Landscapes between the Mountain and the Sea."[11]

For the revised nomination, another technical-evaluation team visited Rio on October 4–8, 2011. Subsequently, ICOMOS wrote to request further information on the management plan, World Heritage criteria, possible boundary extensions, development constraints in the buffer zone, housing conflicts near the Botanical Garden, and other matters. Prior to the visit, in February 2011, the city had already approved a new Master Plan for Sustainable Development, which established the primary importance of Rio's landscapes and included guidelines to promote environmental conservation and land-use policies to preserve the city's identity. The implementation of the new master plan was significant because it recognized the value of protecting the city's larger environmental setting, comprising integrated cultural landscapes, rather than just a series of separate sites. The plan also permitted regulation of urban density, building heights, and economic activities to improve urban quality of life. The World Heritage site's "buffer zones" would become Cultural Environment Protection Areas (APACs) with nuanced management plans. By a decree of December 2011, a management committee chaired by IPHAN would bring together federal, state, and municipal representatives to develop the joint plan for the property and the buffer zone.[12] By virtue of these preparations, the World Heritage Committee inscribed "Carioca Landscapes" as a World Heritage site on July 1, 2012:

> Criterion (v): The development of the city of Rio de Janeiro has been shaped by a creative fusion between nature and culture. This interchange is not the

result of persistent traditional processes but rather reflects an interchange based on scientific, environmental and design ideas that led to innovative landscape creations on a major scale in the heart of the city during little more than a century. These processes have created an urban landscape perceived to be of great beauty by many writers and travelers and one that has shaped the culture of the city.

Criterion (vi): The dramatic landscape of Rio de Janeiro has provided inspiration for many forms of art, literature, poetry, and music. Images of Rio, which show the bay, Sugar Loaf and the statue of Christ the Redeemer have had a high worldwide recognition factor, since the middle of the 19th century. Such high recognition factors can be either positive or negative: in the case of Rio, the image that was projected, and still is projected, is one of a staggeringly beautiful location for one of the world's biggest cities.[13]

These criteria emphasize the preconceived, intentionally planned city, resulting from the efforts of professionally trained architects, landscape designers, scientists, urban planners, artists, writers, and others in shaping the city. This tradition goes back at least to the arrival and residence of the Portuguese royal family in 1808–1821, when the prince regent founded what became the Botanical Garden and other enduring institutions. During the early nineteenth century, European painters and writers often depicted Rio in grandiose terms, as seen earlier. The subsequent influence of the public intellectual, professional, and elite classes continued through the fin de siècle and modernist eras with such famous names as Francisco Pereira Passos, Oscar Neimeyer, Lúcio Costa, Roberto Burle Marx, Oswaldo Cruz, and many others. Such influences undoubtedly reflected Rio's privileged status as Brazil's successive colonial, imperial, and republican capital. But the World Heritage Committee exaggerated in suggesting that the city lacked "traditional processes" of speculative capital and growth-machine politics common to modern urbanization, as numerous authors cited in this book have shown.[14]

While "scientific, environmental and design ideas that led to innovative landscape creations" were no doubt important in Rio, we should not ignore the historical role of urban and environmental activists in organizing for conservation and against excessive development. In their book *Greening Brazil*, Kathryn Hochstetler and Margaret Keck argue that the country's environmental movements arose primarily from domestic political activism as influenced by political institutions and transnational debates. According to their periodization, the "first wave" gained force with conservationist pressures of the mid-twentieth century; the "second wave" reflected political opposition to the environmental problems of the authoritarian military regime from 1964 to 1985; and the "third wave" arose amid neoliberal democratic politics to feature networks of environmentalist organizations with strong social-justice components.[15] In practice, these waves of activism have not occurred in strict linear succession but, rather, have overlapped in time and space. Indeed, for over a century governmental programs have attempted to remedy the environmental issues associated with Rio's urban growth, including water provision, sewage treatment, and deforestation. Despite these efforts, such urban ecological problems have remained evident in the metropolis.

Rio's picturesque Guanabara Bay, for example, illustrates the difficulties of coastal pollution by industry, shipping, oil spills, and untreated sewage. Since the late nineteenth century, urban sanitation and public health have been subject to policy debate. Meanwhile, the once-pristine waters of Guanabara Bay have become unsafe for swimming and questionable sources of fish, crabs, and other seafood. As a result, environmental activism arose to clean up the great bay. Despite some governmental support, progress in bay cleanup has been slow, stifled by inefficiency, political obstacles, and the task's daunting scale. Even so, the growing awareness of urban environmental problems has heightened the city's sense of place, political engagement, and activism. The Carioca Landscapes World Heritage designation of 2012, in my view, arose from long-term concerns over urbanization of the city's bay and lagoons, seashores, mountains and hills, and forests—issues that continue to be debated in Rio.

In archival research for this book, I found that since the 1960s, concerns over the protection of Rio's natural landmarks and endangered environs did indeed form a first wave of urban environmentalism, often led by progressive elites and state agencies. But Hochstetler and Keck's second wave of environmental activism, aimed at the military regime, did not become apparent in my case studies. I can imagine examples nearby that would apply, such as the controversial nuclear-power plant built at Angra dos Reis, a military initiative begun in 1972, but such massive projects were uncommon in the dense city of Rio. In fact, many of the city's early conservationist successes paradoxically occurred during the military governments: under the authoritarian regime, I suspect that progressive Cariocas found their voices in local efforts to landmark the famous hills and mountains, as they did with the implementation of the Cultural Corridor in the historic center. With democratization since 1985, a more socially conscious environmentalism has arisen, given the city's vast disparities of status and wealth. NGOs and neighborhood associations have organized to press authorities on enforcement of laws and to educate the public on socio-environmental problems. This two-pronged analytical framework of movements for both urban conservation and environmental justice typifies contemporary environmentalism in contemporary Rio.

TIJUCA NATIONAL PARK:
ONE PARK, MANY SYMBOLS

Tijuca National Park, which encompasses 15.25 square miles (39.51 km²) within the city of Rio de Janeiro, is widely regarded as the world's largest urban forest. The park is surrounded entirely by the city and is home to 6.7 million residents, as officially estimated for 2019. By way of comparison, Forest Hill Park in Portland, Oregon, widely regarded as the largest U.S. urban forest preserve, covers an area of about 8.08 square miles (20.92 km²)—only half the size of Rio's TNP.[16] The environmental history of Tijuca Forest involves massive deforestation for a series of cash crops, which subsequently led to a pioneering reforestation program in the late nineteenth century and continuing conservation programs thereafter. In fact, the origins and diversities of Rio's environmental activism can be traced back to the struggles over TNP. The park may appear at first glance to be a natural landscape, but on closer inspection, it is clearly a humanized cultural landscape with various uses and groups that lay claim to it. Historically, TNP has experienced many of the same preservation struggles as more densely urbanized spaces of Rio de Janeiro.

The saga of Tijuca Forest's environmental degradation and restoration illustrates the vicissitudes of the city's changing nature-culture relations. With the arrival of the Portuguese royal family in 1808, diplomatic, artistic, and scientific missions from various European countries arrived in Rio. The Tijuca Massif became fashionable with these elites for its temperate "alpine" climate, popularized by Nicolas-Antoine Taunay and other artists. Yet the growth of coffee cultivation, forestry, and agriculture deforested the hills and mountains during the early nineteenth century. In the increasingly barren Tijuca highlands, streams dried up and threatened the city's water supply, so authorities launched a massive reforestation campaign. A serious drought in 1843 caused the imperial governments to expropriate the mountain springs and to replant the forests. With the support of Emperor Pedro II, the planting of tree saplings allowed secondary forests to grow on the denuded hillsides. Major Gomes Archer served as the first administrator of the reforestation scheme from 1861 to 1874. Working initially with six enslaved men, and later with twenty-two paid workers, the team planted 100,000 trees in the first thirteen years. The replanting involved mostly native species, along with notable exotics like eucalyptus. The second administrator, Baron Gastão D'Escragnole, continued the reforestation work from 1874 to 1888, planting some 30,000 more trees, including more exotic species, and turning the forest into a public park. With the help of French landscape designer and botanist

Auguste Glaziou, the forest restoration included the construction of viewpoints, bridges, lakes, fountains, trails, and roads.

After the fall of the monarchy, Tijuca Forest suffered a long period of governmental neglect between 1889 and 1961. Given the extension of the city's watershed to more distant reservoirs, Rio no longer depended on the Tijuca Mountains for its water supply. In addition, fashions and recreational pursuits changed. As the city's beaches became fashionable and attracted both the jet set and the multitudes, authorities virtually abandoned the Tijuca highlands. Restoration efforts only began again in the 1940s, as entrepreneur and art collector Raymundo Ottoni de Castro Maya became administrator of Tijuca Park between 1943 and 1946. With the assistance of Brazilian landscape architect Roberto Burle Marx, the park gained new recreational facilities, hiking trails, restaurants, and historical markers for which it became famous. Part of the Atlantic Forest (Mata Atlântica) that once blanketed coastal Brazil, the city's mountainous forests have largely regenerated and are now mostly of late secondary growth, although there are some remnants of primary forest. Despite the attention given to the 1999 creation of UNESCO World Heritage sites "Discovery Coast Atlantic Forest Reserves" of northeastern Bahia and "Atlantic Forest Southeast Reserves" in São Paulo and Paraná states, the most famous case of Atlantic Forest protection comes from Rio's Tijuca forests. Considered one of the world's models of urban reforestation, the TNP now combines conservationist, recreational, touristic, scientific, illicit residential, and other uses.

The Tijuca National Park and the Carioca Landscapes World Heritage areas also encompass the Botanical Garden. Founded on the lower slopes of the Carioca Mountains by royal decree in 1808, what was initially called the "Royal Garden" (Real Horto) would promote the cultivation of spices and other exotic plants from India. The establishment became the "Royal Botanical Garden" with the coronation of King John VI in 1818. This institution soon began to study plants of scientific, medicinal, and economic utility, while adding an artificial lake, buildings, and other facilities to receive visitors. The Botanical Garden supplied the tree shoots to replant Tijuca Forest during the late nineteenth century. The institution has continued to play an important role in advancing the studies of forestry and botany in Brazil, serving as a center of research on the Atlantic Forest, and providing a national herbarium and research library. For these reasons, the Botanical Garden was listed in Book 1 of the National Registers in 1938.[17]

In 1971, an adjacent and historically related area called the "Forest Garden" (Horto Florestal), officially became part of the Botanical Garden. Listed in the National Register as a "landscape complex" in 1973, the area added a large forest reserve to the Botanical Garden. The institution now comprises an area of 143 hectares (353 acres), including a formal garden of 53 hectares (131 acres), designed in neoclassical style with stately Imperial Palm trees, and a forest reserve of about 90 hectares (222 acres). The garden includes an arboretum with large collections of Amazonian, Brazilian, and international plants. The official name of the Botanical Garden changed in 1998 to "Rio de Janeiro Botanical Garden Research Institute," as part of the federal Ministry of the Environment. Since 2008, the institution has placed greater emphasis on scientific research related to diverse areas of botany, biogeography, ecology and conservation, and related fields. In addition to forty-two permanent and associate scientists, many graduate and postgraduate researchers work on projects funded competitively by government agencies or in partnership with the private sector. According to the institution, a contemporary growth of scientific citations "clearly indicates that the Botanical Garden has come to occupy an increasingly relevant space in the national and international scientific scene." The ICOMOS report of 2012, as part of the Carioca Landscapes World Heritage nomination, proceeded to approve the management plans as "satisfactory. A renovation plan has been drawn up for the arboreal, shrubbery and herbaceous vegetation. For example, the Imperial Palms that are almost dead are to be substituted by other new ones raised in the garden."[18]

Although the ICOMOS evaluation was favorable with regard to the professional revitalization process underway at the Botanical Garden, it asked how "the threat of housing development near the Botanical Garden will be addressed." Referring to the contested land claims of the Horto Favela, which traces its origins back to at least the early nineteenth century, land tenure in the Garden Forest reserve has been disputed for decades. The community has roots in the sugar and coffee plantations that preceded the founding of the Royal Garden in 1808, after which many residents began to work on planting and maintaining the gardens. While allowed to build houses close to work, Horto residents never held legal titles. On the other hand, their ancestors never "invaded" the area: they were already there from early settlement. Active disputes over land tenure began in the 1960s, when conservationist and residential agendas came into direct conflict. In fact, IPHAN's listing of the Garden Forest in the National Register in 1973 observed: "The Garden Forest was incorporated into the Botanical Garden as a natural expansion, very much hindered by several land occupations, and it is being reclaimed as an area of forest reserve and scientific research."[19]

The Botanical Garden relies on an environmental conservation discourse to justify the removal of the Horto population of about two thousand residents, who occupy about 12 percent of the Botanical Garden—17 hectares (42 acres). According to Sérgio Besserman, president of the institution, "The community's presence is not compatible with a functioning research institute." He also maintains that "we are not expanding, we are taking back land which already belongs to the Botanical Gardens." To critics, the high real-estate values and property development in this affluent part of Rio complicate matters: Horto's land has been valued at some US$2.9 billion, which makes property speculation a tempting possibility. The community's counter-narrative is based on long-term residence and stewardship of the environment, as documented by an online archive and demonstrated by regular tours. Like several other informal communities of Rio, Horto maintains an eco-museum with onsite, participatory visitation. Historian Laura Olivieri Carneiro de Souza, who wrote her doctoral dissertation on Horto's project of social memory, has argued that "the community was created to protect the environment, not to destroy it."[20]

Such land disputes, which pit various environmentalist and developmental narratives against each other, have long played out in Tijuca National Park, now a Federal Conservation Unit by Brazilian law. Originally created in 1961 as the Rio de Janeiro National Park, during the mid-1960s, conservationists requested the forest's federal landmarking by the National Heritage Institute to provide a protective measure. The first requests came from Marcelo Moreira of the state's Division of Historic and Artistic Patrimony on August 24, 1965; he wrote to urge IPHAN to list the park in the National Register "so that the forest can be protected and conserved as one of the most beautiful sites of our state."[21] Another endorsement came from Olínio Gomes Paschoal Coelho, head of the state's Service of Landmarking and Protection, who wrote "to promote the protection of the Tijuca Forest region, which constitutes one of the most beautiful corners of our State. Being a place of recreation within the city's protected forests, its preservation is of great social interest." He feared that the reforested area faced renewed pressures, given "the lack of practical policy instruments to patrol and protect it. Landmarking the forest would benefit the city by protecting such an important historical landscape."[22]

As the bureaucratic wheels continued to turn, the federal administrator of the Rio de Janeiro National Park, Alceo Magnanini of the Ministry of Agriculture, became involved in the matter. Not only did Magnanini endorse the park's federal landmarking, but on December 22, 1965, he also proposed protecting an enlarged area of all lands above 80 to 100 meters in elevation, based on local topographic surveys, particularly around the Pedra Dois Irmãos (Two Brothers Rock) and the Pedra da Gávea (Gávea Rock). Then, on January 28, 1966, Paulo Thadim Barreto, head of IPHAN's Art Division, provided another supportive voice for forest conservation. Reporting on the area's history and environment, he noted that the proposed area included forested areas belonging to the federal government, the state of Guanabara, and privately protected areas, largely in the Serra da Carioca. Federal landmarking on the National Register would extend environmental protection over the heterogeneous area.[23]

On April 19, 1966, IPHAN councilor Gilberto Ferrez noted: "Attacks on the natural beauties of Rio de Janeiro and especially on the forests and mountains that surround this city have become increasingly notorious in recent years." He referred specifically to the repeated clearing of forests in Jacarepaguá, Serra da Carioca, Pedra da Gávea, Dois Irmãos, and the Dona Marta Hill. Also, he stressed the proliferation and constant growth of favelas on the hillsides, especially at Corcovado, Dona Marta Hill, and Dois Irmãos, along with formal housing subdivisions that increasingly "made fun of the law" that said areas above 80 to 100 meters of altitude should be exempt from new development. In addition, the television towers on the Serra da Carioca served as a visual obstruction, he argued, as did the lighted signs and billboards that disfigured the slopes of the Sugar Loaf, Urca, and Pasmado peaks. Ferrez noted that the Advisory Council favored the proposal to protect the peaks and hills: "The landmarking proposal is the only act capable of safeguarding this incomparable heritage of our city, of which the Tijuca Forest represents so much effort and sacrifice during the past century, in reforesting it and beautifying it for the delight of current generations."[24]

Finally, on February 8, 1967, a federal decree officially changed the park's name to Tijuca National Park, while the enlarged area gained federal landmark protection. The listing on the National Register occurred in the "Archeology, Ethnography, and Landscape Book" on April 27, 1967. The Ministry of Agriculture remained in charge of the consolidated park, including an enlarged protected area to be achieved by donation and appropriation in the Corcovado Complex, Sumaré-Corcovado, Pedra Bonita, and the Tijuca Massif. At the same time TNP's boundaries were redefined to include several areas above the elevation of 100 meters in the Tijuca Massif, along with the Pedra Bonita, Pedra da Gávea, Corcovado, Alta da Boa Vista, and other sites.[25] With these additions, the park encompassed three highland zones overlooking the city, including the famous Tijuca and Corcovado peaks and the Botanical Garden, along with waterfalls, spectacular viewpoints, sixteen marked trails, and other cultural and natural sites of note.

On August 8, 1973, as part of an effort to further strengthen the protection of Rio's historic hills and mountains, IPHAN listed seven historic hills and mountains on the National Registers: Sugar Loaf, Urca, Babilônia, Dogface (Cara de Cão), Corcovado, Dois Irmãos, and Pedra da Gávea (see table 5.1). During the prior political campaign in favor of the landmarking, Gilberto Ferrez published in the local press a heated editorial that blamed developers and state governments for the environmental damage inflicted on the city: "This is

Table 5.1. Carioca Landscapes between the Mountain and the Sea (18 Heritage Sites)

Bem Tombado (Registered Property)	Registry Book(s)	Listing Number	Year Listed	Formative Period
Aterro do Flamengo/Flamengo Landfill and Park	1	039	1965	1950–2000
Copacabana Palace Hotel	2 3	506 583	1986	1900–1950
Corcovado; Penhasco/Corcovado Peak	1	055	1973	1900–1950
Cristo Redentor, estátua/Christ the Redeemer	1	585	2008	1900–1950
Fortaleza de Santa Cruz (Niteroi)/Santa Cruz Fortress (Niteroi)	2 3	122 274	1939	1550–1600
Fortaleza de São João: Portão/Fortress of Saint John: Gateway	2 3	037 102	1938	1550–1600
Horto Florestal/Forest Park Landscape complex	1	061	1973	1800–1900
Jardim Botânico/Botanical Garden	1	002	1938	1800–1900
Morro Cara de Cão/Dog Face Hill	1	058	1973	n/a
Morro da Babilônia/Babylon Hill	1	054	1973	n/a
Morro da Urca/Urca Hill	1	053	1973	n/a
Morro do Pão de Açúcar/Sugar Loaf Hill	1	052	1973	n/a
Morro Dois Irmãos/Two Brothers Hill	1	056	1973	n/a
Morros da Cidade do Rio de Janeiro/Hills of the City of Rio de Janeiro	2 3	070 151	1938	n/a
Museu do Açude; Chácara do Céu/ Museum of the Dam in Tijuca National Park; and the Museum of the Sky in Santa Teresa	1 2 3	066 450 520	1974	1950–2000
Parque Lage/Lage Park: Landscape Complex	2	322	1957	1850–1900
Parque Nac'l Tijuca/Tijuca N. Park and Forest	1	042	1967	1850–1900
Pedra da Gávea/Rock of Gávea	1	057	1973	n/a

Sources: IPHAN, Arquivo Noronha Santos, http://www.iphan.gov.br/ans/inicial.htm, accessed August 4, 2012; and IPHAN, *Bens móveis e imóveis inscritos nos Livros do Tombo do Instituto do Patrimônio Histórico e Artístico Nacional* (Rio de Janeiro: IPHAN/COPEDOC, 2009); and UNESCO World Heritage Center, http://whc.unesco.org/list/1100.

Note: This list includes 18 properties from the National Registers (*Livros do Tombo*) located in the UNESCO World Heritage site Carioca Landscapes between the Mountain and the Sea. The "Formative Period" refers to when a structure was largely built, a collection gathered, or a cultural landscape shaped. Most listings are in Book 1 (Archeological, Ethnographic, and Landscape) with fewer in Book 2 (Historical) and Book 3 (Fine Arts).

fruit of the unbraked greed of construction companies that completely forget that there is a natural landscape to preserve." He also accused the state government as the second guilty party: "It does not have the good sense to protect its treasures."[26] This accusation suggested that the administration of the state government favored economic development over environmental conservation, given the construction fees, taxes, and other political favors. On June 27, 1973, an editorial in *O Jornal do Brasil* stated: "It is the natural beauty of Rio, along with the happiness of its population, that makes the city different, an attraction. If this heritage is lost there will not be any tourist industry—or any other—that remains. The decision of IPHAN can only be reason for happiness. Rio has begun to find its defenders."[27]

Even with this enhancement of the park's status, boundaries, and protections, the debates among conservationists and others continued. Critics claimed that the TNP continued to suffer from inadequate maintenance, destructive incursions by visitors and nearby residents, criminal activity, and other urban problems. Eliane Velloso, president of the Gávea Neighborhood Association (AMAGAVEA, or "Love Gávea"), complained in a letter dated April 28, 1987, to the IPHAN Advisory Council about the increasing development pressures along the Gávea Highway into the Tijuca National Park. "Four buildings of 25 floors, above the 100-meter elevation," she protested, "assaulting and walling in the natural landscape, cutting down trees, besides increasing the population density, the number of cars, the movement, noise, and air pollution." Velloso argued that such projects have broken federal and municipal conservation laws and have "the general repudiation of the residents and users of Gávea. AMAGAVEA urges you to stop this illegal, disastrous, and scandalous project."[28] This protest suggests that conservationism had come to figure in the political agendas of affluent neighborhood associations, such as Gávea, which reflected a general broadening of Rio's environmentalist constituencies. Yet conservationist elites with homes near the TNP remained most dissatisfied with the protective measures in place. While one might dismiss this case as a "not in my backyard" response, it also speaks to the limitations of a first-wave environmentalism in conflicts with recreational, touristic, residential and commercial development, and other uses.

The most famous of the Carioca Landscapes is the iconic statue *Christ the Redeemer*, with its outstretched arms atop Corcovado Mountain, which is widely visible over the city. It also illustrates the contested uses of the Tijuca National Park. Besides being a symbol of Christianity, the giant statue has become "the symbolic monument of the city of Rio de Janeiro," according to the National Heritage Institute, which listed Corcovado in the National Register in 1973.[29] In fact, for international audiences, the dramatic Corcovado statue has largely come to embody the whole country. The November 2009 cover of the *Economist*, for example, depicted *Christ the Redeemer* taking off like a rocket, while the country boomed economically. By 2013, the country began to slide into an economic recession that provoked massive public demonstrations. Earlier optimism evaporated, and news of government corruption scandals enraged the public. In September 2013, the *Economist* cover depicted Corcovado's *Christ* taking a nosedive into Guanabara Bay, asking, "Has Brazil Blown It?"[30]

The monument itself rises 124 feet (38 meters)—including the 98-foot statue and its 26-foot pedestal—above the steep 2,308-foot (703 meters) summit of Corcovado Mountain. Listed on the National Register in 2008, the massive religious statue has been subject to contemporary controversy over its commercial and touristic uses. Surrounded by Tijuca Forest National Park, the monument lies near the center of the far-flung city of mountains, hills, valleys, bays, and beaches. Declared one of the "New Wonders of the World" in a 2007 Internet poll, Rio's celebrated landmark joined much older (India's Taj Mahal, the Palace Tombs of Petra in Jordan, Peru's Machu Picchu) and larger (Great Wall of China, the Roman Colosseum, and Mexico's Chichén Itzá pyramid) sites around the world. Of these, Rio's statue of Christ is the most overtly religious. Yet Cariocas of famously hedonistic Rio adore it, regardless of their religious faith or lack thereof, according to surveys. The spectacular sight of the statue atop a steep mountain peak certainly contributes to its broad appeal (see photo 5.1). Mark Holston has suggested that other cities do not "come close to combining the magical elements of spirituality and physical beauty that Corcovado boasts in abundance."[31]

Built between 1922 and 1931 in Art Deco style, the statue was the culmination of a long campaign by the city's Roman Catholic hierarchy to build a major religious monument atop Corcovado Mountain. This visibility would reclaim the Church's prestige, after separating from the secular republican state in 1891. In 1903, French-born father Pedro Maria Bos, an enthusiastic advocate, exclaimed, "Corcovado! Here is the most unique pedestal in the world! When will the statue come?"[32] Subsequently, Church officials and lay supporters in the "Catholic Circle," concerned about the "godlessness" of society, mobilized support for a monument. Cardinal Dom Joaquim Arcoverde wanted to show the Church's continuing presence in the secular republic. The statue's design resulted largely from collaboration between Brazilian engineer Heitor da Silva Costa and French sculptor Paul Landowski. Constructed of reinforced concrete, small pieces of resistant soapstone from Minas Gerais covered the statue's exterior. Inaugurated on October 12, 1931, *Christ the Redeemer* also served as a belated monument to the centennial of Brazilian independence in 1922.[33]

Photo 5.1. This panoramic view shows Rio's iconic Corcovado Mountain with *Christ the Redeemer* looming over the Marvelous City, while Sugar Loaf Mountain sits at the entrance to Guanabara Bay. Wikimedia/Mario Roberto Durán Ortiz/Creative Commons.

This case also reveals the multiple, complicated, and contradictory forces that may underlie the construction of cultural landscapes. Despite a separation of church and state in republican Brazil, *Christ the Redeemer* arose as a Roman Catholic monument, built on public land of a national park, and supported by the state at various levels. In fact, governments have funded most of the costs associated with the statue's periodic renovations due to damage from strong winds, erosion, and lightning. By building a religious symbol so visibly in a secular republic, the Church situated the country's traditional religion in the pluralistic modern world. As part of contemporary efforts to restore the monument's religious sense, the Catholic Archdiocese of Rio de Janeiro announced in 2000 that it would no longer permit images of the *Cristo Redentor* statue to appear in commercial advertisements. The Church threatened to prosecute any companies that used the image of the statue without consent.[34] Whether such religious initiatives will fully succeed remains questionable, however, given the way that the city, tourism, and related enterprises have branded the statue as a symbol of Rio de Janeiro and Brazil generally. The great statue on Corcovado Mountain in Tijuca National Park reflects multiple interests and land-use conflicts, so it seems futile to restrict the heritage site to a single stakeholder.

Despite the importance of conserving the Atlantic Forest and fauna, the Tijuca National Park and its many attractions have come under increasing pressure from both visitors and nearby residents. Recent concerns have included deforestation, forest fires, erosion, litter, and loss of species. The listing of the TNP as a national landmark in 1967, besides reflecting federal recognition of Tijuca Forest's historical and environmental importance, served as an attempt to strengthen enforcement of the park's boundaries in the face of such pressures. Yet such a large and varied area as the Tijuca National Park inevitably has many uses, so such a preserved space cannot be expected to serve or symbolize just one purpose. This case suggests that narrowly framed conservationist approaches may suffer from a limited sense of the human role, which in turn contributes to the contemporary rise of movements for environmental justice.

GUANABARA BAY: CONSERVATION TURNS TO ENVIRONMENTAL JUSTICE

Although visitors have long rhapsodized about Rio's great bay, it has served as a dumping ground for centuries. Literally meaning "breast of the sea" in the native Tupí-Guaraní language, Guanabara Bay shrank from 180 square miles (468 km^2) in 1500 to 154 square miles (400 km^2) by 2000—a decrease of 15 percent—due to shoreline expansion. Oval in shape, the bay widens to about 18.6 miles (30 km) and narrows to 1.1 mile (1.8 km) at its entrance. The bay shelters the port from Atlantic storms, but also inhibits the ocean's natural flushing action, particularly in shallow areas beset by landfill, pollution, and sedimentation. Once a river, before postglacial flooding some 12,000 years ago, the bay's central trough now reaches depths of some 164 feet (50 meters). Otherwise, depths on the irregular bottom of this drowned river valley vary from about 56 feet (17 meters) at the entrance, to less than 10 feet (3 meters) away from the navigation channels. As the city's original raison d'être and continuing socioeconomic hub, the bay's margins are highly urbanized and contain much of the metropolitan population, industries, oil refineries, two airports, the seaport and naval base, countless favelas, and the main campus of the Federal University of Rio de Janeiro.[35]

This dense occupation of the bay shore contrasts with an unspoiled natural state upon European arrival five centuries ago, when the bay, lagoons, and mangrove forests teemed with fish and wildlife, including dolphins, whales, birds, and shellfish. Tupí-Guaraní groups, locally called Tupinambás or

Tamoios, clustered in agricultural villages around Guanabara Bay. After the Portuguese founded São Sebastião do Rio de Janeiro at the bay's entrance in 1565, a long process of urbanization ensued—along with deforestation, wildlife extinction, wastewater contamination, and tropical disease. By 1850, when Herman Melville visited and praised "the Bay of all Rivers—the Bay of all Delights—the Bay of all Beauties," overexploitation of the whale population, which once found an ideal breeding ground here, had already ended a flourishing industry in whale meat and oil.[36] Environmental degradation mounted as Rio grew into a megacity: hillside erosion, sedimentation, and landfill steadily encroached on the bay's shorelines, while pollution by industry, shipping, oil spills, and untreated sewage rendered its once-pristine beaches unsafe for swimming. The most polluted beaches of Guanabara Bay are in the port district and along the waterfront of the Maré (Tide) and the Complexo Alemão favelas.[37]

The main concern of the "Carioca Landscapes" heritage program is not the waters of Guanabara Bay, but the preservation of historical structures and landscape designs of the waterfronts close to the bay's entrance, which highlight the close relationship of the city and the sea. In fact, the Portuguese founded their first settlement in 1565 at an improvised fortress on Dogface Hill at the entrance to Guanabara Bay. After expelling the French in 1567, the Portuguese transferred their colony to the bay's west side. But the Fortress of Saint John (Fortaleza de São João) continued to protect the bay from foreign invasion for several centuries. The Portuguese crown resolved in 1618 to expand it into a star-shaped fort with four batteries (São José, São Martinho, São Teodósio, and São Diogo). The Fortress of Santa Cruz, built in 1567, similarly served to protect the other side of the bay's narrow entrance. These fortifications prevented the entrance of a Dutch squadron in 1599 and battled against French invaders in 1711. Since the 1930s, the Fortress of Saint John has served as a military training academy in the Urca district of Rio. Over time, the original battlements deteriorated and were rebuilt, so that the only surviving original part was the impressive entry gate, which was landmarked in 1938. With the modern decline of their strategic military functions, these fortifications remained as historic landmarks, reminiscent of colonial battles.[38]

Extensive land reclamation and waterfront expansion allowed landscape designers to leave their imprints on new places. Flamengo Park arose from the landfill created by the excavation of Santo Antônio Hill in downtown Rio de Janeiro. Beside the fin de siècle seaside boulevard constructed by the Pereira Passos administration, the rubble from the more recent urban renewal created an extensive open space of 1.2 million square meters (see photo 5.2). Built between 1961 and 1965, under Governor Carlos Lacerda, Flamengo Park resulted from the inspiration and organizational efforts of his friend Maria

Photo 5.2. Flamengo Park, built on landfill from Santo Antônio Hill in the early 1960s, with downtown Rio de Janeiro and the Rio-Niterói Bridge (8.25 miles, or 13.2 km long) in the background. Photo by the author, 2004.

Carlota Macedo Soares. The self-trained architect and long-time Brazilian partner of American poet Elizabeth Bishop, "Lota" Soares dedicated the last part of her life to the construction of Flamengo Park, which worsened her depression and resulted in hospitalization for a nervous breakdown; ultimately Lota died from an overdose of tranquilizers in an apparent suicide, on a visit to New York City to see Bishop in 1967.[39] Yet Lota's tragic obsession ensured the park's completion with a team of engineers, architects, and botanists, who followed the landscape design of Roberto Burle Marx. After planting some eleven thousand trees, the park became a vast recreational space that accommodated a new expressway, an enlarged Santos Dumont Airport, a new Museum of Modern Art, and a monument to Brazilian soldiers fallen in World War II. Listed in Book 1 of the National Register in 1965, Flamengo Park is often compared to New York's Central Park in its significance for Rio.

Amid this rush of urban renewal projects, development pressures mounted on the scenic seashores of Rio's South Zone. A major controversy arose over proposed development by the company with the tourist concession for Sugar Loaf Mountain (Cia. do Caminho Aéreo do Pão de Açúcar). Architect

Harry Cole designed a garish three-story tourist complex in the shape of a horseshoe with restaurants, bars, and stores on top of iconic Sugar Loaf Mountain. News of the proposal immediately sparked widespread outrage in Rio and beyond. The *Estado de São Paulo* newspaper thundered on May 9, 1973: "Rio de Janeiro has been, among all large Brazilian cities, the greatest victim of greed allied with stupidity. . . . Let's save Rio de Janeiro from its enemies, beginning by condemning the monstrous "eat-and-drink" on Sugar Loaf."[40] Days later, on May 11, 1973, Rio's *Jornal do Brasil* published an editorial that complained of the neglect of major natural landmarks in Rio, including Sugar Loaf and Corcovado Mountains, and the forests of Tijuca National Park: "Carioca tourism is an orphan falling into a dangerous abyss between the efforts of Embratur and the neglect of tourist attractions."[41] The Director of IPHAN, architect Renato Soeiro, said that the National Heritage Institute could not do anything in defense of Sugar Loaf because it had not been listed on the National Register, although he and others openly expressed their opposition to the development project. The opinion of Governor Chagas Freitas was unclear and the state's Historic Patrimony Council refused to comment, but other prominent Cariocas expressed their opposition, including the president of Riotur, the Urban Development Council, and the Brazilian Education Association.[42]

Although never built, the threat that the gaudy project might irrevocably scar the peak of Sugar Loaf provoked a public outcry that broadened the environmentalist agenda and led to the protection of several major mountains and historic hills in 1973. The sequence of events indicates a process of progressive elite-led environmental conservation. First, Lygia Martins Costa, then head of the IPHAN Art Section, cited her father, the famous architect and planner Lúcio Costa, when she wrote on June 7, 1973: "Sugar Loaf, Corcovado, and Pedra da Gávea are natural monuments of the city." She proposed federal landmarking the historic hills of Sugar Loaf, Urca, Babilônia, and Dogface at the entrance to Guanabara Bay, along with Corcovado, Pedra da Gávea, and Morro Dois Irmãos in Tijuca National Park, noting the latter group's "beautiful and characteristic features, equally exposed to quick and badly oriented development." She also argued that any construction projects be previously submitted for the approval of National Heritage Institute, so as to strengthen the complete and prior defense of the mountains above the level of 100 meters.[43]

Soon thereafter, the director of the National Heritage Institute reported to the state governor that the IPHAN Advisory Committee had approved the listing of the seven historic hills and mountains proposed by Lygia Costa. The landmarking of three of the city's major mountain peaks and four historic hills, inscribed in the Book of Archeology, Ethnography, and Landscape on

August 8, 1973, constituted a major addition in protecting the city's environments from unsightly development.[44] Even so, after Rio's mountains, historic hills, and national forests were declared national landmarks in 1973, Guanabara Bay remained without such protection. During the 1992 Earth Summit in Rio, signatories of the Alternative Treaty famously proposed "that Guanabara Bay and its surrounding environments be declared a World Heritage Site," although no official such protection occurred.[45] After the 1985 presidential election, the switch to democratic politics allowed NGOs to became active in promoting environmental protection. While nongovernmental organizations have played a variety of environmentalist roles, they have certainly increased pressure for the bay's cleanup. For example, the Guanabara Bay Institute, founded in 1993, became one of the most active NGOs working "to study and resolve of the environmental, social, and urban problems of the bay and its watershed."[46]

With democratization came new state programs aimed at sustainable development. In the wake of the 1992 Earth Summit in Rio, authorities launched, in 1994, the massive ten-year Guanabara Bay Cleanup Program with a budget of US$793 million, funded largely by the Inter-American Development Bank and Japan's Overseas Economic Cooperation Fund. Plans called for a 90 percent reduction in industrial pollution by 1999, as well as drastic reductions in untreated domestic sewage discharges. About half of the funds were destined for residential sewage systems, including plans to connect twenty-nine favelas, along with other underserved areas around the bay. The most encouraging results came in better monitoring and reducing pollution from some four hundred polluting industries—including textiles and food-processing plants, the naval and port facilities, shipyards, and several oil refineries. Yet results in the residential sector remained disappointing. Even in the informal communities served by sewerage, residents often could not pay sanitation fees and resisted domestic hookups; without sewers, wastewater drained into the surface runoff—often ending up as dark streaks on public beaches.[47]

The contributing role of informal communities in the bay's degradation cannot be denied, but it raises politically charged debates about causation, culpability, and environmental justice. Created by forces of regional migration, urbanization, and urban renewal, *favelas* arose as a way to house low-income populations whom the formal real-estate market and government programs had not served well. In some ways, favela ecology has favored a healthy circular metabolism, since poverty has meant high levels of recycling, reliance on scavenged and used building materials, collective transport, sharing among households, and community collaboration. Undoubtedly, affluent districts are comparatively wasteful in their use of resources. What favelas have lacked are the vital services and infrastructures necessary to reduce levels of pollution. As a result, it seems cruelly ironic that authorities and elites have so often blamed *favelados* for environmental ills since the turn of the twentieth century.

Although the 1994–2004 cleanup promised the bay's salvation, the program lagged behind schedule and ultimately fell far short of expectations. Pollution continued from various sources. In 1975 and 2000, oil spills befouled the bay's beaches, marine life, and mangroves, but continuing contamination has come primarily from the discharge of domestic and industrial wastewater. As a result, Guanabara Bay's problems of water quality continued to worsen. Given the bay's narrow entrance and shallow depths, it takes two hundred days for the water to be fully renewed outside of deep shipping channels. Environmental agencies and NGOs, while working to save Guanabara Bay, have been frustrated by a lack of both funding and political influence. Despite marginal improvements, the bay still reflected an unhealthy ecology in need of correction.[48] By 2016, despite renewed cleanup efforts, news reports indicated that the "pollution overwhelming Guanabara Bay raised significant concerns about the health of the swimmers and sailors who compete in the bay's water at the Rio Olympics."[49]

Environmental and community activists have protested the lack of more concerted state action in cleaning up the bay, the continuing pollution by the port and petrochemical complex, and the failure to support and protect the fishing population. Since 2009, the Association of Men and Women of the Sea (AHOMAR) has campaigned to protect fishing livelihoods and the environment against the petrochemical complex in the area. Demonstrations and public forums have also advocated infrastructural upgrades to reduce industrial and residential pollution. Another concern has been the rising siltation and eutrophication of the bay, which results from deforestation and erosion. According to Amnesty International, the association's president has survived numerous threats against his life; two members of AHOMAR were shot to death and another two were found drowned. Allied activist groups have included Baía Viva, Casa Fluminense, Association of Free Fishermen of Tubiacanga (APELT), Forum of Fishermen and Friends of the Sea, Goethe-Institut Rio de Janeiro, and the Association of Cyclists of Governor's Island (ACIG). This network of organizations and their support of environmental justice attest to a third wave of activism, no longer reliant on individuals of wealth and influence, but oriented to the politics of community well-being and harmonious socio-nature relations.[50]

Guanabara Bay's degradation has continued largely unabated, as shown during the sailing, rowing, and other aquatic competitions of the 2016 Olympic Games in Rio. The continuing pollution results largely from environmental injustice: the provision of vital urban services in the Zona Norte and its northern suburbs, along with more effective regulation of the port, industry, and the petrochemical complex, would much improve the bay's environmental conditions. The bay's continuing pollution threatens a vital scenic, recreational, and natural resource. It also points to embedded problems that hinder the bay's cleanup. Governmental agencies and community groups have taken steps to address these problems, but more concerted efforts are required to improve the bay's environmental prospects. Although first-wave conservation has largely given way to third-wave movements of environmental justice in and around the bay, the two approaches have much to gain from collaboration. Given the magnitude of the bay's pollution, along with the entrenched industrial and shipping interests opposed to strict regulation of pollution, broadly based environmentalist coalitions undoubtedly will be necessary to save the magnificent bay.

COPACABANA AND IPANEMA: DEMOCRATIC BEACHES?

New Year's Eve is one of the biggest celebrations in Rio de Janeiro. Copacabana Beach, where outdoor stages feature holiday shows, boasts the largest festivities. Since 1976, when the Méridien Hotel first sponsored a beachfront fireworks display, Reveillon has become a major public event in Rio. Once a traditional religious occasion observed by Afro-Brazilian *candomblé* and *umbanda* devotees, the New Year's commemoration now attracts some two million people to the beaches. The revelry mounts as crowds assemble to watch the midnight fireworks, while well-to-do groups attend exclusive parties in high-rise apartments overlooking the beaches. This juxtaposition of elites and masses symbolizes the sharp social contrasts of Brazilian society. Underneath the outward camaraderie, tensions simmer over status, access, and safety. Although affluent elements prefer private settings for their exclusivity and unobstructed views, widespread fears of crime, violence, and other dangers also contribute to a retreat from public space. In fact, tragedy has occasionally marred the New Year's parties: In 1988–1989, a chartered yacht sank while attempting to sail in rough seas from Botafogo Bay to Copacabana, killing fifty-six people on board. In 2000–2001, a Reveillon fireworks explosion hurt fifty spectators and killed one tourist on the beach, subsequently prompting relocating the fireworks to offshore boats. In 2008–2009, Ipanema canceled its festivities for fears of insufficient security. The Ano Novo now mobilizes massive security forces to Rio's beaches.[51]

As in other parts of the Carioca Landscapes heritage program, Copacabana Beach shows the social tensions brought about by widespread use of the city's seashore. Scholarly critiques have focused on the exclusionary forces of social class and race on the beachfronts. James Freeman asserts that the "myth of Rio's democratic beach"—like familiar national myths of the "congenial man" and "racial democracy"—serves to defuse social conflict by obscuring the chasm between rich and poor.[52] Patricia Farias focuses on how persistent systems of racial classification affect the status of Rio's beaches. Although she argues that beaches are recreational and not political, this point depends on how one defines "political."[53] The beachfront is a site of many rallies, parades, and celebrations, although generally they do not take the form of overt protest. The infamous beach riot of 1992 called attention to issues of racial inequality, as we shall see. Exuberant carnival groups (*bandas*) frequently invoke political themes on the beach, and an annual gay parade occurs on Copacabana's Avenida Atlântica. Such events are political in "latent" and "ritualistic" terms, even if not overtly "manifest" forms.[54] Indeed, public policy and land-use regulation broadly set the parameters of social interaction and help to explain contemporary perceptions of "democratic" beaches.

Once a remote fishing village, isolated by coastal mountains from the urban core, Copacabana remained scantily populated until the opening of the Old Tunnel (Túnel Velho) in 1892 and the New Tunnel (Túnel Novo) in 1906. The extension of streetcar lines stimulated real-estate development and rapid urbanization at the turn of the twentieth century. Conceived as the city's first Atlantic beachfront, Copacabana represented cultural change and modernity: "In spite of the rigid laws concerning timetables for sea and sunbathing, established by the municipality to preserve the local moral values, the beach became a habit at once."[55] In 1923, the Copacabana Palace Hotel opened as a luxury resort, and the district became world famous for its glamorous nightlife and casinos. A symbol of the fashionable Carioca seashore, the famous hotel was listed on the National Register in 1986. Avenida Atlântica's black-and-white, wave-patterned sidewalk also became a civic symbol. Between 1930 and 1960, Copacabana's population grew to two hundred thousand, as zoning laws of 1937 allowed high-rise buildings up to twelve stories. Nicknamed the "Princess of the Sea," Copacabana had its heyday in 1958 as the city's cultural epicenter. The beachfront became the city's preferred residential address, a status symbol of tropical living. The growing popularity of the seaside promenade changed the city's social geography and the southern zone "assumed a position at the center of the city's maps."[56]

Public and private investments valorized the Zona Sul. While affluent residents migrated to the fashionable southern beachfronts, governments mounted large-scale planning initiatives to beautify and provide infrastructures for the favored districts. Demolition of hills downtown provided room for new skyscrapers and landfill for expressways and the recreational facilities of Flamengo Beach, landscaped by Roberto Burle Marx and completed in 1960. Subsequent governmental efforts focused on widening the congested beachfronts of Copacabana, Ipanema, and Leblon. The inadequate sanitation and recreational facilities were also problematic. A massive state engineering project, completed in 1970, widened Copacabana and Leme Beaches, installed new drainage and sewerage, enlarged the sidewalks, and separated directional roadways. Burle Marx replicated the original wave patterns on the new beachfront sidewalks and designed a novel pattern for the landward side. The layout of the Copacabana seaside with a wide sidewalk (*calçadão*) along the residential-commercial side, the traffic median, and the beachfront was quite an innovation in its time. The inspiration of Burle Marx has been widely imitated elsewhere. The Carioca Landscapes heritage program recognized about two miles (4.5 km) of the promenade and road, but not the buildings along the built-up side. In 2012, ICOMOS noted that the streetscapes and landscape designs of Burle Marx along Avenida Atlântica in Copacabana "are generally in a good state of conservation. However, ICOMOS notes that the mosaics require leveling and there is a need to reinstate missing pieces. There are also some spaces where trees need replacing to complete the original designs."[57]

If the 1950s were Copacabana's golden years, the 1960s belonged to Ipanema. During the late nineteenth century José Antônio Moreira Filho (popularly known as the Baron of Ipanema) owned what had long been an isolated rural area, but urbanization began with the extension of streetcars from Copacabana. In the early 1960s, composers Tom Jobim and Vinícius de Morães popularized the district with their famous Bossa Nova anthem, "The Girl from Ipanema." With events such as the appearance of a very pregnant actress Leila Diniz in a tiny bikini, or ex-guerrilla and politician Fernando Gabeira in a scandalously small *sunga* bathing suit, *Ipanemenses* gained a reputation as bohemian trendsetters. On Sundays, a popular craft market known as the "Hippie Fair" now thrives on General Osório Square, while thoroughfares generally are full of popular bars and clubs, restaurants, and cafés. The seafront boulevard, Avenida Vieira Souto, serves as the district's preferred address and one of Rio's most expensive.

As opposed to the beaches of heavily polluted Guanabara Bay, where water quality is considered unsuitable for human use, Copacabana and Ipanema beaches are generally safe to swim in. These Atlantic beaches benefit from the natural flushing action of the open ocean, which disperses pollutants more effectively than the closed bay. In addition, offshore discharge systems carry sewage several miles out into the Atlantic Ocean. At various points along the Atlantic beaches, electronic monitors indicate water quality, while flags of different colors fly above the lifeguard stations to indicate riptide and other surf conditions. In periods of heavy rainfall, however, the wastewater from the hills and streets drains onto the beaches. As a result, residents advise visitors not to swim off the southern beaches after rainstorms.

Casual visitors may regard the beach as an undifferentiated human mass, but local residents classify the seaside according to prevalent social groups (*turmas*). In a diverse city like Rio, where beaches are important places for meeting and recreation, stretches of the shoreline are popularly identified with their *turmas*. The Carioca residents of Rio relate these social identities to the lifeguard posts (*postos*), numbered consecutively from Posts 1 to 6 on the Leme-Copacabana beaches and to Posts 7 to 12 on the Ipanema-Leblon beaches. These reputations become self-reinforcing and affect beach status and personality. As a result, Copacabana is a heterogeneous beach of affluent residents, foreign and national tourists, local service employees, *favelados*, and others of modest means. Along with the smaller Leme Beach at the northeastern end, Copacabana's shoreline forms a graceful 2.6-mile, half-moon curve, dramatically framed by the summit of Sugar Loaf and other coastal hills, peaks, and mountains. Near Post 1 in Leme, the beachfront attracts affluent tourists and local residents, along with those from the Babilônia and Chapeu Mangueira Favelas on the hills above. Posts 2 and 3, close to the exclusive Copacabana Hotel, have long been upscale areas. Farther along the shore, residents often associate Post 4 with prostitution, due to the nearby nightclubs. Near Fort Copacabana, Posts 5 and 6 now constitute the district's most desirable residential beachfronts, located near the Arpoador rock formations that divided Copacabana from Ipanema beaches.

Patterns of social segmentation are even more pronounced in Ipanema, which together with neighboring Leblon Beach stretches 2.6 miles below the towering twin peaks of Dois Irmãos (Two Brothers) to the southwest. Close to Copacabana and the Arpoador Point, Post 7 is known for its surfers in search of good waves, marijuana smokers who hide amid the rocks and palm trees, and *favelados* who live on the nearby hills. A daily newspaper recently commented: "The marijuana crowd in Ipanema, which previously whistled to warn of police arrival, has changed its tactic again. Since booing the police may put people in jail for disrespect, the stoners gathered in the coconut grove now stand to applaud when announcing the arrival of the brave men of law."[58] The gay beach at Post 8 (Farme de Amoedo Street) is obvious from the rainbow flags, but this area is also home to another *turma*: young, apparently unemployed men who spend their time on the beach practicing Brazilian jiu-jitsu martial arts, working out, and starting unprovoked fights. Post 9 has become more than a place: it is now a way of life defined by wealth, intellectuality, and good looks—wherever the most beautiful, affluent, and educated young Cariocas lie on the sand. *Ipanemenses* have continued to cultivate a culture of refined difference, often further subdivided by specific identity groups.

Recent beach development programs have uncovered greater differences among beachgoers. In preparation for the 1992 UN Earth Summit in Rio, another major planning initiative reshaped the southern shoreline. The Rio-Orla program of the early 1990s standardized contemporary streetscape design, regulated commerce, and facilitated transit along the southern beaches. Most notably, the program paved a bike path beside the beachfront sidewalk, limited vehicular parking, and replaced informal trailers selling food and drink with uniform commercial kiosks along the seashore. New rules prohibited the selling of glass bottles and fried foods; drinks sold in plastic cups and sandwiches became the norm. Initial efforts to curtail the activities of informal beach venders proved unsuccessful and were abandoned. Although Burle Marx vocally opposed the bike path and parking restrictions, surveys indicated that most city residents approved of the measures and regarded the new kiosks as aesthetic and sanitary improvements. Nonetheless, the beachfront plans provoked lawsuits by displaced local businesses and protests by neighborhood associations accustomed to a more relaxed, informal beachfront. In response, a leading newspaper solemnly editorialized: "Democracy is good, but not the perversion of democratic practice."[59] Given project delays, most of the planned kiosks were not ready for the June 1992 UN Conference; while awaiting commercial operations, several suffered damage or occupation, reportedly by homeless and unemployed street people.

Also controversial has been the privatization of Rio's beachfronts in the South Zone. A good example is the historic Copacabana Fort; built in 1908–1914 to protect the Brazilian capital, it has long been subject to debates (see photo 5.4) As the fort lost its military importance, schemes to build a five-star hotel on the spectacular oceanfront property sparked widespread local opposition. After the Brazilian Army decided to create a visitor center and museum open to the public in 1986, the State Institute of Cultural Heritage landmarked Copacabana Fort in 1990, only to have the designation partially removed in 1991 to allow for construction of new facilities. In 1994, the site became part of an Environmental Protection Area. In 1996–2000, the fort inaugurated exhibition spaces and commercial partnerships (cafés, restaurants, and shops) open to the public at a small charge. Similar to the "festival marketplaces" common in urban waterfront revitalization, this endeavor illustrates the way entrepreneurial urbanism has involved degrees of privatization within a context of public-private partnership.

Another public-private partnership has involved the construction of new commercial kiosks on the sidewalks of Leme and Copacabana Beaches, originally planned to coincide with the 2007 Pan-American games. As opposed to

Photo 5.3. The Copacabana beachfront sidewalk, showing the commercial kiosks along Avenida Atlântica, along with the *barraca* stands for the sale of drinks and the rental of umbrellas and beach chairs. Photo by the author, 2010.

the cramped, rustic kiosks installed in the early 1990s, the recent mega-kiosks boast a curved, transparent design to highlight the scenic seaside setting (see photo 5.3). Presented as environmentally conscious, the redesign featured wood-paneled seating areas over the sand and occupied less space on the sidewalk. The new kiosks also include such new amenities as subterranean bathrooms, kitchens, and garbage areas to maintain the seaside views. Built by the RIO-TUR agency and leased to corporate chains rather than independent operators, the new operations often feature specific themes—such as Bahian, Arab, or seafood cuisines—and are more formal and expensive than formerly, making low-income residents less likely to patronize them and threatening the livelihood of the current employees. Together with Fort Copacabana, the renovated beachfront indicated a commercial gentrification and incipient social displacement on the beaches of Copacabana and Ipanema. Asked what would happen to him with installation of the new sleek model, one kiosk owner simply answered: "unemployed."

Despite these upscale improvements, the specter of public disorder intensified with a highly publicized riot and robbery by a group of assailants—nicknamed *arrastão*, literally a "dragnet" or "sweep." This phenomenon began on Copacabana Beach in the 1980s, but the most infamous one occurred

Photo 5.4. The entrance to historic Fort Copacabana. Photo by the author, 2009.

on a crowded Ipanema Beach as the subequatorial summer approached on Sunday, October 18, 1992. What apparently began as a gang fight among young people from Rio's working-class suburbs escalated into a collective attack on beachgoers, which quickly provoked a panic among the crowds on the beach. In the resulting stampede, groups of teenagers stole valuables left behind, mugged local residents, vandalized property, and looted businesses. Even the Hippie Fair on the nearby General Osório Square suffered an *arrastão* later that day. The rampage continued all afternoon along Ipanema and Copacabana Beaches. Although isolated incidents had occurred previously, this *arrastão* received widespread attention in the national and international press, which provoked widespread fears of social disorder and class warfare on the beach. To elites of the Zona Sul, it seemed that poor populations of color from the northern suburbs had not only invaded their fashionable beachfront, but had also wreaked havoc along it. In response, a heightened police presence sought to prevent a recurrence of such disturbing events. Christened "Operacão Anti-Arrastão," public-safety efforts featured patrols by municipal guards and military police to secure the beaches and adjacent streets. This security campaign and the Rio-Orla program jointly represented an assertion of governmental control over public space: the southern beachfronts were "branded" as legible landscapes, recognizable by the black-and-white stone sidewalks, uniform kiosks, and intensified policing.

Further concerns about public security led to implementation of the "Shock of Order" (Choque de Ordem) program in 2010, created by the city's Secretary of Public Order (SEOP). Identifying itself as a "regulator and inspector of economic activity and municipal areas," SEOP claims that social "disorder" causes public insecurity and facilitates crime. The Shock of Order program monitors events, regulates economic activities, and enforces rules on the beach, sidewalks, and other public spaces. Implementation began in Ipanema and Leblon during September 2009, and it continued to Leme and Copacabana Beaches in March 2010. The program includes eighty municipal guards, who patrol the shoreline daily, regulate the playing of beach games, and enforce prohibitions on the sale of informally prepared food. The Shock of Order also monitors activities of the venerable beach tents (*barracas*) set up on the sand to sell drinks and rent beach umbrellas and chairs. Authorities have replaced the older informal tents with 175 standardized models, each licensed and numbered, for a fee at specific locations. The city government has justified the program as "combating the small crimes on the principal corridors, contributing decisively to the improvement of our city" and "achieving the return of order to the city."[60]

Although the local press and public generally regard the Shock of Order program as a positive force for organization, uniformity, and general well-being on Rio's beaches, critics see it as an authoritarian measure to appropriate and control public space. Since the program's inception, some residents lament the enforcement of new rules, such as specific hours for soccer, volleyball, and other activities. The program also has removed homeless people from city streets and placed them in city shelters. Sale of home-prepared foods is now prohibited, and venders selling souvenirs must be authorized. Such strict official regulations may eliminate sources of income for many informal venders. Choque de Ordem raises important questions about how truly "public" the beachfronts should be.

To gain insights into people's attitudes toward, and uses of, Rio's beaches, Olivia Arguinzoni and I interviewed forty-seven residents of diverse ages, neighborhoods, races, and social classes in July of 2010 and January of 2011.[61] We began interviews among friends and associates who lived in the Copacabana and Ipanema districts, using a "snowball" method of social networking for about a third of those interviewed. For the other two-thirds, we approached people at random on the seaside boulevards and beaches of these districts to ensure a wide diversity of backgrounds. Respondents ranged from fifteen to eighty years old with a median age of thirty-five. About half lived in affluent southern districts, while the others were generally of modest means and lived in local favelas, the northern districts, or other parts of the metropolis. Half of those interviewed considered themselves people of color and the rest as white. This method ensured a broad cross-section of Carioca residents, workers, and visitors to the beaches.

We asked questions about security in public spaces, the role of the beach in urban life, whether interviewees attended public events there, recent beachfront planning and security initiatives, and whether the beaches were "democratic" by welcoming all types of people, and we asked for suggestions for improving the city beaches. Several patterns quickly became apparent. When queried about favorite public places, the vast majority of respondents mentioned the beaches and seaside avenues. Reasons given for this strong beach preference included the opportunity to stroll and exercise, sunbathe or take in views, swim, and relax out of doors. Most respondents occasionally attended public events on the beach, such as New Year's Eve or Carnival celebrations, musical shows, and cultural events. Frequently, the exuberance Cariocas are known for became apparent. One sixty-year-old domestic worker, a married mother (and grandmother), particularly enjoyed attending the annual LGBTQ parade on Avenida Atlântica, which she felt showed such "marvelous style." Another finding of note was that those we interviewed on the beach tended not to live nearby. Local residents use the beachfront selectively, often avoiding holidays and other times when crowds gather. Affluent residents have more options about where to spend leisure time, including various types of commercial venues.

The people we interviewed heartily agreed that the beach was important for the city's social life. Besides acknowledging its importance for general enjoyment and tourism, many felt that the beach was an excellent place to meet friends without necessarily having to pay. When asked if the beach was a welcoming place for everyone, virtually everyone concurred and acknowledged their enjoyment of watching people from diverse backgrounds. Referring to this social diversity and apparent freedom, one man excitedly exclaimed: "You can't own a beach in Brazil!" With some further questioning, some of those interviewed conceded that different types of people remained largely separate and did not interact significantly. A young man argued: "There are many separations on the beach: gays are separate from heterosexuals and old are separate from young." A middle-aged Afro-Brazilian man, who worked as a security guard nearby but lived in the Zona Norte, claimed that "all of the city's racism and classism is present on the beach." Still, the vast majority of the initial thirty interviewees maintained that the beaches were democratic and accessible to all residents and visitors.

Appreciation for social diversity is mixed with concern over public security and wariness over potential danger. Most respondents admitted that they did not feel entirely safe on the beach, and this concern mounted with age. One older resident recalled that she used to enjoy evenings on the beach with friends and family, but that for many years she has not dared stay out past sundown. An affluent local physician, whose apartment recently had been burglarized, said that while the beach remained a place of enjoyment, he was constantly on the alert for danger. People commonly felt a lack of police protection on the beach. They held city and state governments largely responsible for not taking preventive measures to ensure public safety. On the other hand, an Afro-Brazilian interviewee, who worked as a doorman in the Zona Sul but lived in a working-class suburb, said he felt unsafe because of widespread class and racial intolerance.

With regard to the new kiosks on Copacabana Beach, almost everyone liked them. Many said they found the new structures more attractive, while others found them "modern" and "hygienic," presumably due to the addition of public restrooms. Still, several people did question the formality and expense of the new businesses. Two young women from the nearby Cantagalo favela complained that the new establishments were too expensive. The doorman who claimed that the beach was unsafe because of intolerance also did not like the new kiosks because they were elitist and "took away from the natural beauty of the beach." This topic revealed some underlying issues of social class: less affluent residents and local service employees disliked the higher prices of the food and drink, which catered to a more restricted clientele than before and created a greater sense of beachfront exclusivity.

We also probed more deeply into whether residents considered the beaches to be welcoming and accessible to all types of people. In seventeen additional interviews, randomly selected on Ipanema Beach, nearly all respondents agreed that the beach constituted a democratic space. Although five people admitted that class prejudice was present, even four of these felt that the beach was a democratic space. For example, one person said that although he believed that the beach was a democratic space, "of course the beach is classist, people who live in the Zona Sul don't want others here. They would prefer the beach to be private." Likewise, a municipal guard noted that beachgoers were aware of those with high status and those without it. Both respondents agreed that the beach was democratic, despite the evidence of class bias.

Sensitive issues of race relations on the beach also arose. Most interviewees said that racism, like classism, was not evident. Of the minority who noted the presence of racial bias, most claimed it was of a subtle nature. Perceptions of subtle racism fit into Rio's easy-going beach culture and general ideology of the "racial democracy." For example, occasional claims by respondents that sections of the beach with large proportions of people of color were somehow "ugly" or "dangerous" supported common stereotypes about social status, criminality, and race. Similarly, preferred etiquette about how to act on Ipanema Beach—such as bringing only a few essential personal possessions, renting beach chairs and umbrellas, and buying food and drink from local venders rather than transporting a picnic prepared at home—reflects class biases that often intersect racial lines. Such subtle racism allows people to agree with the notion of a democratic beach, while still adhering to established social structures and biases. In fact, people were more reluctant to talk about race than social class or subcultural groupings. Despite occasional reports of bias on the beach, our respondents overwhelmingly regarded social diversity in positive terms.

These interviews suggest that beaches are complicated public spaces in Rio, as elsewhere. At the seashore, egalitarian aspirations confront social privileges. Still, Rio's residents generally consider their beaches to be democratic: overall, 90 percent of the Cariocas we interviewed agreed with this assertion, often emphasizing public accessibility and social diversity. In a city stratified by class and race, where widespread fears of urban crime prompt increasing fortification of places, Cariocas are struck by the relative freedom of the beachfronts. On the other hand, residents readily admit to the prevalence of social segmentation, class-consciousness, and even subtle racism on the beach. Although the press and public may embrace contemporary governmental discourses of beachfront planning, regulation, and policing, critics lament the erosion of traditional freedoms for informal venders and casual sports. In this sense, debates over Rio's beaches echo concerns in other global cities, where authorities have emphasized public order, community policing, and the removal of informal activities.

Historically, Rio's southern beaches have displayed a complex relationship of public and private spheres, mediated by institutional forces of governmental policy, urban planning, policing, and commercial activity. Public investments in transportation, recreation, and urban services favored the rise of affluent beachfronts in the Zona Sul, although paradoxically these same programs also made Copacabana and Ipanema accessible to the masses. Streetcar lines promoted the early urbanization, while recent subway lines have valorized real estate in the districts; extension of relatively inexpensive bus service has met the most resistance from local elites. Modern urban renewal included the beach widening, improved sewerage systems, and new boulevards of the late 1960s. A new phase of public investment and regulation began with the approach of the 1992 Earth Summit. Despite political controversy, the Rio-Orla program of the early 1990s succeeded in standardizing the beachfront kiosks and strengthening state authority on the southern shoreline.

More recently, the public-private ventures of Fort Copacabana and the sleek new mega-kiosks illustrate a shift to a neoliberal style of commercial revitalization, which favors large companies over small businesses. Similarly, the UNESCO World Heritage designation encouraged upscale renovation of selected beachfronts—the commercial kiosks on the sidewalks, *barraca* tents for venders on the beach, and the heightened security—and thereby favored affluent populations. Renovation of historic stretches of sand and sidewalk calls into question whom and what preservation is for. On the surface, the beachfront of the South Zone still appears to be a paradise of diversity, but with the contemporary tide of neoliberal development non-elites feel less welcome. In my opinion, policy goals should include fidelity to historic designs on the beachfront, along with the provision of adequate public security, while being mindful of the social diversity and accessibility implicit in democratic ideals of Rio's beaches.

ENVIRONMENTAL HERITAGES: PROTECTING CARIOCA LANDSCAPES

While heritage studies traditionally have emphasized cultural and historical concerns, the growing appreciation for urban environments has opened new areas of interdisciplinary study. Environmental heritage complements historic preservation by broadening placemaking beyond architecture and built form to include the urban cultural landscape. Although historic sites have been preserved since the 1930s, cultural environments gained similar protections only in the late twentieth century, given public pressure to save Rio's scenic locations from development. Over time, urban environmental activism has taken various forms in Rio, ranging from early elite-led conservationism to more community-based movements for environmental justice. Each approach favors a particular discourse, but they are broadly complementary for many environmentalist causes. Yet there are conflicts that seem irreconcilable, particularly those involving the expansion of favelas on forest lands. The case of the Botanical Garden and the Horto community, for example, has resisted resolution for decades, although a compromise aimed at reconciling the rights of both sides would appear beneficial to all concerned. Yet the continued impasse suggests that a narrow conservationist perspective proves inadequate to address the multiple uses and users of a forest preserve.

The Tijuca National Park is anything but a natural landscape, given its history of destruction, reforestation, and contemporary pressures from various sources. Listing of the TNP on the National Register in 1967 reflected an environmental conservationism in Rio, followed by IPHAN's landmarking to protect the city's historic hills and mountains in 1973. The UNESCO World Heritage site Carioca Landscapes between the Mountain and the Sea further expands the collective memory to encompass the heritages of urban cultural landscapes. While environmental conservation has largely succeeded at protecting Rio's natural landmarks, it has been less successful at incorporating the human element in equitable terms. The previous chapter shows how environmentalism has become an important rallying point for favela resilience, while this chapter indicates the way in which environmental activism has expanded beyond elite-led conservation of natural landmarks to include community-based activism. The protests of the AHOMAR and its many allies, for example, have attempted to protect fishing livelihoods and their environments against the petrochemical complex in Guanabara Bay. In this case, environmental heritage does not represent merely a scenic view but also a productive resource for working people and an important context of human health and well-being. As such, the great bay's continuing pollution has become a matter of life and death, and is well worth a socially just environmental resolution.

Rio's famous beachfronts are also more than scenic panoramas, as they provide public space for exercise and recreation, commerce, political activity, and social interaction. Although Rio's historic beaches have long been viewed as "democratic spaces," where social diversity and tolerance for difference prevails, the state has responded to perceived threats of public disorder and insecurity by redesigning the iconic beachfronts, installing heightened security measures, and commodifying the beach-going experience. At Copacabana and Ipanema Beaches, many visitors appreciate the heightened security, but many local residents, young people, and informal vendors express concerns about the high prices and increased regulation of the space. While the beaches attract socially diverse clienteles, the crowds are segmented by identities and unequal in racial and social status. Historic preservation programs, while important for the sense of place and identity, should be mindful of commercial upgrading that reduces social diversity. Rio's experience shows that preservation of historic urbanism, nature, and placemaking can be highly beneficial, but it requires special attention to socioeconomic equity and access.

NOTES

1. Maria Graham, *Journal of a Voyage to Brazil; and Residence there during part of the Years 1821, 1822, 1823* (London: Longman, Hurst, Rees, Orme, Brown and Green, 1824), 159.

2. Editorial, *O Jornal do Brasil,* June 27, 1973.

3. Juan Mauricio Rugendas [Johann Moritz Rugendas], *Viaje pintoresco a través del Brasil* (Buenos Aires: Emecé Editores, 1947); Ruy Castro, *Rio de Janeiro: Carnival under Fire* (New York: Bloomsbury, 2003), 13.

4. United Nations, "The Rio Declaration on Environment and Development" (New York: United Nations Documentation Center, 1992), 2.

5. World Commission on Environment and Development, *Our Common Future* (Oxford University Press, 1987); and Stephen M. Wheeler and Timothy Beatley, *The Sustainable Urban Development Reader* (London and New York: Routledge, 2006), 58–65.

6. Brian J. Godfrey, "Urban Sustainability: Teaching at the Interface of Environmental and Urban Studies," *Ometeca: Science and Humanities* 14–15, special issue "Educating for Ecological Sustainability," February 2010, 274–93.

7. United Nations (UN), "The Earth Summit and Agenda 21," New York, United Nations Documentation Center, 1992, 3.

8. United Cities and Local Governments (UCLG), Committee on Culture, *Agenda 21 for Culture*, 2008; *Culture: Fourth Pillar of Cultural Development*, 2014; *Culture, Climate Change and Sustainable Development*, 2016; and *Culture in the Sustainable Development Goals: A Guide for Local Action*, 2018, http://www.agenda21culture.net/.

9. Denis E. Cosgrove, *Social Formation and Symbolic Landscape* (University of Wisconsin Press, 1998); and Andrew Sluyter, *Colonialism and Landscape: Postcolonial Theory and Applications* (Lanham, MD: Rowman & Littlefield, 2001).

10. World Heritage List, "Rio de Janeiro: Carioca Landscapes between the Mountain and the Sea," http://whc.unesco.org/en/list/1100; and Advisory Body Evaluation (ICOMOS), "Rio de Janeiro (Brazil), No. 1100rev," March 14, 2012, World Heritage List, http://whc.unesco.org/en/list/1100/.

11. Advisory Body Evaluation (ICOMOS), "Rio de Janeiro (Brazil), No. 1100rev."

12. IPHAN, *Site Management Plan, Rio de Janeiro: Carioca Landscapes between the Mountain and the Sea*, February 2014.

13. World Heritage List, "Rio de Janeiro, Carioca Landscapes."

14. See, for instance, Maurício de A. Abreu, *Evolução do Rio de Janeiro* (Rio de Janeiro: IPP/Instituto Municipal de Urbanismo Pereira Passos, 4.a Edição, 2006).

15. Kathryn Hochstetler and Margaret E. Keck, *Greening Brazil: Environmental Activism in State and Society* (Duke University Press, 2007).

16. "Forest Park," Official Guide to Portland, www.travelportland.com › attractions › forest-park; *Trilhas: Parque Nacional da Tijuca* (Rio de Janeiro: Instituto Terra Brasil, 2006); Instituto Brasileiro de Geografia e Estatística (IBGE), Cidades@, https://cidades.ibge.gov.br.

17. Arquivo Notonha Santos, "Horto Florestal: Conjunto Paisagístico" (Rio de Janeiro, RJ), IPHAN Archives (Processo 0633-T-61) Rio de Janeiro, http://portal.iphan.gov.br/ans/inicial.htm.

18. Jardim Botânico do Rio de Janeiro, "Equipe de Pesquisa," retrieved Aug. 6, 2020, http://www.jbrj.gov.br; and Advisory Body Evaluation (ICOMOS), "Rio de Janeiro (Brazil), No. 1100rev."

19. Arquivo Notonha Santos, "Horto Florestal: Conjunto Paisagístico" (Rio de Janeiro, RJ), IPHAN Archives, (Processo 0633-T-61) Rio de Janeiro, http://portal.iphan.gov.br/ans/inicial.htm.

20. Laura Olivieri Carneiro de Souza, *Horto Florestal: um lugar de memória da cidade do Rio de Janeiro—A construção do Museu do Horto e seu correspondente projeto social de memória.* (PhD diss. in history, Pontífica Universidade Católica, Rio de Janeiro, 2012).

21. Marcelo Moreira, Of. 193, Proc. 03/300 399, Tijuca National Park and Forest (IPHAN Process 0762-T-65), Arquivo Noronha Santos, IPHAN Archives, Rio de Janeiro.

22. Olínio Gomes Paschoal Coelho, Memo T.02/65, Tijuca National Park and Forest (IPHAN Process 0762-T-65), Arquivo Noronha Santos, IPHAN Archives, Rio de Janeiro.

23. Alceo Magnanini, Of. No. 205, Dec. 22, 1965; and Paulo Thadim Barreto, Chefe da Seção de Arte, report to the IPHAN Director, Jan. 28, 1966, Tijuca National Park and Forest (IPHAN Process 0762-T-65), Arquivo Noronha Santos, IPHAN Archives, Rio de Janeiro.

24. Councilor Gilberto Ferrez, April 19, 1966, Tijuca National Park and Forest (IPHAN Process 0762-T-65), Arquivo Noronha Santos, IPHAN Archives, Rio de Janeiro.

25. Renaming and historic preservation of the Tijuca National Park in 1967 (Process 0762-T-65), landmarked April 27, 1967, IPHAN, http://www.iphan.gov.br/.

26. Gilberto Ferrez, "Os Morros Tombados," *O Jornal do Brasil*, Rio de Janeiro, June 27, 1973.

27. Renato Soeiro, IPHAN Director, Of. No. 1725, July 19, 1973, to the governor of the state of Guanabara; and IPHAN (Instituto do Patrimônio Histórico e Artístico do Brasil), Livro Arqueológico, Etnográfico e Paisagístico, Processo 869-T-73, Inscrição 055, Aug. 8, 1973.

28. Eliane Velloso, president of the Neighborhood Association of Gávea (AMAGA-VEA), letter to the IPHAN Advisory Council, April 28, 1987, Tijuca National Park and Forest (IPHAN Process 0762-T-65), Arquivo Noronha Santos, IPHAN Archives, Rio de Janeiro.

29. IPHAN (Instituto do Patrimônio Histórico e Artístico do Brasil), Livro Arqueológico, Etnográfico e Paisagístico, Inscrição 55, Processo 0869-T-73 (Rio: Arquivo Noronho Santos).

30. Hattie Hartman, "Seeds of Change: Urban Transformation in Brazil," *Architectural Design* 86, 3 (May 2016).

31. Mark Holston, "Statue of Christ the Redeemer," *Americas* (English edition), 60, 3 (May/June 2008): 613.

32. Holston, "Statue of Christ the Redeemer," 613.

33. Larry Rohter, "Rio Is Easing the Way to Corcovado's Summit," *New York Times*, September 23, 2001; and "Christ the Redeemer," *Time*, Oct. 26, 1931.

34. Emerson Giumbelli, "A modernidade do Cristo Redentor," *Dados* (Rio de Janeiro) 51, 1 (2008), https://doi.org/10.1590/S0011-52582008000100003.

35. Victor Coelho, *Baía de Guanabara: Uma História de Agressão Ambiental* (Rio de Janeiro: Casa da Palavra, 2007); Eliane Canedo de Freitas Pinheiro, *Baía de Guanabara: Biografia de uma Paisagem* (Rio de Janeiro: Andrea Jakobsson Estúdio, 2005).

36. Melville, *White-Jacket; or, The World in a Man-of-War*; and Coelho, *Baía de Guanabara*, 19.

37. Brian J. Godfrey, "Urban Renewal, *Favelas*, and Guanabara Bay: Environmental Justice and Sustainability in Rio de Janeiro," in *Sustainability: A Global Urban Context*, ed. Igor Vojnovic (Michigan State University Press, 2013), 359–86.

38. IPHAN, Livro de Belas Artes, Inscrição 102, May 24, 1938; and Livro Histórico, Inscrição 037, May 24, 1938—N° Processo 0101-T-38, http://portal.iphan.gov.br/ans/, accessed Aug. 11, 2016.

39. Carmen L. Oliveira, *Rare and Commonplace Flowers: The Story of Elizabeth Bishop and Lota de Macedo Soares*, trans. Neil K. Besner (Rutgers University Press, 2002).

40. "Salvemos o Rio," *Estado de São Paulo*, May 9, 1973.

41. "Turismo e Ostracismo," *Jornal do Brasil*, Rio de Janeiro, May 11, 1973.

42. "Um prédio como este, no alto do Pão de Açúcar? Alguns Cariocas são contra," *Jornal da Tarde*, São Paulo, May 3, 1973; "Pão de Açúcar: As Quatro Críticas ao Projeto," *Jornal da Tarde*, São Paulo, May 9, 1973.

43. Lygia Martins Costa, Chefe da Seção de Arte, IPHAN, Info. no. 134, June 7, 1973.

44. IPHAN (Instituto do Patrimônio Histórico e Artístico do Brasil), Livro Arqueológico, Etnográfico e Paisagístico, Processo 869-T-73, Inscrição 055, Aug. 8, 1973.

45. Information Habitat, *The NGO Alternative Treaties from the Global Forum at Rio de Janeiro*, 1992. Despite the "alternative treaty," Guanabara Bay still does not figure in the list of 127 natural and cultural landscapes for Rio de Janeiro, http://www.iphan.gov.br/.

46. Instituto da Baía de Guanabara, http://www.portalbaiadeguanabara.com.br/sitenovo/.

47. Coelho, *Baía de Guanabara*, 68–70.

48. Coelho, *Baía de Guanabara*, 62–68; Pinheiro, *Baía de Guanabara*, 263.

49. Ken Belson, "Sailors on Guanabara Bay Are Adept at Dodging Debris and Skirting Sewage," *New York Times*, Aug. 2, 2016.

50. Raine Robichaud, "Boat Ride for a Living Guanabara Bay Calls Attention to Defining Element of Rio's Iconic Landscape," RioOnWatch, Aug. 10, 2017.

51. This material on Copacabana Beach first appeared in an article that I coauthored with a former student and research assistant, Olivia M. Arguinzoni. We thank the American Geographical Society for allowing us to reprint passages from "Regulating Public Space on the Beachfronts of Rio de Janeiro." *Geographical Review* 102, 1 (Jan. 2012): 17–34.

52. James Freeman, "Democracy and Danger on the Beach: Class Relations and Public Space in Rio de Janeiro," *Space and Culture: International Journal of Social Spaces* 5, 1 (2002): 9–28; and "Great, Good, and Divided: The Politics of Public Space in Rio de Janeiro," *Journal of Urban Affairs* 30, 5 (2008): 529–56.

53. Patricia Farias, *Pegando uma Cor na Praia: Relações Raciais e Classificação de Cor na Cidade do Rio de Janeiro* (Rio de Janeiro: Coleção Biblioteca Carioca, 2006).

54. Setha Low, *On the Plaza: The Politics of Public Space and Culture* (University of Texas Press, 2000), 183.

55. C. Pereira, "Copacabana: Um Passeio no Tempo / A Stroll in Time" (Rio de Janeiro: Prefeitura da Cidade, 2007), 5.

56. Joaquim Ferreira dos Santos, *Feliz 1958, O Ano Que Não Devia Acabar* (Editora Record, 1998); and B. Carvalho, "Mapping the Urbanized Beaches of Rio de Janeiro: Modernization, Modernity and Everyday Life," *Journal of Latin American Cultural Studies: Travesia* 16, 3 (2007): 325–39.

57. Advisory Body Evaluation (ICOMOS), "Rio de Janeiro (Brazil), No. 1100rev," March 14, 2012, World Heritage List, http://whc.unesco.org/en/list/1100/.

58. J. F. Santos, "Gente Boa," *O Globo*, July 29, 2000, 5.

59. *Jornal do Brasil*, "Confusão na Orla," June 17, 1991; and "A Polêmica cerca Rio-Orla," Aug. 23, 1991.

60. City of Rio de Janeiro, "Choque de Ordem," posted on September 16, 2009, at http://www.rio.rj.gov.br/web/guest/exibeconteudo?article-id=87137.

61. Brian J. Godfrey and Olivia M. Arguinzoni, "Regulating Public Space on the Beachfronts of Rio de Janeiro," *Geographical Review* 102, 1 (Jan. 2012): 17–34.

Chapter 6

Remembering Rio
The Politics of Memory

> After all, the act of remembering is always in and of the present, while its referent is of the past and thus absent. Inevitably, every act of memory carries with it a dimension of betrayal, forgetting, and absence.
>
> —Andreas Huyssen, 2003[1]

Long imagined as the "land of the future," Brazil has belatedly experienced a contemporary fascination with its collective memory and heritage.[2] Brazilian cities now actively promote historic landmarks and districts, monuments and memorials, and parks and nature preserves as strategies of placemaking—the social, spatial, and symbolic processes that create distinctive places. Rio de Janeiro has been a leader in this trend because of its long-term role as national capital, its large concentration of historic sites, and its ongoing economic restructuring. Within the country's historical and political contexts, processes of selective remembrance (and forgetting) have sculpted the urban landscapes that give Rio its sense of place. The right to remember—in my view, a logical correlate of the right to the city—now shapes social identities, community profiles, and popular cultures in this spectacular, if highly stratified, city. Heritage designation has become another battleground for human rights.

This book maintains that collective memory serves present-day purposes: heritage programs alternately maintain or challenge the status quo, depending on their respective social standings, narratives, and political alliances. In Brazil, innovative legislation to recognize historic sites and artistic works of national importance started in the 1930s. Over time, historic placemaking has gained legitimacy at national, state, and local levels. At times, the pressures of urban development trumped landmark protection—a fact that underscores the centrality of political power in the debates and planning processes involved in historic preservation, even if behind-the-scenes struggles over heritage sites are hidden from public view. While the literature on historic preservation often emphasizes the aesthetics of authenticity or the roles of influential leaders and stakeholders in reclaiming a built heritage, I suggest that political-economic relations also help to explain a city's historic places.[3] I ask: Whose city has been preserved, by whom, and what have been the consequences for Rio de Janeiro?

Although Brazilians now largely agree that historic places should be preserved for future generations, the success of any preservation project depends on the appeal of favored narratives and images. The National Heritage Institute (IPHAN is its Portuguese acronym), the federal agency charged with protecting historic sites and artistic works, has suggested that it "does not preserve the past, but works to make it part of the future."[4] But whose conceptions of the past should prevail? Conflicts occur as different institutions and interest groups lay claim to places of memory. Historic placemaking is seldom if ever politically neutral, since it inevitably raises questions about whose history is to be remembered and whose heritage is to be conserved. Contemporary cultural lenses filter any remembrance of the past, which makes assertions of authenticity problematic. Given the broad sweep of history, the search for a pure, authentic past proves elusive. A historic district celebrates an architectural style, a local social history, a particular memory—but not others. As we preserve a built heritage, we simultaneously erase other legacies of the past. Thus, historic preservation of cities reinvents them in terms of their cultural meanings, socioeconomic functions, and political symbolism. Diverse narratives have repeatedly "reinvented" Rio, promoted by memory brokers of elite society, while marginalized communities have increasingly responded with counter-narratives to reclaim their heritage, promote social change, and enhance environmental resilience. As David Harvey suggests, "Struggles over representation are, as a consequence, as fiercely fought and as fundamental to the activities of place construction as bricks and mortar."[5]

For several decades after its establishment in the late 1930s, the National Heritage Institute (initially, "Service") was the main symbolic banker for successive federal governments intent on consolidating their power and legitimizing their authority. Sites listed on the national registry books (Livros do Tombo) provided the cultural capital for nationalist state-building regimes. Heritage designations were concentrated in the most important former colonial cities, most notably Rio de Janeiro and Salvador da Bahia, along with the colonial mining towns of Minas Gerais. But the rise of neoliberalism since the 1970s has altered power relations somewhat in favor of corporate interests, which now renovate and brand historic centers in partnership with city governments. Furthermore, with the demise of the military-authoritarian regime in 1985 and the subsequent rise of democratic politics and economic liberalization in Brazil, grassroots social movements and neighborhood associations have also promoted memory of distinctive local identities. These trends explain how and why particular heritages—including their social, racial, and environmental identities—become anchored in places through governmental regulation, manipulated by commercial purposes, and contested by communities struggling for governmental recognition, infrastructures, and services.

Instead of questioning placemaking narratives in terms of their historical accuracy, I interrogate them as projects of social promotion and political power. This approach broadens and differentiates the array of heritage projects: official historic sites most often rebrand the city according to a glorious past, while local grassroots organizations adopt counter-memories that strive for a more inclusive society with more opportunity and a better quality of life. Although this book could not reasonably cover more than a representative sample of the preservation projects in Rio, I analyze selective cases with regard to three main types of memory. First, historic districts may celebrate the city's past elites and important institutions, as does November 15th Square for the Cultural Corridor program in the city center. Second, grassroots sites of counter-memory strive for a more inclusive society, such as the African Heritage Circuit and the favelas' community museums. Third, Rio has promoted environmental heritage through the listing of landscapes on both the IPHAN National Registers and the UNESCO World Heritage program, along with protective legislation.

Early historic preservation in Brazil, beginning in the late 1930s, was largely about the ruling class and dominant institutions. Heritage designations for the most part recalled colonial, imperial, and early republican powers. Most of the 1,362 registry listings commemorate historic sites from before the turn of the twentieth century—historic churches, palaces and mansions, public buildings, fortifications, and public squares.[6] Rio's Cultural Corridor also stressed social elites and powerful institutions from these eras, but the political-economic context of the program had changed by the time of its onset circa 1980. As urban planning shifted gears to focus on historic sites and quality of life, the Cultural Corridor represented a heritage-based revitalization program to promote tourism, the arts, and commercial upgrading. As the program got underway in the early 1980s, it reflected the interests of entrepreneurial regimes that rebranded the city center as a place of heritage and cultural capital.

The Cultural Corridor's favored historical styles refer primarily to the "imperial" (1808–1889) or "old republican" (1889–1930) periods. Mandating specific styles from these eras, planners directed the historic center's renovation in an innovative, if top-down fashion: while property owners and commercial interests financed the historically themed building renovation (largely reimbursed by tax abatements), behind the refurbished built heritage was a public-private revitalization program, designed to revive the business sector and social status of the city center. The built heritage largely highlights the collective memory of institutional power and elite society. The Imperial Palace, the Municipal Theater, the National Library, the Fine Arts Museum, the old cathedral of Our Lady of Mount Carmel, innumerable ornate colonial churches, and venerable structures of all kinds grace Rio's historic center. While often depicted as a democratic and participatory form of historic preservation, the Planning Department cleverly selected and imposed particular themes for each of four historic districts of the Cultural Corridor. This project has experienced notable upgrading of the November 15th Square, Cinelândia, and Lapa districts, while the São Francisco and SAARA districts remain unevenly affected.

The Cultural Corridor fits what Boyer has called the "city of collective memory," which lost its earlier historic coherence and became "a patchwork of incongruous leftover pieces alongside a set of artfully designed compositions."[7] As the political-economic contexts of historic sites have changed, however, revitalization campaigns have renovated and repurposed them. The conservation of dilapidated buildings, social inclusion of low-income residents, public safety, and economic fortunes remain uneven, although the results have been impressive in places like the Imperial Palace, restored to its circa–1818 appearance. Still, the collaboration of municipal, state, and federal authorities in coordinating their land-use, transportation, and historic preservation policies, along with public-private partnerships and tax incentives for building renovation, has largely succeeded in renewing the urban core's sense of place and reversing its general decline. A continuing task for the future will be to provide for more socially inclusive policy and representation in the Cultural Corridor.

The rediscovery of the Valongo Slave Wharf, along with other related heritage sites, reactivated the memory of what was once, and is now increasingly again, called "Little Africa." The sudden rediscovery of Rio's old slave wharf in early 2011, and subsequent archeological dig, sent shock waves through the city and the world. The Cemetery of New Blacks had been rediscovered in 1996, but it was on private property and less visible to the general public. The slave wharf, on the other hand, became the subject of intense media attention. In a city with a preponderance of historic monuments dedicated to wealthy, white, male leaders, people of color had been largely excluded. The Valongo site dramatically contested that tendency. Acknowledging the history of enslaved Africans and their heritage in Rio by showing what both royal and republican regimes had crushed and ignored, rather than burying and hiding the tragic past, was the diametrical opposite of previous practices.

Despite initial resistance from the city's port renewal program, the broad political efforts of community activists, Afro-descendants, and public intellectuals prevailed in saving and memorializing Valongo Wharf. Former mayor Eduardo Paes signaled accommodation when he endorsed the project and even called it "Rio's Roman ruins." The site became a UNESCO World Heritage site in 2017.[8] One of the lessons here is that in today's entrepreneurial city of Rio, the politics of memory turn on the most marketable branding campaigns with broad shareholder support. While the cultural reinvention of Little Africa has affirmed Afro-Brazilian identities, contemporary place branding constitutes less of a sociocultural rupture for civil rights than an accommodation to prevailing neoliberal policies of urban revitalization, heritage tourism, and multiculturalism. While the visibility of the African Heritage Circuit has been beneficial in promoting awareness of the history of slavery and racial diversity, further political efforts will be needed to achieve social equality.

Another remarkable case of counter-memory is the contemporary celebration of community heritage in Rio's favelas, which in my view serves as a form of resistance to displacement and a promotion of human rights. Despite their continuing place stigma and problems of organized crime in favelas, residents struggle to retain their rights to housing, security, and remembrance. There has been a contemporary explosion of interest in favela heritage, as shown in the many community open-air museums, walking tours, political activity, and historical documentation. In other words, *favelados* increasingly now speak for themselves. Local activists and their supporters have created their own historical and political narratives, often at odds with the largely negative images of the news media and authorities. In fact, the entrepreneurial potential of Favela Chic raises issues of cultural commodification and social class polarization, especially in conjunction with the beginnings of gentrification in better situated communities. The collective memory and built heritage of favelas—their urban landscapes of struggle—often display beneficial, if often ignored or overlooked, aspects of sustainable urbanism in Rio. In terms of their livable scales, density, and walkability, favelas can even be reimagined as a form of "New Urbanism."

Not surprisingly, tourism has spawned a powerful "growth machine" of governmental agencies, merchants, developers, journalists, hotels, and others. Yet grassroots activism, energized by oppositional counter-memory, has also informed public affairs. The thousands of residents who faced displacement from their homes to make way for Olympic facilities in 2016, for example, were vocal in their opposition. Environmentalists protested the pollution of

Guanabara Bay, which first became an international cause célèbre during the 1992 Earth Summit. The long-stalled cleanup efforts sparked demonstrations by local fishing groups and environmentalists before the 2016 Olympics, as concerns mounted about aquatic events in the polluted bay. As a result, this book extends the study of historic preservation and collective memory to include urban environmental heritages. With the growth of an environmentalist consciousness, the battle has been to recognize the city's strong connections to nature and to protect the natural landmarks and cultural landscapes.

Given how various interest groups have sliced apart Rio's heritages, acknowledgement of the urban environment's importance helps to focus on a larger common goal. While the city's environs have been contested like built forms, of course, there is still the prospect of finding a cohesive whole in city-nature relations. Although historic sites downtown have been preserved since the late 1930s, only in the late twentieth century did the city's environments gain protection, as a result of mounting public pressure to save scenic locations from development. Taking the 2012 UNESCO World Heritage site Rio de Janeiro: Carioca Landscapes between the Mountain and the Sea as a point of departure, I examine its origins, components, and impacts of environmental conservation and environmental-justice movements in Rio. Rio's environmental heritages have become arenas for public debate and policy formulation that engage the city's diverse stakeholders. The city illustrates the importance of environmentalism as a form of collective memory and a source of identity, thereby linking the city, nature, and sense of place.

The rise of elite-led environmental conservation efforts gained momentum in the 1960s, particularly by listing environmental landmarks on the National Register as a strategy for environmental protection. On the other hand, grassroots movements for environmental justice proliferated with democratization in the 1980s. While the two approaches are often compatible, sometimes the conservationist quest for a pristine nature conflicts with the social-justice embrace of human betterment—such as resolving land-tenure conflicts for favelas in forested areas, or cleaning up pollution in low-income neighborhoods. While there are notable problems still to be effectively addressed, such as the pollution of Guanabara Bay and the provision of land titles for favelas, generally Rio has made steady improvements over the years in the protection of its spectacular site. Although much remains to be done, the historical record indicates long-term progress in reconciling economic development, environmental conservation, and public access to Rio's mountains, hills, and seashores.

As Rio's diverse heritages have become sites of struggle over human rights, subject to both official and grassroots efforts to shape the historic narratives, the broadening of political participation challenges the city's continuing inequalities. Extending the right to remember to new groups inevitably involves a degree of conflict and contestation, but it also raises new possibilities for collaboration and understanding. Historical memory serves as a surrogate for social status and political power: official, state-sponsored historic preservation first arose in the early twentieth century as a patrimonial project to centralize federal power and build nationalism. Contemporary political pressures to expand the right to remember have steadily incorporated novel social, ethnic, and environmental heritages, while the entrepreneurial city encourages place branding in promotional campaigns. Amid all this social diversity, collective memory may serve as a great equalizer. Given the city's democratic aspirations, expansion of the right to remember raises the possibility of a more inclusive, egalitarian, and compassionate Rio de Janeiro.

NOTES

1. Andreas Huyssen, *Present Pasts: Urban Palimpsests and the Politics of Memory* (Stanford University Press, 2003), 3–4.
2. Stefan Zweig, *Brazil: A Land of the Future* (Riverside CA: Ariadne Press, 2000).
3. Diane Barthel, *Historic Preservation: Collective Memory and Historic Identity* (Rutgers University Press, 1996), 152.
4. IPHAN, *Normatização de Cidades Históricas: Orientações para a elaboração de diretrizes e Normas de Preservação para áreas urbanas tombadas*, ed. Anna Finger and Yole Medeiros (Brasília: Ministério da Cultura, 2011), 6.
5. David Harvey, "From Space to Place and Back Again: Reflections on the Condition of Postmodernity," in *Mapping the Futures: Local Cultures, Global Change*, ed. J. Bird, B. Curtis, T. Putnam, G. Robertson, and L. Tickner (London: Routledge, 1993), 23.
6. IPHAN, *Bens móveis e imóveis inscritos nos Livros do Tombo do Instituto do Patrimônio Histórico e Artístico Nacional* (RJ: IPHAN/COPEDOC, 2009); and http://www.iphan.gov.br/.
7. M. Christine Boyer, *The City of Collective Memory: Its Historical Imagery and Architectural Entertainments* (Cambridge, MA: MIT Press, 1994), 9–11.
8. International Committee on Monuments and Sites (ICOMOS), "Valongo Wharf (Brazil)," *World Heritage List* (UNESCO, March 10, 2017), 337, http://whc.unesco.org/en/list/1548/documents/.

Bibliography

Abreu, Mauricio de Almeida. *Evolução Urbana do Rio de Janeiro*. Rio de Janeiro: IPLANRIO/ZAHAR, 1987.
———. *Geografia Histórica do Rio de Janeiro (1502–1700)*. 2 Vols. Rio de Janeiro: Andrea Jakobsson Estúdio & Prefeitura do Rio de Janeiro, 2010.
———. "Reconstruindo uma história esquecida: Origem e expansão das favelas do Rio de Janeiro." *Revista Espaço & Debates* 37 (1994): 34–46.
———. "Sobre a Memória das Cidades." *Revista da Facultade de Letras—Geografia*, Porto, XIV, 1 (1998): 77–97.
African Origins Project. *Voyages: Trans-Atlantic Slave Trade Database*. Emory University. http://www.slavevoyages.org (accessed September 13, 2020).
Alencar, Emanuel. *Baía de Guanabara: Descaso e Resistência*. Rio de Janeiro: Fundação Heinrich Bôll/Mórula, 2016.
Amaral, Bráz Hermenegildo do and Jean-Baptiste Debret. "Valongo, a Notorious Slave Market." In *The Rio de Janeiro Reader: History, Culture, Politics*, edited by Daryle Williams, Amy Chazkel, and Paulo Knauss, 42. Durham, NC: Duke University Press, 2016.
Anjos, Ana Maria de la Merced, and Júlio Medeiros da Silva. *Saga dos Pretos Novos*. Rio de Janeiro: Prefeitura do Rio de Janeiro, 2015.
Araújo, Ana Lucia. *Shadows of the Slave Past: Memory, Heritage, Slavery*. New York: Routledge, 2016.
Arquivo da Cidade. "Memória da Destruição: Rio-Uma História que se Perdeu." Program of the exhibition from December 17, 2001 to February 15, 2002, Rio de Janeiro.
Assefa, Haimy [Director]. "Providência: 115 Anos de Luta." Produced by RioOnWatch, posted on August 10, 2012. https://www.youtube.com/watch?v=it=bdOXxq14 (accessed April 15, 2020).
Associated Press. "Unearthing of Rio Slave Port Sparks Debate Over Black Space." *New York Times*, December 28, 2015.
Attoh, Kafui A. "What Kind of Right Is the Right to the City?" *Progress in Human Geography* 35, 5 (2011): 669–85.

Bandeira, Olivia. "Derrubada da Perimetral Reformulará Sistema Viário do Centro do Rio." *Infraestrutura Urbana*, June 2012.
Barbassa, Julia. "Brazil's Black History, Uncovered." *Americas Quarterly* 11, 1 (2018). https://www.americasquarterly.org/fulltextarticle/brazils-black-history-uncovered/ (accessed September 13, 2020).
Barcellos, Caco. *Abusado—the Owner of Morro Dona Marta.* Rio de Janeiro: Record, 2003.
Barreto, Afonso Henriques de Lima. *Revista Careta*, August 28, 1920. Quoted in exhibition "O Paço, a Praça e o Morro." Paço Imperial, Rio de Janeiro, June 23–August 28, 2016.
Barthel, Diane. *Historic Preservation: Collective Memory and Historical Identity.* New Brunswick, NJ: Rutgers University Press, 1996.
Belson, Ken. "Sailors on Guanabara Bay Are Adept at Dodging Debris and Skirting Sewage." *New York Times*, August 2, 2016.
Bentes, Ivana. "The Sertão and the Favela in Contemporay Brazilian Film." In *The New Brazilian Cinema*, edited by Lúcia Nagib. New York: I. B. Tauris/The Center for Brazilian Studies, University of Oxford, 2003, 121–37.
Bezerra, Kátia da Costa. *Postcards from Rio Favelas and the Contested Geographies of Citizenship.* New York: Fordham University Press, 2017. Kindle edition.
Bin, Daniel. "Rio de Janeiro's Olympic Dispossessions." *Journal of Urban Affairs*, 39 no. 7 (2017): 924–38.
Bishop, Elizabeth. *The Complete Poems, 1927–1979.* New York: Farrar, Straus, Giroux, 1983.
Boyer, M. Christine. *The City of Collective Memory: Its Historical Imagery and Architectural Entertainments.* Cambridge, MA: MIT Press, 1994.
Boym, Svetlana. "Nostalgia and Its Discontents." In *The Collective Memory Reader*, edited by J. K. Olick, V. Vinitzky-Seroussi, and D. Levy, 452–57. Oxford and New York: Oxford University Press, 2011.
Braga, Damião. "Uma Palavra da Comunidade Quilombola Pedra do Sal." Facebook, January 18, 2017. https://www.facebook.com/notes/quilombo-pedra-do-sal/uma-palavra-da-comunidade-quilombola-pedra-do-sal/757175007770605/ (accessed September 13, 2020).
Bueno, Alexei, Augusto da Silva Teles, and Lauro Calvacanti. *O Patrimonio Construído: As 100 Mais Belas Edificações do Brasil.* São Paulo: Editora Capivara, 2002.
Bueno, Eduardo. *Náufragos, Traficantes e Degredados: As Primeiras Expedições ao Brasil, 1500–1531.* Editora Objetiva, 1998.
Bullard, Robert D. *Dumping in Dixie: Race, Class, and Environmental Quality.* New York: Westview Press, 2008.
Burns, E. Bradford. *A History of Brazil.* Second edition. New York: Columbia University Press, 1980, 317.
"Cabeça de Avestruz." *Jornal do Brasil*, February 13, 1998, 8.
Caldeira, Teresa P. R. "From Modernism to Neoliberalism in São Paulo." In *Other Cities, Other Worlds: Urban Imaginaries in a Globalizating Age*, edited by Andreas Huyssen, 51–78. Durham, NC: Duke University Press, 2008.

Calvino, Italo. *Invisible Cities.* New York: Harcourt, 1974.
Caminha, Pero Vaz de. "Letter to King Manuel." In *The Voyage of Pedro Alves Cabral to Brazil and India*, edited by William B. Granlee, 3–33. London: Hakluyt Society, 1938.
Cardoso, José Luis. "The Transfer of the Court to Brazil, 200 Years Afterwards." *E-Journal of Portuguese History* 7, 1 (Summer 2009). http://www.brown.edu/Departments/Portuguese_Brazilian_Studies/ejph/index.html (accessed September 13, 2020).
Carneiro, Julia. "Brazil's Hidden Slavery Past Uncovered at Valongo Wharf." BBC Brasil. Rio de Janeiro, December 25, 2014.
Casa Pública. "Museu do Ontem." https://apublica.org/museu-do-ontem/ (accessed September 13, 2020).
Castriota, Leonardo. "Living in World Heritage Site: Preservation Policies and Local History in Ouro Preto, Brazil." *Traditional Dwellings and Settlements Review: Journal for the International Association for the Study of Traditional Environments* 10, 2 (1999): 7–19.
Castro, Ruy. *Rio de Janeiro: Carnival under Fire.* New York: Bloomsbury, 2003.
Cavalcanti, Lauro. "1982 a 1992: Dez Anos na História Recente do Paço Imperial." In *Paço Imperial*, edited by Sergio Pagano, Heloísa Buarque de Hollanda, and Lauro Cavalcante, 14–27. Rio de Janeiro: Sextante Artes, 1999.
———. "Vinte Anos do Paço Imperial como Centro Cultural do IPHAN." In *Paço Imperial/Centro Cultural do IPHAN*, edited by Lauro Cavalcante, 11–16. Rio de Janeiro: MNC/IPHAN, 2005.
Cavalcanti, Nireu. *O Rio de Janeiro Setecentista: A Vida e a Construcção da Cidade, da Invasão Francesa até a Chegada da Corte.* Rio de Janeiro: Jorge Zahar Editores, 2004.
———. *Rio de Janeiro: Centro Historico, 1808–1998.* Rio de Janeiro: Dresdner Bank Brasil, 1998.
Centro Cruzeiro: Um Comunitário de Providência. "Um pouco de história." http://www.casacruzeiro.org/ (accessed September 13, 2020).
Chacoff, Alejandro. "Brazil Lost More Than the Past in the National Museum Fire." *New Yorker,* September, 16, 2018.
Chamberlain, Henry. *Views and Costumes of the City and Neighbourhood of Rio de Janeiro, Brasil.* London: Thomas McLean, 1822.
Chisholm, Jennifer. "A Sustainable Favela? How Favela Residents in Rio Are Fighting Back against Threats of Eviction by Forging New Identities Based on Ecological Preservation." NACLA, November 10, 2017, 1–7.
"Christ the Redeemer." *Time*, October 26, 1931.
Cicalo, André. "From Public Amnesia to Public Memory Rediscovering Slavery Heritage in Rio de Janeiro." In *African Heritage and Memories of Slavery in Brazil and the South Atlantic World*, edited by Ana Lucia Araujo. Amherst, NY: Cambria Press, 2015. Kindle edition.
"Uma Cidade Despreparada." *O Globo*, February 21, 1998, 12.

Coelho, Victor. *Baía de Guanabara: Uma História de Agressão Ambiental*. Rio de Janeiro: Casa da Palavra, 2007.
Cohen, Alberto A., and Sergio A. Fridman. *Rio de Janeiro: Ontem e Hoje 2*. Rio de Janeiro: Rioarte 2004.
Cosgrove, Denis, and S. Daniels, eds. *The Iconography of Landscape: Essays on the Symbolic Representation Design and Use of Past Environments*. Cambridge, UK: Cambridge University Press, 1988.
———. *Social Formation and Symbolic Landscape*. Madison: University of Wisconsin Press, 1998.
Costa, Lúcio. *Lúcio Costa: Documentos de Trabalho*. Second edition, edited by José Pessôa. Brasília: IPHAN, 1998.
Crossa, Veronica. "Resisting the Entrepreneurial City: Street Vendors' Struggle in Mexico City's Historic Center." *International Journal of Urban and Regional Research* 33, 1 (March 2009): 43–63.
Cummings, Jake. "Confronting Favela Chic: The Gentrification of Informal Settlements in Rio de Janeiro, Brazil." In *Global Gentrifications: Uneven Development and Displacement*, edited by Loretta Lees, Hyun Bang Shin, Ernesto López-Morales, 81–99. Bristol: Bristol University Press/Policy Press, 2015.
Curry, Michael. *The Work in the World: Geographical Practice and the Written Word*. Minneapolis: University of Minnesota Press, 1996.
Davis, Mike. *Magical Urbanism: Latinos Reinvent the US City*. Updated edition. London: Verso, 2012.
Dean, Warren. *With Broadax and Firebrand: The Destruction of the Brazilian Atlantic Forest*. Berkeley: University of California Press, 1995.
Debret, Jean-Baptiste. *Voyage Pittoresque et Historique au Brésil*. Paris: Actes Sud, 1834.
Delson, Roberta Marx. *New Towns for Colonial Brazil: Spatial and Social Planning of the Eighteenth Century*. Syracuse University: Delplaine Latin American Series, 1979.
Demos, T. J. "Sites of Collective Counter-Memory," *Scribd*, 2012. https://www.scribd.com/document/103447935/Sites-of-Collective-Counter-Memory-by-T-J-Demos (accessed September 13, 2020).
Dias, Veronica Ferreira. "A Cinema of Conversation: Eduardo Coutinho's Santo Forte and Babilônia 2000." In *The New Brazilian Cinema*, edited by Lúcia Nagib. London: I.B. Tauris, 2006.
Dickenson, John. "The Future of the Past in the Latin American City: The Case of Brazil." *Bulletin of Latin American Research* 13, 1 (1994): 13–25.
Dolff-Bonekamper, Gabi. "Cultural Heritage and Conflict: The View from Europe," *Museum International* 62, 1–2 (2010): 14–19.
Douglas, Bruce. "The Story of Cities #15: The Rise and Ruin of Rio de Janeiro's First Favela." *Guardian*, April 5, 2016.
Duncan, James. "The Superorganic in American Cultural Geography." *Annals of the Association of American Geographers* 70 (1980): 181–94.
Edmundo, Luiz C. *Rio in the Time of the Viceroys*. Rio de Janeiro: J.R. Oliveira, 1936.

Fabricius, Daniela. "Resisting Representation: The Informal Geographies of Rio de Janeiro." *Harvard Design* 28 (2008): 4–17.
Farias, Patricia. *Pegando uma Cor na Praia: Relações Raciais e Classificação de Cor na Cidade do Rio de Janeiro*. Rio de Janeiro: Coleção Biblioteca Carioca, 2006.
Favela Faces. "A Tale of Two Cities: The Asphalt and the Favela." http://www.favelafaces.org/intro_eng.html (accessed July 20, 2016).
Favela Tem Memória. "Depoimentos." http://www.favelatemmemoria.com.br/ (accessed February 13, 2018).
Ferreira de Mello, João Batista, "Roteiros Geográficas: Roteiros gratuitos em defesa da cidade do Rio de Janeiro." https://roteirosgeorio.wordpress.com/nossos-roteiros/roteiros-diurnos/ (accessed May 25, 2020).
Ferrez, Gilberto. *O Paço da Cidade do Rio de Janeiro*. Rio de Janeiro: Fundação Nacional Pró-Memória, 1984.
Figueiredo, L. H. M. *Problemas Ambientais Globais: Conceitos Fundamentais e Instrumentos de Análise Ambiental*. Programa de Despoluição da Baía de Guanabara, Capacitação em Educação para a Gestão Ambiental. Rio de Janeiro: CEPUERJ/UERJ, 1997.
Fischer, Brodwyn. *A Century in the Present Tense*. Durham, NC: Duke University Press, 2014. Kindle edition, 11.
Foggin, Sophie. "Brazil's 14 UNESCO World Heritage Sites in Need of Extra Funding, Say Local Governments." *Brazil Reports*, August 24, 2018. https://brazilreports.com/brazils-14-unesco-world-heritage-sites-in-need-of-extra-funding-say-local-governments/ (accessed July 15, 2017).
Frank, Zephyr, and Whitney Berry. "The Slave Market in Rio de Janeiro circa 1869: Movement, Context, and Social Experience." *Journal of Latin American Geography* 9, 3 (2010), 85–110. https://doi.org/10.1353/lag.2010.0033.
Freeman, James. "Democracy and Danger on the Beach." *Space and Culture* 5, 1 (2000): 9–28.
———. "Great, Good, and Divided: The Politics of Public Space in Rio de Janeiro." *Journal of Urban Affairs* 30, 5 (2008): 529–56.
Freire, Rafael de Luna, and Leticia de Luna Freire. "The Rio *Favela* in Musical Comedy Films: From Cradle of Sample to Public Problem." *Comun. Mídia Consumo*, Sao Paulo, 15, 43 (2018).
Freire-Medeiros, Bianca. "The Favela and Its Touristic Transits." *Geoforum* 40 (2009): 580–88.
———. "Favela Como Patrimônio da Cidade? Reflexões e Polêmicas em Torno de Dois Museus." *Estudos Históricos* 38 (2006): 49–66.
Freitas, S. R., C.L. Neves, and P. Chernicharo. "Tijuca National Park: Two Pioneering Restorationist Initiatives in Atlantic Forest of Southeastern Brazil." *Brazilian Journal of Biology* 66, 4 (2006): 975–82.
Freyre, Gilberto. *The Masters and the Slaves: A Study in the Development of Brazilian Civilization*. Berkeley: University of California Press, 1986.
Fridman, Fania, and Eduardo Cézar Siqueira. "O Bairro Judeu no Rio de Janeiro." International Seminar on Urban Form. *Conference Proceedings* (CD format), Ouro Preto, Brazil, August 2007.

Fuks, Mario. "Environmental Litigation in Rio de Janeiro: Shaping Frames for a New Social Problem." *International Journal of Urban and Regional Research* 22, 3 (1998): 394–408.

Gaffney, Christopher Thomas. "Gentrifications in Pre-Olympic Rio de Janeiro." *Urban Geography* (2015): 1–22.

———. "Mega-Events and Socio-Spatial Dynamics in Rio de Janeiro, 1919–2016." *Journal of Latin American Geography* 9, 1 (2010): 7–29.

Gay, Robert. *Popular Organization and Democracy in Rio de Janeiro: A Tale of Two Favelas.* Philadelphia: Temple University Press, 1994.

Gilligan, Melanie. "Slumsploitation: The Favela on Film and TV." *Mute* 2, 3 (September 5, 2006).

Giumbelli, Emerson. "A Modernidade do Cristo Redentor," *Dados* 51, 1 (2008). https://doi.org/10.1590/S0011-52582008000100003.

Godfrey, Brian J. "Remembering Rio: From the Imperial Palace to the African Heritage Circuit." In *The City as Power: Urban Space, Place, and National Identity*, edited by A. Diener and J. Hagan, 105–20. Lanham, MD: Rowman & Littlefield, 2018.

———. "Spanish and Portuguese Colonial Cities in the Americas: A Historical-Geographical Approach to Urban Morphology." In *Cities and Urban Geography in Latin America*, edited by Vicent Ortells Chabrera, Robert B. Kent, and Javier Soriano Martí, 15–38. Castelló de la Plana, España: Publicacions de la Universitat Jaume I, 2005.

———. "Urban Renewal, *Favelas,* and Guanabara Bay: Environmental Justice and Sustainability in Rio de Janeiro." In *Sustainability: A Global Urban Context*, edited by Igor Vojnovic, 359–86. East Lansing: Michigan State University Press, 2012.

———. "Urban Sustainability: Teaching at the Interface on Environmental and Urban Studies," *Ometeca: Science and Humanities* 14–15, special issue "Educating for Ecological Sustainability," February 2010, 274–93.

Godfrey, Brian J., and Olivia M. Arguinzoni. "Regulating Public Space on the Beachfronts of Rio de Janeiro." *Geographical Review* 102, 1 (2012): 17–34.

Gomes, Isabelle Macedo. "Dois Séculos em Busca de uma Solução: Esgotos Sanitários e Meio Ambiente na Cidade do Rio de Janeiro." In *Rio de Janeiro: Formas, Movimentos, Representações—Estudos de Geografia Histórica Carioca*, edited by Maurício de Almeida Abreu, 56–71. Rio de Janeiro: Da Fonseca Comunicação, 2005.

Graham, Brian, G. J. Ashworth, and J. E. Tunbridge. *A Geography of Heritage: Power, Culture, and Economy.* London: Arnold/Oxford University Press, 2000.

Graham, Kelly. "The Asphalt and the Favela: A Critical Examination of Contemporary Urban Segregation." Senior thesis in geography-anthropology, Vassar College, 2007.

Graham, Maria. *Journal of a Voyage to Brazil; and Residence There During Part of the Years 1821, 1822, 1823.* London: Longman, Hurst, Rees, Orme, Brown and Green, 1824.

Green, J. N. *Beyond Carnival: Male Homosexuality in Twentieth-Century Brazil.* Chicago: University of Chicago Press, 1999.

Goulart, Gustavo. "Milícia Domina 45% das Favelas Cariocas, Revela Pesquisa." *O Globo*, December 3, 2013.

Guimarães, Roberta Sampaio. "O Patrimônio Cultural na Gestão dos Espaços do Rio de Janeiro." *Estudos Históricos* 29, 57 (January–April 2016): 149–68.

———. "Urban Interventions, Memories and Conflicts: Black Heritage and the Revitalization of Rio de Janeiro's Port Zone." *Vibrant* 10, 1: 208–27.

Halbwachs, Maurice. "From *The Collective Memory*." In *Collective Memory Reader*, edited by Jeffrey K. Olick, Vered Vinitzky-Seroussi, and Daniel Levy, 139–49. New York: Oxford University Press, 2011.

———. *On Collective Memory*. Edited by Lewis A. Coser. Chicago: University of Chicago Press, 1992.

Halnon, Karen. "Poor Chic: The Rational Consumption of Poverty." *Current Sociology* 50 (2002): 501–16. https://doi.org/10.1177/0011392102050004002.

Harvey, David. "From Managerialism to Entrepreneurialism: The Transformation in Urban Governance in Late Capitalism." *Geografiska Annaler* 71B, 1 (1989): 3–17.

———. From Space to Place and Back Again: Reflections on the Condition of Postmodernity. In *Mapping the Futures: Local Cultures, Global Change*, edited by J. Bird, B. Curtis, T. Putnam, G. Robertson, and L. Tickner, 3–29. London: Routledge, 1993.

———. "Monument and Myth: The Building of the Basilica of the Sacred Heart." In *Consciousness and the Urban Experience*, 221–49. Oxford: Oxford University Press, 1985.

———. "The Right to the City," *International Journal of Urban and Regional Research*, 27, 4 (2003): 939.

———. "The Right to the City," *New Left Review* 53 (September–October 2008): 23–40

Hobsbawm, Eric. "Introduction: Inventing Traditions." In *The Invention of Tradition*, edited by E. Hobsbawn and Terrence Ranger, 1–14. New York: Cambridge University Press, 1983.

Hochstetler, Kathryn, and Margaret E. Keck. *Greening Brazil: Environmental Activism in State and Society*. Durham, NC: Duke University Press, 2007.

Holanda, Sergio Buarque de. *Raizes do Brazil*. Rio de Janeiro: J. Olympio, 1936.

Hollenbach, Lisa. "A Groundbreaking App Exposes the Nefarious History of Rio de Janeiro's Port." Rio on Watch: Community Reporting in Rio, July 19, 2017 http://www.rioonwatch.org/ (accessed September 13, 2020).

Holston, Mark. "Statue of Christ the Redeemer." *Americas* (English edition) 60, 3 (May/June 2008): 613.

Honorato, Claudio de Paula. "Valongo: O Mercado de Escravos do Rio de Janeiro, 1758–1831." Master's thesis in history, Universidade Federal Fluminense, Niterói, 2008.

Huyssen, Andreas. *Present Pasts: Urban Palimpsests and the Politics of Memory*. Stanford, CA: Stanford University Press, 2003.

ICOMOS (International Council on Monuments and Sites). "The Burra Charter: The Australia ICOMOS Charter for the Conservation of Places of Cultural Significance." Last modified 2008. http://www.icomos.org/australia/burra.html.2008.

IBGE (Instituto Brasileiro de Geografia e Estatística). Census of Population. http://www.ibge.gov.br/, various years.

———. "Cidades@." http://www.ibge.gov.br/cidadesat/topwindow.htm (accessed July 20, 2012).

———. "IBGE lança Mapa da Pobreza e Desingualidade." http://www.ibge.gov.br/ (accessed July 12, 2012).

Information Habitat. *The NGO Alternative Treaties from the Global Forum at Rio de Janeiro. Resolution 34: Concerning Guanabara Bay: Humankind's Heritage.* 1992.

Instituto da Baía de Guanabara. http://baiadeguanabara.org.br/site/ (accessed September 14, 2020).

IPHAN (Instituto do Patrimônio Histórico e Artístico Nacional). "Area Central da Praça Quinze de Novembro." Processo 1213-T-86. Rio de Janeiro: Arquivo Central, 1986.

———. *Bens móveis e imóveis inscritos nos Livros do Tombo do Instituto do Patrimônio Histórico e Artístico Nacional, 1938–2009.* Rio de Janeiro: IPHAN/COPEDOC, 2009.

———. "Casas á Praça Quinze de Novembro, 32 e 34—Arco de Teles." Processos 55-T-38, 56-T-38, 99-T-38. Rio de Janeiro: Arquivo Central, 1938.

———. "Livros do Tombo." Arquivo Noronha Santos. http://portal.iphan.gov.br/ans/inicial.htm (accessed September 13, 2020).

———. *Normatização de Cidades Históricas: Orientações para a elaboração de diretrizes e Normas de Preservação para áreas urbanas tombadas.* Brasília, D.F.: Ministério da Cultura, 2011.

———. "Paço Imperial." Processo 159-T-38. Rio de Janeiro: Arquivo Central, 1938.

———. "Pesquisa Histórica: Formulário Geral do Sítio Urbano—Praça XV de Novembro." Rio de Janeiro: Arquivo Central, April 2004.

Ivester, Sukari. "Removal, Resistance and the Right to the Olympian City: The Case of Vila Autódromo in Rio de Janeiro." *Journal of Urban Affairs*, 39, 7 (2017): 970–85.

Jaguaribe, Beatriz. "Cities without Maps: Favelas and the Aesthetics of Realism." In *Urban Imaginaries: Locating the Modern City*, edited by Alev Cinar and Thomas Bender, 114. Minneapolis: University of Minnesota Press, 2007.

Jaguaribe, Beatriz, and Kevin Hetherington. "Favela Tours: Indistinct and Mapless Representations of the Real in Rio de Janeiro." In *Tourism Mobilities: Places to Play, Places in Play*, edited by Mimi Sheller and John Urry, 155–66. London: Routledge, 2004.

João do Rio. *As Religiões no Rio*. Editora Nova Aguilar, 1976. Originally published in 1904.

Jordão, Rogério Pacheco. "Machado's Valongo in Rio de Janeiro's cartography: Urban Slavery in Motion." *Machado de Assis em Linha* 8, 16 (December 2015). http://dx.doi.org/10.1590/1983682120158166 (accessed July 15, 2018).

JR. "Women Are Heroes." Vimeo, 2012. https://vimeo.com/42286795 (accessed September 15, 2020).

Karasch, Mary. *Slave Life in Rio de Janeiro, 1808–1850.* Princeton: Princeton University Press, 1987.

Khatchadourian, Raffi. "In the Picture: An Artist's Global Experiment to Help People Be Seen." *New Yorker*, November 28, 2011.

Kimmelman, Michael. "A Divided Rio de Janeiro, Overreaching for the World." *New York Times*, November 25, 2013.

———. "What Is Lost When a Museum Vanishes? In Brazil, a Nation's Story." *New York Times*, September 16, 2018.

King, John J. *Magical Reels: A History of Cinema in Latin America.* London and New York: Verso, 1990.

Kugel, Seth. "So, You Were Maybe Expecting Carmen Miranda?" *New York Times*, August 27, 2008,

Lamego, Alberto Ribeiro (ed.). *O Homem e a Guanabara.* Rio de Janeiro: IBGE, 1964.

Lessa, Carlos. *O Rio de Todos os Brasis (Uma Reflexão em Busca de Auto-Estima).* Rio de Janeiro and São Paulo: Editora Record, 2000.

Lima, Tania Andrade, Glaucia Malerba Sene, and Marcos André Torres de Souza. "Em busca do Cais do Valongo, Rio de Janeiro, Século XIX." *Anais do Museu Paulista* 24, 1 (January–April 2016), 299–391.

Lin, Zhongjie, Fernando Diniez Moreira, and Aline de Melo Nascimento. "Changing Informality: Gentrification in the Favelas of Rio de Janeiro." In *Rio de Janeiro: Urban Expansion and the Environment*, edited by José L. S. Gámez, Qhongjie Lin, Jeffrey S. Nesbit, chapter 4. New York: Routledge, 2020, Kindle edition.

Lobato, José Bento Monteiro. "Não arrasen o morro do Castelo" in *Rio de Janeiro em Prosa e Poesia*, edited by Manuel Bandeira and Carlos Drummond de Andrade, 413–14. Rio de Janeiro: José Olympio, 1965.

Low, Setha M. *On the Plaza: The Politics of Public Space and Culture.* Austin: University of Texas Press, 2000.

Maranhão, Ricardo. *Cinelândia: Retorno ao fascínio do passado.* Rio de Janeiro: Letra Capital Editora, 2003.

Marra, Livia. "Traficante Marcinho VP é assassinado no complexo do Bangu." *Folha de São Paulo*, July 28, 2003.

Martin, Anne Spencer. "Cultural Conservation in Brazil: Saving Pelourinho." PhD diss., University of Florida, 1993.

Martins, Luciana L. and Maurício A. Abreu. "Paradoxes of Modernity: Imperial Rio de Janeiro, 1808–1821." *Geoforum* 32, 4 (2001): 533–50.

Marx, Murillo. *Cidade Brasileira,* São Paulo: Editora da Universidade de São Paulo, 1980.

Massey, Doreen. "Power-Geometry and a Progressive Sense of Place." In *Mapping the Futures: Local Cultures, Global Change*, edited by J. Bird, B. Curtis, T. Putnam, G. Robertson, and L. Tickner, 59–69. London: Routledge, 1993.

McNally, James. "Favela Chic: Diplo, Funk Carioca, and the Ethics and Easthetics of the Global Remix." *Popular Music and Society* 40, 4 (2017).

Meade, Teresa A. *"Civilizing" Rio: Reform and Resistance in a Brazilian City, 1889–1930.* University Park: Pennsylvania State University Press, 1997.

Melville, Herman. *White-Jacket; or, The World in a Man-of-War.* New York: Harper & Brothers, 1850. http://www.melville.org/hmwjack.htm (accessed July 15, 2009).

Moraes, Camila. "A Invenção da Favela Ecológica: Um Olhar Sobre Turismo e Meio Ambiente no Morro Babilônia." *Estudos sociológicos* 18, 35 (July–December 2013): 459–74.

Moura, Roberto. *Tia Ciata e a Pequena África no Rio de Janeiro.* Rio de Janeiro: Secretaria Municipal de Cultura, 1995.

Museu Comunitário da Providência. "Olimpíada da exclusão—A luta e resistência das favelas," July 18, 2016. https://www.facebook.com/museuprovidencia/ (accessed May 25, 2020).

Museu Nacional. "Arquitetura e História—Exposição de 1922." Rio de Janeiro, June 13, 2016.

National Park Service. "National Historic Sites Registry." http://www.nps.gov/nr/index.htm (accessed July 20, 2012).

Needell, Jeffrey D. "The Revolta Contra Vacina of 1904: The Revolt against 'Modernization' in Belle-Epoque Rio de Janeiro." *Hispanic American Historical Review* 67, 2 (May 1987): 233–69.

———. "Rio de Janeiro and Buenos Aires: Public Space and Public Consciousness in Fin-de-Siecle Latin America." *Comparative Studies in Society and History* 37 (1995): 519–40.

———. "Rio de Janeiro at the Turn of the Century: Modernization and the Parisian Ideal." *Journal of Interamerican Studies and World Affairs* 25, 1 (2003): 83–103.

———. *A Tropical Belle Epoque: Elite Culture and Society in Turn-of-the-Century Rio de Janeiro.* Cambridge; Cambridge University Press, 1987.

O'Hare, Greg, and Michael Barke. "The Favelas of Rio de Janeiro: A Temporal and Spatial Analysis." *GeoJournal* 56 (2002): 225–40.

Olick, Jeffrey K., Vered Vinitzky-Seroussi, and Daniel Levy (eds). *The Collective Memory Reader.* New York: Oxford University Press, 2011.

Olick, Jeffrey K., and Joyce Robbins. "Social Memory Studies: From 'Collective Memory' to the Historical Sociology of Mnemonic Practices." *Annual Review of Sociology* 24, 1 (1998): 105–41.

Oliveira, Carmen L. *Rare and Commonplace Flowers: The Story of Elizabeth Bishop and Lota de Macedo Soares*, translated by Neil K. Besner. New Brunswick, NJ: Rutgers University Press, 2002.

Pagano, Sergio, Heloísa Buarque de Hollanda, and Lauro Cavalcanti. *Paço Imperial.* Rio de Janeiro: Sextante Artes, 1999.

Pamplona, Nicola. "Aumenta Desigualdade Salarial Entre Brancos e Pretos, diz IBGE: Diferença Nos Rendimentos Atingiu o Maior Patamar desde 2016." *Folha de São Paulo,* May 6, 2020.

Passos, F. P. *Melhoramentos da Cidade Projetadas pelo Prefeito do Distrito Federal*, Governo do Rio de Janeiro, 1903.

Patel, Gitanjali. "Museums of Counternarratives and Resistance. Part 3: Maré Museum." RioOnWatch, May 16, 2018. https://www.rioonwatch.org/?p=43384 (accessed September 13, 2020).

———. "Museums of Counternarratives and Resistance. Part 5: The Evictions Museum," RioOnWatch, May 18, 2018. https://www.rioonwatch.org/?p=43516 (accessed September 13, 2020).

Pechman, Sérgio, and Lilian Fritsch. "A Reforma Urbana e Seu Avesso." *Revista Brasileira de História* 8, 9 (1985), 148–49.
Peregrino, Miriane. "Museu Aberta do Morro da Providência Competa 11 Anos." *O Cidadão*, February 4, 2020. http://jornalocidadao.net/museu-aberto-do-morro-da-providencia-completa-11-anos/ (accessed September 13, 2020).
———. "Museu das Remoções é inaugurado na Vila Autódromo," *O Cidadão*, May 26, 2016. http://jornalocidadao.net/museu-das-remocoes-e-inaugurado-na-vila-autodromo/ (accessed September 13, 2020).
———. "Tram, Tourism, History and Resistance in Santa Marta: 'Each Brick Has Its Story.'" *Rio onWatch*, March 6, 2015.
Pereira, Anthony W. "Is the Brazilian State 'Patrimonial'?" *Latin American Perspectives* 43, 2 (March 2016): 135–52.
Pereira, C. *Copacabana: Um Passeio no Tempo / A Stroll in Time.* Rio de Janeiro: Prefeitura da Cidade, 2007.
Perlman, Janice E. *Favela: Four Decades of Living on the Edge in Rio de Janeiro.* New York: Oxford University Press, 2011.
———. "The Metamorphosis of Marginality: Four Generations in the Favelas of Rio de Janeiro." *Annals of the American Academy of Political and Social Science* 606 (2006): 154–77. https://doi.org/10.1177/0002716206288826.
———. *The Myth of Marginality: Urban Poverty and Politics in Rio de Janeiro.* Berkeley and Los Angeles: University of California Press, 1976.
Phillips, Tom. "Brazil: How *Favelas* Went Chic." *Brazzil*, December 2003. http://brazzil.com/2003/html/news/articles/dec03/p105dec03.htm (accessed September 14, 2020).
Pinheiro, Augusto Ivan de Freitas. "Aprendendo com o Patrimônio." In *Cidade: História e Desafios*, ed. L. L. Oliveira, 141–55. Rio de Janeiro: Ed. Fundação Getulio Vargas, 2002.
———. "A Cidade e o Tempo." In *Rio de Janeiro: Cinco Séculos de História e Transformações Urbanas*, edited by A. I. de Freitas Pinheiro, 21–42. Rio de Janeiro: Casa da Palavra, 2010.
———. "Novas Experiências em urbanismo: Barra da Tijuca e Corredor Cultural." In *Capítulos da Memória do Urbanismo Carioca: Depoimentos ao CPDOC/ FGV*, ed. A. Freire and L. L. Oliveira, 202–21. Rio de Janeiro: Folha Seca, 2002.
Pinheiro, Augusto Ivan, and Vicente Del Rio. "Cultural Corridor: A Preservation District in Downtown Rio De Janeiro, Brazil." *Traditional Dwellings and Settlement Review* IV, 11 (1993): 51–84.
Pinheiro, Eliane Canedo de Freitas. *Baía de Guanabara: Biografia de uma Paisagem.* Rio de Janeiro: Andrea Jakobsson Estúdio, 2005.
Price, Marie, and Martin Lewis. "Reinventing Cultural Geography." *Annals of the Association of American* Geographers 83 (1993): 1–17.
Pulido, Laura. "Rethinking Environmental Racism: White Privilege and Urban Development in Southern California." *Annals of the Association of American Geographers* 90, 1 (2000): 12–40.
Rede Favela Sustaintável. *Guia de Museus e Memórias.* Rio de Janeiro, Novembro de 2020.

Reis Filho, Nestor G. *Contribuição ao Estudo da Evolução Urbana do Brasil*, São Paulo: Editora da Universidade de São Paulo, 1968.
Rezende, Maria Beatriz, Bettina Grieco, Luciano Teixeira, and Analucia Thompson. "Fundação Nacional Pró-Memória, 1979–1990." *Dicionário IPHAN do Patrimônio Cultural*. Rio de Janeiro and Brasília: IPHAN/DAF/Copedoc, 2015.
Ribeiro, Duanne. "A Shattered City: Eco-Limits and Rio de Janeiro." *Latismo*, September 21, 2009, http://www.latismo.com/a-shattered-city-eco-limits-and-rio-de-janeiro (accessed July 15, 2020).
Riley, Mathew Francis. "Counterwitnessing the Visual Culture of Brazilian Slavery." In *African Heritage and Memories of Slavery in Brazil and the South Atlantic World*, edited by Ana Lucia Araujo. Amherst, NY: Cambria Press, 2015. Kindle edition.
RIOARTE (Instituto Municipal de Arte e Cultura, Rio de Janeiro). *Corredor Cultural: Como Recuperar, Reformar ou Construir seu Imóvel*. Fourth edition. Rio de Janeiro: Prefeitura da Cidade/Instituto Pereira Passos, 2002.
"Rio dá Primeiro Passo para a Derrubada da Perimetral." *Veja*, September 21, 2011. http://veja.abril.com.br/noticia/brasil/rio-da-o-primeiro-passo-para-a-derrubada-da-perimetral/ (accessed September 13, 2020).
Rio, Vicente del. "Restructuring Inner-City Areas in Rio de Janeiro: Urban Design for a Pluralistic Downtown." *Journal of Architectural and Planning Research* 14, 1 (1997): 20–34.
Rio, Vicente del, and Denise de Alcantara. "The Cultural Corridor Project: Revitalization and Preservation in Downtown Rio de Janeiro." In *Contemporary Urbanism in Brazil: Beyond Brasília*, edited by V. del Rio and W. Siembieda, 125–43. Gainesville: University of Florida Press, 2009.
Robichaud, Raine. "Boat Ride for a Living Guanabara Bay Calls Attention to Defining Element of Rio's Iconic Landscape." *Rio on Watch*, August 10, 2017.
Roett, Riordan. *Brazil: Politics in a Patrimonial Society.* Westport, CT: Praeger, 1999.
Rohter, Larry. "Rio Is Easing the Way to Corcovado's Summit." *New York Times*, September 23, 2001.
Romero, Simon. "Rio's Race to Future Intersects Slave Past." *New York Times*, March 8, 2014.
———. "Slum Dwellers Are Defying Brazil's Grand Design for Olympics." *New York Times*, March 4, 2012.
Rossiter, Brian. "'They Don't Care about Us': Michael Jackson's Black Nationalism." *Popular Music and Society* 35, 2 (2012): 203–22.
Rugendas, Johann Moritz. *Voyage pittoresque dans le Brésil*. Paris: Engelman, 1835.
———. *Viagem Pitoresca através do Brasil*. São Paulo: Livraria Martins, 1940.
———. *Viaje pintoresco a través del Brasil*. Buenos Aires: Emecé Editores, 1947.
Santos, Joaquim Ferreira dos. *Feliz 1958, O Ano Que Não Devia Acabar.* Editora Record, 1998.
———. "Gente Boa." *O Globo*, July 29, 2000, 5.
Sauer, Carl. "The Morphology of Landscape." Reprinted in 1925. *Land and Life: A Selection of the Writings of Carl Ortwin Sauer*, edited by John Leighly, 315–50. Berkeley and Los Angeles: University of California Press, 1963.

Scarpaci, Joseph. *Plazas and Barrios: Heritage Tourism and Globalization in the Latin American Centro Histórico.* Tucson: University of Arizona Press, 2005.

Schemo, Diana Jean. "Rio Frets as Michael Jackson Plans to Film Slum." *New York Times*, February 11, 1996.

Schultz, Kirsten. *Tropical Versailles: Empire, Monarchy, and the Portuguese Royal Court in Rio de Janeiro, 1808–1821.* New York and London: Routledge, 2001.

Secretaria Municipal de Habitação (SMH), *Cadernos Favela-Bairro Comunidades: A Brief History.* Rio de Janeiro: Prefeitura da Cidade, 2007.

Silva, Maria Lais Pereira. "Favelas do Rio de Janeiro: Localização e Expansão Através do Espaço Urbano (1928–1964)." In *Rio de Janeiro: Formas, Movimentos, Representações—Estudos de Geografia Histórica Carioca*, edited by Maurício de Almeida Abreu, 176–201. Rio de Janeiro: Da Fonseca Comunicação, 2005.

Skidmore, Thomas A. *Black into White: Race and Nationalism in Brazil.* Oxford University Press, 1974.

Sluyter, Andrew. *Colonialism and Landscape: Postcolonial Theory and Applications.* Lanham, MD: Rowman & Littlefield, 2001.

Smith, Cynthia E. *Design with the Other 90%.* New York: Cooper-Hewitt Museum, Smithsonian Design Museum, 2011.

Smith, Robert C. "The Seventeenth- and Eighteenth-Century Architecture of Brazil." *Proceedings of the International Colloquium of Luso-Brazilian Studies*, Washington, DC, October 15–20, 1950. Nashville, TN: Vanderbilt University Press, 1953.

Soares, Carlos Eugênio Líbano. *Valongo, Cais dos Escravos: Memória da Diáspora e Modernizaçao Portuária na Cidade do Rio de Janeiro, 1668—1911.* Programa de Pós-Graduação em Arqueologia, Museu Nacional and Universidade Federal do Rio de Janeiro, Depto. de Antropologia, 2013.

Soares, Fabio, and Yuri Soares. "The Socio-Economic Impact of Favela-Bairro: What Do the Data Say?" Working Paper OVE/WP-08. Washington, DC: Inter-American Development Bank, August 4, 2005.

Souza, Carla. "The Urban Agroforestry Unfolding in Providência, Brazil's First Favela." RioOnWatch, February 28, 2020. https://www.rioonwatch.org/?p=57952 (accessed September 13, 2020).

Souza, Laura Olivieri Carneiro de. *Horto Florestal: Um lugar de memória da cidade do Rio de Janeiro—A construção do Museu do Horto e seu correspondente projeto social de memória.* PhD diss., Pontífica Universidade Católica, Rio de Janeiro, 2012.

Spayde, Jon. "Monumental Changes: New Thinking about Historical Monuments Is Embracing Inclusivity—and Ambiguity." *Public Art Review* 29, 57 (2018): 40–49.

Stam, Robert. "Slow Fade to Afro: The Black Presence in Brazilian Cinema." *Film Quarterly* 36, 2 (Winter 1982–1983): 16–32.

State Institute for Cultural Heritage (INEPAC). "Pedra do Sal." Process Number E-18/300.048/84. http://www.inepac.rj.gov.br/index.php/bens_tombados/detalhar/20 (accessed September 13, 2020).

Steiner, Eric, and Zephyr Frank. "Tenement Housing in Rio de Janeiro, 1870s–1880s." Stanford University, Spatial History Project, 2019, http://web.stanford.edu/group/spatialhistory/cgi-bin/site/viz.php?id=45&project_id=0 (accessed September 13, 2020).

Thomas, June M. "The Role of Ethnicity and Race in Supporting Sustainable Urban Environments." In *Urban Sustainability: A Global Perspective*, edited by Igor Vojnovic, 475–508. East Lansing: Michigan State University Press, 2012.

Tocqueville, Alexis de. *Democracy in America.* New York: J. & H. G. Langley, 1841.

Torres, Antonio. "The Palace, Step by Step." In *Paço Imperial*, edited by Lauro Cavalcanti, 77–104. Rio de Janeiro: Editora Index, 2005.

Trilhas: Parque Nacional da Tijuca. Rio de Janeiro: Instituto Terra Brasil, 2006.

Underwood, David. *Oscar Niemeyer and Brazilian Free-Form Modernism.* New York: George Braziller, 1994.

UNESCO (United Nations Educational, Scientific, and Cultural Organization)."The Evaluations of Nominations of Cultural and Mixed Properties of the World Heritage List." Report for the 36th session of the World Heritage Committee, June–July, 2012. St. Petersburg, Russian Federation. http://whc.unesco.org/en/sessions/36COM/.

———. "The Slave Route: Preservation of Memorial Sites and Places." http://www.unesco.org/new/en/social-and-human-sciences/themes/slave-route/spotlight/preservation-of-memorial-sites-and-places/ (accessed September 13, 2020).

———. "World Heritage List." World Heritage Center. http://whc.UNESCO.org/en/list2008. (accessed July 12, 2012).

United Cities and Local Governments (UCLG). Committee on Culture, *Agenda 21 for Culture*, 2008. http://www.agenda21culture.net (accessed September 13, 2020).

———. *Culture, Climate Change and Sustainable Development*, 2016. http://www.agenda21culture.net (accessed September 13, 2020).

———. *Culture: Fourth Pillar of Cultural Development,* 2014. http://www.agenda21culture.net (accessed September 13, 2020)

United Nations. *Agenda 21: Programme of Action for Sustainable Development.* New York: United Nations Dept. of Public Information, 1993.

———. "The Rio Declaration on Environment and Development." New York: United Nations Documentation Center, 1992.

Valladares, Licia. "A gênese da favela carioca." *Revista Brasileira de Ciências Sociais* 15, 44 (2000): 5–34.

———. *A Invenção Da Favela: Do Mito de Origem A Favela.Com.* Rio De Janeiro: Fundação Getúlio Vargas, 2005.

Vargas, Getúlio. President of the Republic of Brazil. "Decree Law No. 25 of November 1937." Rio de Janeiro, November 30, 1937, 1. [Published by the Union's *Dally Journal* of December 6, 1937 and republished on December 11, 1937.]

Ventura, Zuenir. *Cidade Partida.* São Paulo: Companhia das Letras, 1994.

Vertical Shopping, Rio de Janeiro, http://verticalshopping.com.br (accessed September13, 2020).

Weiner, Eric. "Heads Up: Poverty Tours—Slum Visits: Tourism or Voyeurism?" *New York Times*, March 9, 2008.

Wheeler, Stephen M., and Timothy Beatley. *The Sustainable Urban Development Reader.* London and New York: Routledge, 2006.

Wilcken, Patrick. *Empire Adrift: The Portuguese Court in Rio de Janeiro, 1808–1821.* London: Bloomsbury, 2004.

Williams, Daryle. *Culture Wars in Brazil: The First Vargas Regime, 1930–1945.* Durham, NC: Duke University Press, 2001.

———. "Rio's Favelas: The Power of Informal Urbanism." In *Perspectiva 50: Urban Divides*, ed. Meghan McAllister and Mahdi Sabbagh, 213–28. Cambridge, MA: MIT Press, 2017.

Williamson, Theresa. "Community Land Trusts in Rio's Favelas." *Land Lines*, Lincoln Institute of Land Policy 30, 3 (July 2018): 8–23.

Williamson, Theresa, and Maurício Hora, "In the Name of the Future, Rio Is Destroying Its Past," *New York Times*, August 12, 2012.

Worcman, Susane. *SAARA.* Rio de Janeiro: Relume Dumará, 2000.

World Commission on Environment and Development. *Our Common Future.* Oxford University Press, 1987.

World Cup and Olympics Popular Committee of Rio de Janeiro. *Mega-Events and Human Rights Violations in Rio de Janeiro Dossier*, December 2015.

Young, James. "Memory and Counter-Memory: The End of the Monument in Germany." *Harvard Design* 9 (Fall 1999): 1–10.

Zweig, Stefan. *Brazil: A Land of the Future.* Adriadne Press, 1941 [republished, 2000].

Index

abolitionists, 87, 89–91, 107–8
abolition of slavery, in 1888, xi, 15, 66, 68, 91–92, 100, 120
Abreu, Maurício, 9–10, 12, 17, 127
Abusado (Oliveira), 139–40
adaptive reuse, of Imperial Palace, 65–71
African Americans, 93–94
African Burial Ground, in Lower Manhattan, 93–94
African diaspora, 81, 83–84, 93, 95–96
African Heritage Circuit, 79, 96, 132; Little Africa and, 99–109, 201; map of historic sites, 107–8, *108*; official support for, 109–10
African slaves: disembarkation in or near Rio, 84–86, 91, 121; disembarkations in Brazil, *83*, 83–85; freed, in late eighteenth century, 84; in informal settlements, 119; male and female, 101–2; as New Blacks, 84–91; race in Brazil and, 92; in Rio population, 1821, 84–85; sanitarist segregation of, 86, 91; Valongo Cove and, 85–88; Valongo Wharf and, 77–79, 84–85, 89–92; Valongo Wharf Archaeological Site and, 19, 80, 200–201
Afro-Brazilian identities, 106–7, 201

Afro-Brazilians: in Brazilian histories, 82; on Cemetery of the New Blacks, 95; cultures, in favelas, 138; Filhos de Gandhi cultural and spiritual group, 97, *98*; history and culture, in Rio, 29–30; in Little Africa, 77, 80, 100–110; population of, 83, 100; in Providência Hill favela, 120–22; religion of, 106; in Revolt of the Vaccine, 103; in Rio, 29–30, 36, 38, 41; Saint Benedict Catholic Church and, 103–4; spiritual rites, 102; Valongo Wharf, heritage and, 79–80; on Valongo Wharf, 96–97, 99–100
Afro-descendant identities, 29–30, 108–9, 201
After Dinner Refreshments on the Palace Square (painting), 61
Agache, Donat-Alfred, 42–43, 127
Agache Plan, 42–43
Agenda 21, 158–59
AHOMAR. *See* Association of Men and Women of the Sea
Alpoim, José Fernandes, 58–59, 66–67
AMAGAVEA. *See* Gávea Neighborhood Association
Amaral, Bráz Hermenegildo do, 88
Amaral, Tarsila do, 43
Anderson, Benedict, 6

221

Index

Andrade, António Gomes Freire de, 66
Andrade, Carlos Drummond de, 43
Andrade, Rodrigo, 62
anti-displacement networks, 149
APACS. *See* Cultural Environment Protection Areas
Araújo, Ana Lucia, 87
Arches of Lapa, 53
Arch of Teles (Arco de Teles), 51, *59*, 59–64
Arguinzoni, Olivia, 187–88
arrastão, 185–86
As Religiões no Rio (Barreto, P.), 101
Association of Men and Women of the Sea (AHOMAR), 179, 192
Association of Residents and Fishermen of Vila Autódromo, 132–35
Atlantic Forest (Mata Atlântica), 142, 166, 174
Aunt Ciata (Tia Ciata), 104–5
authoritarianism, 16, 36–37, 132
Avenida Atlântica, 181–82, *185*, 188
Avenida Central (Rio Brando Boulevard), 41
Azevedo, Aluísio, 39–40

Bahia, 83, 120–21, 166
bailes funk, 145
Barcellos, Caco, 139
Barreto, Afonso Henriques de Lima, 42
Barreto, Paulo, 101
Barreto, Paulo Thadim, 168
Barthel, Diane, 24
Basic Urbanist Plan (Plano Urbanístico Básico), 48
beach riot, of 1992, 181, 185–86
Becker, Cristina, 138–39
Benedictines, 58
Bentes, Ivana, 138
Besserman, Sérgio, 167–68
Betancur, John, 99
Bishop, Elizabeth, 127, 176
Black communities, urban renewal programs and, 78–79
Black Orpheus, 47–48

Black social movements, of Rio, 95
blocos (Carnival blocks), 122
Bolsa de Valores do Rio de Janeiro (BVRJ), 63–64
Bos, Pedro Maria, 172
Botanical Garden, 18–19, 118, 160–63, 166–69, 191
Botofogo district, 41, 135, 140
Boutique de la Rue du Val-Longo (painting), 88, *89*
Boyer, M. Christine, 3, 24, 64, 200
Boym, Svetlana, 25. 70
Bragança dynasty, 1, *2*, 3, 11–14
branding, 27, 48, 144–45
Brasília, 16, 35
Brazil, 1; African slave disembarkations in, *83*, 83–85; Buenos Aires and, 15; cities in, ix–x; colonial, 10–11, 13–14, 16, 19, 83; Decree-Law n° 25, 45, 62; democratization since 1980s, 37; First and Second Empires, 1822–1889, 14–15; first republican period, 1889–1930, 29, 38, 50, 199; heritage legislation in, 45; Historic Cities program, 47; historic monuments, 69; as "land of the future," 16–22; military regime of, 1964–1985, 16, 45, 47, 49–50, 55–56, 128, 149, 164, 198–99; modern art and architecture, 16–18; Old Towns of, x; republican government in, 1889, 15; Revolution of 1930, 42–43, 127–28; UNESCO World Heritage program, cultural tourism and, 47; urbanization, ix–x, 43; Zweig on, 16. *See also* Rio de Janeiro; *specific locations*; *specific topics*
Brazil: A Land of the Future (Zweig), 16
Brazilian scholarship, in English language, xi
Buenos Aires, 15, 40
built heritage, 4, 16, 26, 35, 38, 201
Burle Marx, Roberto, 43, 166, 176, 181–82, 184

Burns, E. Bradford, 83, 121
Burra Charter, 22
BVRJ. *See* Bolsa de Valores do Rio de Janeiro
"By the Telephone," 104–5

Cabeça de Porco ("Pig's Head" tenement), 40
Cabral, Pedro Alvares, 6–7
Cabral, Sérgio, 140–43
Caldeira, Teresa, 145
Calvalcante, Lauro, 69
Calvino, Italo, ix
Caminha, Pedro Vaz de, 7–8
Campbell, Glauco, 69
Campo de Santana, 36
candomblé, 102, 104, 107, 180
Capanema, Gustavo, 43
Cardoso, José Luis, 1
Carioca Landscapes. *See* Rio de Janeiro: Carioca Landscapes between the Mountain and the Sea
Carioca River, 7
Cariocas, 20–21, 70, 77, 164, 172, 177, 188–90
Carlota Joaquina (queen), 11, 13–14
Carmelites, 58
Carnival, Rio, 1, 100, 102, 104–5, 122
A Casa Amarela (The Yellow House), 125
Casa Pública, 100
casas de cómodos (rooming houses), 101, 104
Castle Hill (Morro do Castelo), 9–10, 12, 18, 41–43, 58
Castriota, Leonardo, 43
Castro, Ruy, 17, 28–29, 157
Castro Maya, Raymundo Ottoni de, 166
Catacumba (Catacombs), 129–31
Cavalcanti, Nireu, 12
Cemetery of New Blacks, 81, 94–95, 100, 200
Chamberlain, Henry, 10, 13, 84, 88
Children of Gandhi (Filhos de Gandhi), 97, *98*

CHISAM. *See* Coordination of Social Interest Housing of the Greater Rio Metropolitan Area
Chisholm, Jennifer, 118
Choque de Ordem (Shock of Order) program, 187
Christ the Redeemer statue, 147, 160, 163, 171–73, *173*
Church of Our Lady of Mount Carmel, 58
Cidade de Deus (City of God), 137
Cidade Partida (Ventura), 115
Cinelândia district, 51, 53, 71, 200
Cinema Novo (New Cinema), 8, 138
City Archives, Rio, 18, 78–79
City of God (Cidade de Deus), 137
City of God (film), 137
City of Men, 137
civil rights, 29–30
classism, 188–89
climate change, 159
Coelho, Gonçalo, 7
Coelho, Olínio Gomes Paschoal, 168
Cole, Harry, 176–77
collective identity, 4, 81
collective memory, 20; Carioca Landscapes site and, 191–92; city of, Boyer on, 24; Cultural Corridor and, 200; cultural identity and, 55; of favelas, 116, 201; Halbwachs on, 22–23; places in, 26; power, memory brokers and, 24–25; of Rio, x–xi, 30–31; social diversity and, 203
collective rights, 4
colonial Brazil, 10–11, 13–14, 16, 19, 83
colonial Rio, 8–14, 19, 58, 67, 84
colonization and colonialism, 6–11, 81
Comando Vermelho (Red Command), 123, 125, 139
commercial kiosks, at Copacabana Beach, 184–85, *185*, *186*, 190
Commission for the Eradication of Favelas, 128

community-based environmental activism, 160, 192
community identity, cultural politics and, 109–10
Conçalves Ledo Street, 54, *55*
Conceição Hill, 106–7
Congress of New Urbanism, 150–51
Conselheiro, Antônio, 120–21
Convention on Biological Diversity and the Climate Change Convention, 158
Coordination of Social Interest Housing of the Greater Rio Metropolitan Area (CHISAM), 128–29
Copacabana Beach, 180–92, *185*, *186*
Copacabana Palace Hotel, 181
Corcovado Mountain, 160, 169, 171–74, *173*, 177
O Cortiço (Azevedo), 39–40
cortiços (tenements), of Rio, 38–41, 101, 120
Costa, Almerinda da, 122–23
Costa, Lúcio, 16, 43, 54, 62
Costa, Lygia Martins, 177
Costa, Telma da, 122
Council of Europe, 5
counter-memory, 8, 20, 29–30; colonialism and, 81; cultural reinvention and, 80–83; favelas and, 118, 149, 201; Little Africa and, 81, 109; official memory and, 82; racial democracy discourse *versus*, 108; Revolt of the Vaccine and, 103; Valongo Wharf and, 100
counter-narratives, 29, 103, 132, 198
Coutinho, Eduardo, 136–37
COVID-19, ix, 151
critical preservationist stance, 3
Cruz, Oswaldo, 102
Cultural Corridor Law, of 1984, 49
Cultural Corridor program, in Rio, x, 17, 36, 109–10; APACS and, 49; Cinelândia district in, 51, 53; collective memory and, 200; as entrepreneurial preservation, 57, 70–71; gentrification and, 63, 65, 71; historic districts created by, *50*, 50–51, 53–54; historic placemaking and, 51, 56, 66; historic preservation and, 54–57, 63, 199–200; Imperial Palace and, 69; influence on other Brazilian cities, 57; Lapa district in, 53–54; local organizations in, 49–50; Maia on, 54; November 15th Square district and, 51, 57–58, 64; police actions in, 57; public-private partnerships in, 16, 29, 37–38, 54–57; reinvention, continuity and, 70–71; SAARA district in, 53–54, *55*, 71; São Francisco district in, 53–54, 57, 71; sense of place and, 51, 66, 70, 200; urban design in, 56; urban revitalization and, 50–51, 55; Vertical Shopping in, 64
cultural difference, social status and, 12
Cultural Environment Protection Areas (APACS), 48–49, 162
cultural geography, 26–27
cultural heritage, 5, 16, 25–26, 43, 47
cultural identity, 5, 55
cultural landscapes, 4, 23–24, 81, 165, 173, 202; Carioca Landscapes site, 18–19, 160–64, 191–92
cultural politics, community identity and, 109–10
cultural reinvention, 80–83
cultural tourism, 23, 47, 96, 100, 108
"cultural turn" in academia, xi
culture, 158–60
Culture 21, 159
Culture in Sustainable Cities: Learning with Culture 21 Actions program, 159
Cunha, Euclides da, 121
Curry, Michael, 6

Débarkment (lithograph) (Rugendas), 87
Debret, Jean-Baptiste, 13–14, 61, 88–89, *89*
deforestation, 117, 141–42, 164–65, 169, 174–75, 179

Democracy in America (Tocqueville), xi
democratic beaches, 181, 184, 188–90, 192
Demos, T. J., 81
D'Escragnole, Gastão, 165
Dias, Verônica Ferreira, 136
Dickenson, John, 17
Diniz, Leila, 182
distantiation, 145–46
Dogface Hill (Morro Cara de Cão), 8
Dolff-Bonekamper, Gabi, 5
Dona Marta Hill, 135, 137–38, 169

Earth Summit in Rio, UN, 1992, 157–59, 178, 184, 190, 201–2
eco-barriers, 141–43, *142*
ecological favelas, 117–18
Economist, 172
Economy, Equity, and Environment, Agenda 21 on, 158
ecotourism, 117–18
eco-walls, 141–43, *142*
Edmundo, Luiz, 13–14, 19, 58, 67
Empress Wharf, 77, 90, 92, 95
enslaved Africans. *See* African slaves
entrepreneurial city, 37–38, 70–71, 80, 109, 132, 201, 203
entrepreneurial preservation, 37–38, 47–51, 53–57, 70–71
entrepreneurial urbanism, 37–38, 184
environmental conservation, 158, 162–63, 167, 171, 177, 191–92, 202
environmental heritage, 30, 159–61, 191–92, 199
environmental injustice, 118, 179–80
environmentalism, 160, 164, 192, 202
environmental justice, 160, 164, 174–80, 191, 202
environmental movements in Brazil, three waves of, 163–64, 171, 179, 191
environmental problems: *favelados* unfairly blamed for, 117, 124, 179; favelas and, 117, 123–24, *124*, 141–42, 178–79; from growth of Rio, 175; pollution of Guanabara Bay, 178–80, 182, 201–2
environmental restoration and activism, 125–26
Ernesto, Pedro, 105
Estado de São Paulo, 177
ethnic-racial identity, 106–7
Eurocentric "civilization," 121
Evictions Museum (Museu das Remoções), 134–35

Fabricius, Daniela, 122
Farias, Patricia, 181
Favela-Bairro (Favela-Neighborhood) program, 126, 140
Favela Bar, 145
Favela Chic, 138, 143–50, 201
Favela da Maré (Favela of the Tide), 116–17
favelados, 115, 183, 201; on eco-walls, 142; environmental problems unfairly blamed on, 117, 124, 179; on Favela Chic, 148–49; Favela Tourism and, 148–50; in films, 137–38; integration into society, favela removal and, 130–31; on marginality, 131, 137; of Vila Autódromo, 132–34
Favela Hype restaurant, 146
Favela-Neighborhood (Favela-Bairro) program, 126, 140
Favela of My Loves (Favela dos Meus Amores), 122
Favela of the Tide (Favela da Maré), 116–17
Favela Painting project, 140–41
Favela Rising, 137–38
favelas, of Rio, 30, 38–39, 41, 101–2, *119*; branding, 144–45; Catacumba removal, 129–31; CHISAM on removal, 128–29; Cidade de Deus, 137; collective memory of, 116, 201; Commission for the Eradication of Favelas on, 128; community organizing in, 149;

contested origins of, 119–27; counter-memory and, 118, 149, 201; counter-narratives of activists, 132; Cunha and, 121; eco-barriers around, 141–43, *142*; ecological, 117–18; environmental problems and, 117, 123–24, *124*, 141–42, 178–79; Evictions Museum on, 134–35; expansion of, official numbers, 127; Favela Chic and, 138, 143–50, 201; gentrification and, 146, 149–50; Horto, 167–68, 191; marginalization and, 19, 30, 118, 137–38, 143; neoliberal displacement of, 132; New Urbanism and, 149–51, 201; in North Zone, 115–16, 131, 141; pollution and, 178–79; population of, 116, 123, 128, *129*; Praia do Pinto removal, 130; at Providência Hill, 120–27, *124*; remembrance and heritage in resiliency of, 118; removal and resistance, 127–35; Santa Marta, 135–43, *136*, *142*, 145, 147; at Santo Antônio Hill, 120; social geography and, 115–16; in South Zone, 116, 129–31, 135, 141–43, 150; as spectacle, 135–43; tourism in, 126, 144, 146–50; UPPs and, 123, 140–41, 143; urban ecology, environmental problems and, 117, 141; urbanization and, 116, 119–27; urban renewal and, 127; Vila Autódromo against removal, 132–35; voters in, 131–32; War of Canudos and, 120–21

Favelas Have Memory program (Favela Tem Memória), 116

Favela Tours, 146–47

Favella Hill, 120–21

Federal District, 36, 38–40, 128

Felippsen, Cosme, 126

Ferreira de Mello, João Baptista, 20–21, *21*

Ferrez, Gilberto, 35, 169, 171

FIFA World Cup, 2014, 79, 132, 140

Filho, José Antônio Moreira, 182

Filhos de Gandhi (Children of Gandhi), 97, *98*

First and Second Empires (1822–1889), 14–15

first republican period (1889–1930), 29, 38, 50, 199

Fischer, Brodwyn, 119

Flamengo Beach, 181–82

Flamengo Park, 175–76, *176*

Fort Coligny, 8

Fort Copacabana, 183, 185, *186*, 190

Foucault, Michel, 22, 40, 80

Framework Convention on the Value of Heritage for Society, Council of Europe, 5

La France Antarctique, 8

Freeman, James, 181

Freireyss, G. W., 94

Freitas, Chagas, 177

French-Portuguese battles, 8–9, 11

Freyre, Gilberto, 92

Fribourg Declaration on Cultural Rights, 5

Fuks, Mario, 117

Fundação Pro-Memória (Heritage Foundation), 69

funk carioca, 144–46

Gabeira, Fernando, 182

Gamboa district, Rio, 94, 100

Gávea Neighborhood Association (AMAGAVEA), 171

General Mines (Minas Gerais), 10, 84, 86, 129, 172, 198

General Services Administration, U.S. (GSA), 93

gentrification, 63, 65, 71, 99, 146, 149–50

"Geographic Itineraries" walking tours (Roteiros Geográficos), 20–21, *21*

Gilligan, Melanie, 137

"The Girl from Ipanema," 182

Glaziou, Auguste, 165–66

globalization, 22, 27, 159
Golden Law (Lei Aurea) of 1888, 68, 91
Graham, Brian, 3
Graham, Kelly, 137
Graham, Maria, 11–12, 14, 157
Greenberg, Miriam, 27
Greening Brazil (Hochstetler and Keck), 163–64
green urbanism, 159
Grupo Cultural AfroReggae, 137–38
GSA. *See* General Services Administration, U.S.
Guanabara Bay, 3, 7–8, 10, 63, 160–62, 164, 192; from conservation to environmental justice in, 174–80; pollution of, 178–80, 182, 201–2
Guimarães, Roberta, 56
Guran, Milton, 93, 97–98
Gustavo Capanema Palace, 43

Halbwachs, Maurice, 22–23
Halnon, Karen, 144
Harvey, David, 4, 37, 65, 198
Haussmann, George-Eugene, 40
Henry II (king), 8
Herald Sun, 141
heritage, 19–20; built, 4, 16, 26, 35, 38, 201; construction of, 5; cultural, 5, 16, 25–26, 43, 47; in cultural reinvention, 81; cultural tourism and, 23; environmental, 30, 159–61, 191–92, 199; institutionalization of, 45; legislation, Brazilian, 45; memory, preservation and, 22–26; nationalism and, 23; politics of, 24; power and, 23–24; remembrance and, 4–5, 16, 118, 197; urban, 48, 71. *See also* African Heritage Circuit; National Historic and Artistic Heritage Service; UNESCO World Heritage sites
heritage conservation, 22–23, 26, 30, 43, 79
Heritage Foundation (Fundação Pro-Memória), 69

heritage management, 22–23
heritage sites: memory and, 3; place memory and, 6; power and, 24; preservation or restoration of, 4; of Rio, 5–6, 29–30; social justice and, 4. *See also* UNESCO World Heritage sites
heritage tourism, 17, 19–20, 27, 47, 80, 99, 201
historical memory, 80–81
Historic Cities program, Brazil, 47
historic placemaking, 197–98; African Heritage Circuit and, 99; in city, *28*; Cultural Corridor program and, 51, 56, 66; dynamics of, 5–6; memory, power and, 35; narratives of, 6–12; in Rio, 19–22, 27–30, 47, 51, 56; in Valongo Wharf, 99–100
historic preservation, x–xi; built heritage and, 26, 35; campaigns, 25; community participation in, 56, 70; controversies, 45; critical perspective on, 26; Cultural Corridor and, 54–57, 63, 199–200; environmental heritages and, 159–60; favelas and, 30; heritage conservation and, 22, 30; identity and, 26, 192; IPHAN and, 43–45, 54; local organizations in, 49–50; memory and, 24; Pinheiro on, 48; power and, 4, 24, 26, 197–98; in sense of place and identity, 192; urban development *versus*, 197–98; of Valongo Wharf, 95–97
historic sites, branding campaigns for, 27
history, memory and, 22, 198
Hobsbawm, Eric, 4
Hochstetler, Kathryn, 163–64
Hollant-Denis, Nicole, 94
Holston, Mark, 172
Hora, Maurício, 125
Horto Favela, 167–68, 191
How Tasty Was My Little Frenchman, 8
human rights, 4–5, 197
Huyssen, Andreas, 23, 80–81, 197

ICOMOS. *See* International Council on Monuments and Sites
identity: Afro-Brazilian, 106–7, 201; Afro-descendant, 29–30, 108–9, 201; collective, 4, 81; community, 109–10; cultural, 5, 55; ethnic-racial, 106–7; in historic preservation, 26, 192; nature-culture, 161–62; place, 82, 192; place, power and, *28*; place memory and, 26–31, *28*; racial, 92, 106–8; social, 22
Imperial Palace (Paço Imperial), 35, 41, 51, 58, 63; adaptive reuse of, 65–71; Alpoim building, 66–67; as cultural center, *66*, 70; Cultural Corridor and, 69; Heritage Foundation ownership of, 69; IPHAN and, 68–69; protests at, 82; renovations, 69–70
Independence Centenary International Exposition, 42
"I ♥ New York" campaign, 48
informal communities, 115, 128–29, 132, 141, 143, 149–50, 178. *See also* favelas, of Rio
informal urbanism, 127, 149, 151
informal urbanization, 116, 120
Institute for Research on the New Blacks (IPN), 94–95
Intelligent Garden project, 125–26
Interior Department, U.S., 93–94
International Council on Monuments and Sites (ICOMOS), 22, 161–62, 167, 182
invention of tradition, 4
Invisible Cities (Calvino), ix
Ipanema Beach, 180, 182–92
IPHAN. *See* National Historic and Artistic Heritage Service
IPN. *See* Institute for Research on the New Blacks
Isabel (princess), 68
Ivester, Sukari, 134

Jackson, Michael, 138–40, 145, 147
James, Preston, 11

Jewish community, in June 11th Square, 104
João Ricardo Tunnel, 125–26
João VI (king), 11, 13–14, 69, 166
Joaquim, Leandro, 59–60, *60*
Jobim, Tom, 182
Jornal do Brasil, 177
O Jornal do Brasil, 141, 171
José Bonifácio Cultural Center, 107–8
JR, 125
June 11th Square (Praça Onze), 36, 104–5

Karasch, Mary, 82, 84
Keck, Margaret, 163–64
Kimmelman, Michael, 99
King, Rodney, 138
knowledge construction, power in, 22
Koolhaas, Jeroen, 140–41

Lacerda, Carlos, 62, 175–76
Lagoa Rodrigo de Freitas, 129
Lagoinha (Little Lagoon), 132
"land of the future," Brazil as, 16–22
Land of the True Cross (Terra de Vera Cruz), 7
Landowski, Paul, 172
Lapa district, 53–54
Latin America, 27, 40
Lavradio, Marquess of, 86–87
Laws of the Indies, Spanish, 9–10
Le Corbusier, 42–43
Lee, Spike, 138
Lefebvre, Henri, 4
Lei Aurea (Golden Law) of 1888, 68, 91
Leme Beach, 182–84
Leon, Rodney, 94
Lessa, Carlos, 48
"Letter of Pedro Vaz de Caminha to King Manuel," 7
Liberal Revolution of 1820, 13
Lima, Negrão de, 130
Lima, Tania Andrade, 95
Lins, Paulo, 137
Lisboa, Antônio Francisco, 11

Lisbon, 10–11, 13–14
Little Africa: African Heritage Circuit and, 99–109, 201; Afro-Brazilians in, 77, 80, 100–110; Afro-descendant identities and, 29–30, 108–9, 201; Aunt Ciata and, 104–5; community identity, cultural politics and, 109–10; counter-memory and, 81, 109; June 11th Square in, 104–5; place identity of, 82; place memory of, 80; poverty and living conditions of, 101; quilombo and, 105–7; Salt Point Square in, 100, 105–7; samba schools in, 105; tenements in, 101; Valongo Wharf and, 82; Yoruba language in, 101
Little Lagoon (Lagoinha), 132
Lobato, José Bento Monteiro, 42
Lund, Katia, 137, 139–40

Macedo, Joaquim Manuel de, 67–68
Machado de Assis, 91–92
Madonna, 140
Magnanini, Alceo, 168
Maia, César, 54, 126, 133
Mangueira Social Project, 148
Manuel (king), 7
MAR. *See* Museum of Art of Rio de Janeiro
marginality, myth and reality of, 131, 137
marginalization, of favelas, 19, 30, 118, 137–38, 143
Maria I (queen), 11, 13, 58
Marinho, Roberto, 126
Mário, José, 147
Martins, Luciana, 12
Marx, Murillo, 40
Massey, Doreen, 27
The Masters and the Slaves (Freyre), 92
Master Valentim Fountain, 51, 60–61
Mata Atlântica (Atlantic Forest), 142, 166, 174
McNally, James, 145

Meirelles, Fernando, 137
Melville, Herman, 175
memory: cultural identity and, 5; environmental heritage and, 30, 199; heritage, human rights and, 4–5; historical, 80–81; in historic placemaking, power relations and, 35; historic preservation and, 24; history and, 22, 198; in nationalism, 22; nostalgic, 25; politics of, 160; preservation, heritage and, 22–26; right to, 106; Rio and, 3, 17, 19–20, 29; of slavery, 90, 95, 97; social, 22, 116, 168; subjective, official history and, 22; types of, 199. *See also* collective memory; counter-memory; place memory
"memory boom," 22
memory brokers, 4, 24–25, 30, 198
memory formation, x–xi
"Memory of Destruction: Rio—A History of What Was Lost (1889–1965)" exhibition, 18, 78–79
memory sites, of Evictions Museum, 134–35
Mendes, Armando, 49
Merced, Ana Maria de la, 94
Military Review on the Palace Square (painting), 59–60, *60*
Minas Gerais (General Mines), 10, 84, 86, 129, 172, 198
mining, 10–11, 16
Miranda, Carmen, 63
Miss Favela restaurant, 144–45
Mitchell, Don, 27
Modern Art Week, of 1922, 43
modernism, 43, 163
monarchy, Portuguese: bicentennial of arrival in Rio, 1, *2*, 3; fall of, 38
Monroe Palace, 18, 45, 53
Morães, Vinícius de, 82
Moreira, Marcelo, 168
Morro Cara de Cão (Dogface Hill), 8
Morro da Providência. *See* Providence Hill (Morro da Providência)

Morro do Castelo (Castle Hill), 9–10, 12, 18, 41–43, 58
multiculturalism, 18, 26–27, 37
Museu das Remoções (Evictions Museum), 134–35
Museu do Amanhã (Museum of Tomorrow), 18, 79, 100
Museu do Ontem (Museum of Yesterday), 100
Museum of Art of Rio de Janeiro (MAR), 79
Museum of Tomorrow (Museu do Amanhã), 18, 79, 100
Museum of Yesterday (Museu do Ontem), 100
myth of marginality, 131, 137

Napoleon, 11
Napoleon III (emperor), 40
National Cathedral, in Rio, 35
National Historic and Artistic Heritage Service (IPHAN), 36, 43–45, 198; Carioca Landscapes and, 161–62; on *Christ the Redeemer* statue, 171; Conçalves Ledo Street buildings preserved by, 54, *55*; on historical hills and mountains of Rio, 169, 177–78; on Imperial Palace, 68–69; on November 15th Square, 58, 61–64; TNP and, 168–69, 171, 191; Valongo Wharf site, UNESCO World Heritage designation and, 97, 99
National Historic Register: Botanical Garden in, 166; Cinelândia district sites in, 51; Copacabana Palace Hotel on, 181; Decree-Law n° 25 on, 62; November 15th Square district sites in, 51, *52–53*, 58, 61–64; SAARA district sites in, 54; São Francisco district sites in, 54; Sugar Loaf Mountain and, 177; TNP in, 168–69, 191
National History Museum, 51
nationalism, 6, 22–23, 108, 203
National Library, in Rio, 41–42

National Museum, in Rio, 17–18
National Register of Historic Places, U.S., 43
Natural City Park of Catacumba, 130
nature-culture identities and relations, 161–62, 165
Needell, Jeffrey, 101, 103
neoliberal cities, 27, 110
neoliberalism, 198; environmental policy and, 160; in favela displacement, 132; historic districts and, 23–24; public-private partnerships in, 23, 56, 110, 132; of Rio rebranding strategy, 48; socioeconomic inequality and, 37
neoliberal policies, of urban revitalization, 17, 29–30, 37, 56, 108, 191, 201
neoliberal urbanism, 37
neoliberal urban renewal programs, 99
New Blacks: African slaves as, 84–91; Cemetery of New Blacks, 81, 94–95, 100, 200; IPN, 94–95
New Cinema (Cinema Novo), 8, 138
News from a Personal War, 139–40
New Urbanism, favelas and, 149–51, 201
New Year's Eve celebrations, in Rio, 180
New York City, 64; African Burial Ground site, 93–94; branding campaigns in, 27; "I ♥ New York" campaign, 48; Miss Favela restaurant in, 144–45; Pennsylvania Station demolition in, 45; urban revitalization in, 27
New York Times, 133, 144
NGOs. *See* nongovernmental organizations
Niemeyer, Oscar, 16, 43
"Noble Savage" trope, 7
nongovernmental organizations (NGOs), 30, 116, 148–49, 164, 178–79
North America, slave disembarkations in Brazil and, 83, *83*

North Zone (Zona Norte), 101, 115–16, 131, 141
nostalgia, 3, 24–25, 27, 70
November 15th Square district, 1, 35, 48, 103; Arch of Teles in, 51, *59*, 59–64; BVRJ in, 63–64; in Cultural Corridor, 51, 57–58, 64; as Imperial Capital, 57–58, 64–65; Imperial Palace in, 58, 63, 65, 70; IPHAN on, 58, 61–64; National Historic Register sites in, 51, *52–53*, 58, 61–64; Palace Square in, 59–61, *60*, 65; placemaking on, 57–65; public-private partnerships in, 58; Vertical Shopping in, 64

Old Republic (1889–1930), 29, 38, 50, 199
Olick, Jeffrey, 22
Oliveira, Márcio Amaro de, 139–40
Olympic Games, 2016, 3, 79, 132–34, 140, 146, 179, 201–2
Olympic Park and Athlete's Village, 133
"100 Resilient Cities" network, 118
Operacão Anti-Arrastão, 186–87
Oratory of the Cross, 122, 126
Osório, Manuel Luís, 68
Our Lady of the Penha Church, 126–27
Ouro Preto, 47

Pacifying Police Unit (UPP), 123, 140–41, 143
Paço Imperial. *See* Imperial Palace
Paes, Eduardo, 79, 96, 107, 133, 140, 201
Palace at São Cristóvão, 67
Palace of Tirandentes, 51
Palace Square, 10, 14, 59–61, *60*, 65, 68
Pan American Games, 2007, 132
Paraná, 166
Paris, 40, 65, 69
Pedro I (emperor), 14–15, 67, 69
Pedro II (emperor), 14–15, 66–67, 69, 77, 90, 107–8, 165

Pequena Africa. *See* Little Africa
Pereira dos Santos, Nelson, 8
Pereira Passos, Francisco, 40, 115
Perlman, Janice E., 130–31, 146
Petrópolis, 16
Phillips, Tom, 144
"Pig's Head" tenement (Cabeça de Porco), 40
Pilot Plan, of Brasília, 16
Pinheiro, Augusto, 48
place: "authenticity" of, 26–27; constructing, 6; identity, power and, *28*; identity and, 82, 192; politics of, 25–26. *See also* sense of place
place-based identities, 27
place-based imaginaries, 6
place branding, 29–30
place identity, of Little Africa, 82
placemaking: colonial, 7; community organizing in, 149; European colonization and, 6; favelas and, 121; narratives of, 6, 199; on November 15th Square, 57–65. *See also* historic placemaking
place memory: built heritage and, 4; heritage sites, landmark preservation and, 6; identity and, 26–31, *28*; of Little Africa, 80; narratives, power brokers and, 35–36; recovery of, 110; remembrance, heritage and, 5; in Rio, 19–20; of Valongo Wharf, 90–91, 97–98
Plano Urbanístico Básico (Basic Urbanist Plan), 48
Pombal, Marquis of, 10–11
Poor Chic, 144–45
Portugal, Napoleonic invasion of, 11
Portuguese exploration and colonization, in South America, 6–11
Portuguese founding of Rio, 1565, x–xi, 1
Portuguese monarchy, 1, *2*, 3, 38
Portuguese urbanism, 9–10
postcolonial urbanism, in Rio, 38–45, *46*, 47, 119–20

The Posthumous Memoirs of Brás Cubas (Machado de Assis), 91–92
power: heritage and, 23–24; in historic placemaking, memory and, 35; historic preservation and, 4, 24, 26, 197–98; in knowledge construction, 22; memory brokers and, 24–25; place, identity and, *28*
power brokers, narratives of, place memory and, 35–36
Praça Cantão, 140–41
Praça da Pedra do Sal (Salt Point Square), *21*, 100, 105–7
Praça Onze (June 11th Square), 36, 104–5
Praça XV. *See* November 15th Square
Praia do Pinto, 130
Prazeres, Heitor dos, 100
preservation, 4, 18; entrepreneurial, 37–38, 47–51, 53–57, 70–71; memory, heritage and, 22–26; politics of, built heritage and, 35. *See also* historic preservation
President Vargas Boulevard, Rio, 36–37, 42–43, 45, 54, 104
Providence Hill (Morro da Providência), 30, 102; Afro-Brazilians and, 120–22; Carnival blocks, 122; crime and, 122–23; environmental problems at, 123–24, *124*; environmental restoration and activism in, 125–26; Favela-Neighborhood program and, 126; growth of, 123; 120th anniversary of, 127; urban renewal and, 124–25; "Women Are Heroes" art exhibition, 125
Providência Community Museum, 126–27
public participation, 4
public-private partnerships: in Cultural Corridor program, 16, 29, 37–38, 54–57; entrepreneurial urbanism and, 184; Imperial Palace and, 69; in neoliberalism, 23, 56, 110, 132; in November 15th Square district, 58

public space, 4
Punitions publiques; sur la Place Ste. Anne (painting), 87

quilombo, 105–7

race-blind nationalism, 108
racial democracy, 29, 92, 108, 138, 181, 189–90
racial identity, 92, 106–8
racism, 138, 188–89
Real Horto (Royal Garden), 166–67
reality of marginality, 131, 137
Red Command (Comando Vermelho), 123, 125, 139
reflective nostalgia, 25
Regina, Sandra, 135
remembrance, heritage and, 16; as human rights, 4–5, 197; in resilience of favelas and, 118
Republic Square, 36
resistance, to favela removal, 127–35
restorative nostalgia, 25
Revolt of the Vaccine, 1904, 41, 82, 102–3
Revolution of 1930, 42–43, 127–28
Ribeiro, Barata, 40
right to heritage, 5
right to memory, 106
the right to the city, 4, 197
Riley, Mathew, 87
Rio, Vicente del, 56
Rio+20 summit, 159
Rio Branco law, of 1871, 91
Rio Brando Boulevard (Avenida Central), 41
Rio Declaration, 1992, 158
Rio de Janeiro, ix–xi; African slaves disembarking in or near, 84–86, 91, 121; Agache Plan for, 42–43; Art Deco buildings in, 43; automobiles and traffic in, 47–48; Bragança dynasty, Portuguese rule in Brazil and, 1, *2*, 3, 11–14; Carnival, 1, 100, 102, 104–5, 122; City Archives,

Index

"Memory of Destruction" exhibition, 18, 78–79; "civilizing" through urban design, 12–15; colonial, 8–14, 19, 58, 67, 84; diversity and diverse narratives of, 19, 26; as entrepreneurial city, 37–38, 70–71, 80, 132, 201, 203; "Geographic Itineraries" walking tours of, 20–21, *21*; as global city, 1, 3, 132; gold and, 11; ground plan of, 1812, *9*; historic landmarks and federally protected sites, 5; historic places, lost in twentieth century, 41–42; historic waterfront, heritage-based redevelopment of, 4–5; imaginaries of, 28–29; landscape and topography of, 9–10, 13, 16, 19, 35, 157; major periods of urban transformation in, 45, *46*; migration to, 119–21, 128; naming of, 7–8; past of, demolishing, 17–18; Planning Department, 48–49, 55, 200; Portuguese founding, 1565, x–xi, 1; Portuguese refugees in, 11; post-abolition, 101–2; public-health campaign, 41; Roman Catholic religious orders, in colonial public spaces, 58; slave markets, 60, 82, 85, 87–89, 91, 100, 107, 120; as slave port, 82–92; spatial irregularity of, 40; trade in, 10–12, 15; urban poverty, 19; view from São Bento, 14, *15*; waterfront expansion, 77, *78*, 90, 92; waterfront renewal program, 77–79; World's Fair, 1922-1923, 42. *See also specific locations*; *specific topics*

Rio de Janeiro, population of: African slaves in, 1821, 84–85; of Afro-Brazilians, 83, 100; during Bragança dynasty, 12–13; of Copacabana Beach, 181; in 1872, 38; in favelas, 116, 123, 128, *129*; of Providência Hill favela, 123; in 2019, 19

Rio de Janeiro: Carioca Landscapes between the Mountain and the Sea, 30, 47, *161*, 166–67, *170*, 202; *Christ the Redeemer* statue in, 171–73; collective memory and, 191–92; Copacabana Beach in, 180–82; as cultural landscape, 18–19, 160–64, 191–92; environmental heritage of, 161, 191–92

Rio de Janeiro: Carnival under Fire (Castro), 17

Rio de Janeiro National Park, 168–69

Rio in the Time of the Viceroys (Edmundo), 19

Rio-Niterói bridge, 122

Rio Summer Olympics, 2016, 3, 79, 132–34, 140, 146, 179, 201–2

ritualistic cannibalism, of Tupinambás, 8

Robbins, Joyce, 22

Rocinha district, 143, 148

Rodriguez Alves, Francisco, 40, 102

Roman Catholic Church, 58, 105–6, 172–73

rooming houses (*casas de cómodos*), 101, 104

Roteiros Geográficos ("Geographic Itineraries"), 20–21, *21*

Royal Garden (Real Horto), 166–67

Rugendas, Johann Moritz, 13–14, *15*, 67, 87, 157

Sá, Estácio de, 8

SAARA. *See* Society of Friends of Alfândega Street and Vicinity

Sacré-Cœur, 65, 69

Saint Benedict Catholic Church, 103–4

Salles, João Moreira, 139–40

Salt Point Square (Praça da Pedra do Sal), *21*, 100, 105–7

Salvador da Bahia, 82, 198

samba, *21*, 36, 100, 104–7, 146

samba schools, 1, 102, 105, 122, 147

Sampaio, Carlos, 42

sanitarist segregation, 86, 91

Santa Marta, 135–43, *136*, *142*, 145, 147

Santa Marta: Two Weeks on the Hill, 136–37
Santo Antônio Hill, 120, 175, *176*
Santos, Eron César dos, 126
Santos Dumont Airport, 42, 176
São Bento, 14, *15*
São Francisco district, 53–54, 57, 71
São Paulo, 15–16, 35, 43, 64, 145–46, 166
São Sebastião, 8, 175
Saraiva-Cotegipe law, of 1885, 91
Saramago, José, 142
SARCA. *See* Society of the Friends of Carioca Street
Saúde district, 41
Sauer, Carl O., 26–27
Scarpaci, Joseph, 27
Schlee, Andrey, 99
Secretary of Public Order (SEOP), 187
sense of place, x, 1, 3–6, 28–29; Cultural Corridor and, 51, 66, 70, 200; favela, 118; historic preservation programs in, 192; of Little Africa, 80; urban landscapes in, 197
SEOP. *See* Secretary of Public Order
Os Sertões (Cunha), 121
Shock of Order (Choque de Ordem) program, 187
Silva Costa, Heitor da, 172
slave markets, of Rio, 60, 82, 85, 87–89, 91, 100, 107, 120
slave port, Rio as, 82–92
Slave Routes project, UNESCO, 93, 96
slavery, 19, 81; abolition of, xi, 15, 66, 68, 91–92, 100, 120; memory of, 90, 95, 97. *See also* African slaves
slave trade: middle passage, 83, 87; transatlantic, 19, 29, 83–86, 89–91, 97; UNESCO Slave Routes project on, 93, 96; at Valongo Cove, 85–90, 120
Slum, Poverty, or Reality Tourism, 146
smallpox vaccination, 102–3

Smith, Robert C., 10
Soares, Maria Carlota Macedo, 175–76
social diversity, ix, 65, 71, 143, 188–92, 203
social elites, 4, 199
social groups (*turmas*), 183
social identity, 22
social justice, 4–5
social memory, 22, 116, 168
social status: at Copacabana and Ipanema Beaches, 188–89, 192; cultural difference and, 12; political-economic power, historic preservation and, 4, 24, 26
Society of Friends of Alfândega Street and Vicinity (SAARA), 50, 53–54, *55*, 71
Society of the Friends of Carioca Street (SARCA), 50
Soeiro, Renato, 177
South America, Portuguese exploration and colonization in, 6–11
South Zone (Zona Sul), 146, 176; beaches in, 181, 184, 186–87, 190–91; favelas in, 116, 129–31, 135, 141–43, 150
Souza, Laura Olivieri Carneiro de, 168
Spain, 9–10
subjective memory, official history and, 22
Sugar Loaf Mountain, 160–62, 176–77, 183
Summer Olympic Games, 2016, 3, 79, 132–34, 140, 146, 179, 201–2
sustainable development, 157–58, 162, 178
sustainable urbanization, 159
symbolic bankers, 24, 28, 35, 159, 198

Tamoios, 8, 174–75
Taunay, Nicolas-Antoine, 165
Teles de Menezes family, 58–59
tenements (*cortiços*), of Rio, 38–41, 101, 120
Tereza Cristina (princess), 77, 90

Terra de Vera Cruz (Land of the True Cross), 7
"They Don't Care About Us," 138
Tia Ciata (Aunt Ciata), 104–5
Tijuca Forest, 30, 141, *142*, 161–62, 165–66, 168–69, 174
Tijuca National Park (TNP), 30, 165–69, 171–74, 177, 191
Tip Top Tour Project, 147–48
Tiradentes Square, 39, 54, 59–60
TNP. *See* Tijuca National Park
Tocqueville, Alexis de, xi
transatlantic slave trade, 19, 29, 83–86, 89–91, 97
Transatlantic Slave Trade Database, 83, *83*
Tupí-Guaraní, 7, 174–75
Tupinambás, 7–8, 174–75
turmas (social groups), 183

UCLG. *See* United Cities and Local Governments
umbanda, 102, 180
Underwood, David, 15
UNESCO Slave Routes project, 93, 96
UNESCO World Heritage Committee, 97, 161–63
UNESCO World Heritage sites, x–xi, 16, 29, 190; Carioca Landscapes between the Mountain and the Sea, 18–19, 30, 47, 160–64, *161*, 166–67, *170*, 171–73, 180–82, 191–92, 202; criterion for selection, 97, 162–63; cultural tourism in Brazil and, 47; Valongo Wharf Archaeological Site, 19, 47, 80, 91–100, 108–10, 200–201
United Cities and Local Governments (UCLG), 158–59
United Nations Conference on Environment and Development, 1992, 157–58, 178, 184, 190, 201–2
United Nations "Habitat III" conference, 159
UPP. *See* Pacifying Police Unit
urban design, 12–15, 56

urban ecology, 117, 141
urban environmentalism, 160, 164
urban heritage, 48, 71
urbanism: Agenda 21, sustainable management and, 158; entrepreneurial, 37–38, 184; green, 159; informal, 127; neoliberal, 37; new, 149–51, 201; Portuguese, 9–10; postcolonial, in Rio, 38–45, *46*, 47, 119–20
urbanization, ix–x, 19, 43, 116, 119–27, 159–60
urban landscape, 4–5, 122, 197
urban planning, 127, 199
urban reforms, 82, 102
urban renewal: Black communities and, 78–79; favelas and, 127; first program, in 1902, 40–41, 102, 115; June 11th Square destroyed in, 105; neoliberal programs, 99; Providência Hill and, 124–25; Sugar Loaf Mountain tourism and, 176–77
urban revitalization: Cultural Corridor project and, 50–51, 55; cultural tourism and, 108; entrepreneurial preservation in, 57; heritage-based programs of, 16; heritage tourism and, 17, 80, 201; neoliberal policies of, 17, 29–30, 37, 56, 108, 191, 201; in New York City, 27; place branding and, 29–30; as uneven, 24
urban space, democratic engagement, in design and use of, 4
urban transformation, in Rio, major periods of, 45, *46*
Urhahn, Dre, 140–41

Valladares, Lícia, 121
Valongo Cove, African slaves and slave trade in, 85–90, 120
Valongo Wharf, 60, 132; African slaves and, 77–79, 84–85, 89–92; Afro-Brazilian heritage and, 79–80; Afro-Brazilians on, 96–97, 99–100; in Afrocentric cultural tourism and

counter-memory, 100; Cemetery of New Blacks and, 81, 94–95, 100, 200; Empress Wharf and, 77, 90, 92, 95; heritage conservation of, 79; historic placemaking in, 99–100; historic preservation of, 95–97; Little Africa place identity and, 82; memorial, design of, 99; place memory of, 90–91, 97–98; rediscovered, 96, 110; in UNESCO Slave Routes project, 93, 96
Valongo Wharf Archaeological Site, 19, 47, 80, 91–100, 108–10, 200–201
Vargas, Getúlio, 29, 36, 42–43, 45, 127–28
Veja, 142
Velho, Gilberto, 61–62
Velloso, Eliane, 171
Ventura, Zuenir, 115
Vespucci, Amerigo, 7
Vila Autódromo, 132–35
Vila Autódromo Neighborhood Association Building, 134–35
Villegagnon, Nicolas Durant de, 8
"Viva Rio" NGO, 116

Voyage Pittoresque dans le Brésil (Rugendas), 87

War of Canudos, 120–21
We of the Hill program, 148
West Zone (Zona Oeste), 115–18, 143
Williamson, Theresa, 150, 151
"Women Are Heroes" art exhibition, 125
Wonderful Port program, 79, 95, 98, 107, 109–10, 124
World Heritage sites. *See* UNESCO World Heritage sites
World's Fair in Rio, 1922-1923, 42
World War II, 16, 51, 129, 176

The Yellow House (A Casa Amarela), 125
Yoruba language, 101
Young, James, 99

Zona Norte (North Zone), 101, 115–16, 131, 141
Zona Sul. *See* South Zone (Zona Sul)
Zweig, Stefan, 16

About the Author

Brian J. Godfrey is professor of geography at Vassar College, where he participates in the multidisciplinary programs in environmental studies, Latin American and Latinx studies, and urban studies. Brian teaches courses on global geography, urban geography, global urbanization, public space, neighborhood change, and historic preservation and memory. He received his BA in history from Pomona College, and his MA and PhD in geography from the University of California at Berkeley. Favoring the analytical lens of historical geography, he has carried out research on urban and regional change in both the United States and Latin America, resulting in the books *Neighborhoods in Transition* (1988), *Rainforest Cities: Urbanization, Development, and Globalization of the Brazilian Amazon* (with John Browder, 1997), and *Cidades da Floresta* (with John Browder, 2006). Brian has contributed recent book chapters to *Cities of the World: Regional Patterns and Urban Environments* (2020); *The City as Power: Urban Space, Place, and National Identity* (2018); *Contemporary Ethnic Geographies in America* (2016); and *Sustainability: A Global Urban Context* (2013). His articles and reviews have appeared in such journals as the *Annals of the AAG*, *Geographical Review*, *Journal of Cultural Geography*, *Journal of Latin American Geography*, and *Urban Geography*.

www.ingramcontent.com/pod-product-compliance
Lightning Source LLC
Chambersburg PA
CBHW050325020526
44117CB00031B/1801